AF739183

This book is a must-read for anyone who wants to learn about the evolution of private credit and asset-backed lending, and how the structural shock of the 2008 financial crisis, innovation, and technology spawned the development of the non-bank lending market that is now genuinely transformative for borrowers and investors alike.

—Christian Faes, co-founder, LendInvest; CEO, Faes & Co

Here is a book that explains clearly the workings of new and exciting world of real estate finance and how it is completely transformed by technology. I highly recommend it to anyone who is engaging with real estate. I will definitely be using it in my class.

—Nir Vulkan, Associate Professor, Said Business School, Oxford, Director of the Oxford Fin Tech programme.

BEYOND BANKS

The Wiley Finance series contains books written specifically for finance and investment professionals as well as sophisticated individual investors and their financial advisors. Book topics range from portfolio management to e-commerce, risk management, financial engineering, valuation and financial instrument analysis, as well as much more. For a list of available titles, visit our Web site at www.WileyFinance.com.

Founded in 1807, John Wiley & Sons is the oldest independent publishing company in the United States. With offices in North America, Europe, Australia and Asia, Wiley is globally committed to developing and marketing print and electronic products and services for our customers' professional and personal knowledge and understanding.

BEYOND BANKS

THE RISE OF PRIVATE DEBT IN REAL ESTATE FINANCE

ROXANA MOHAMMADIAN-MOLINA

WILEY

This edition first published 2027

© 2027 John Wiley & Sons, Ltd

All rights reserved, including rights for text and data mining and training of artificial intelligence technologies or similar technologies. No part of this publication may be reproduced, stored in a retrieval system, or transmitted, in any form or by any means, electronic, mechanical, photocopying, recording or otherwise, except as permitted by law. Advice on how to obtain permission to reuse material from this title is available at http://www.wiley.com/go/permissions.

The right of Roxana Mohammadian-Molina to be identified as the author of this work has been asserted in accordance with law.

Registered Offices
John Wiley & Sons, Inc., 111 River Street, Hoboken, NJ 07030, USA
John Wiley & Sons Ltd, New Era House, 8 Oldlands Way, Bognor Regis, West Sussex, PO22 9NQ, UK

For details of our global editorial offices, customer services, and more information about Wiley products visit us at www.wiley.com.

The manufacturer's authorized representative according to the EU General Product Safety Regulation is Wiley-VCH GmbH, Boschstr. 12, 69469 Weinheim, Germany, e-mail: Product_Safety@wiley.com.

Wiley also publishes its books in a variety of electronic formats and by print-on-demand. Some content that appears in standard print versions of this book may not be available in other formats.

Trademarks: Wiley and the Wiley logo are trademarks or registered trademarks of John Wiley & Sons, Inc. and/or its affiliates in the United States and other countries and may not be used without written permission. All other trademarks are the property of their respective owners. John Wiley & Sons, Inc. is not associated with any product or vendor mentioned in this book.

Limit of Liability/Disclaimer of Warranty

While the publisher and the authors have used their best efforts in preparing this work, including a review of the content of the work, neither the publisher nor the authors make any representations or warranties with respect to the accuracy or completeness of the contents of this work and specifically disclaim all warranties, including without limitation any implied warranties of merchantability or fitness for a particular purpose. Certain AI systems have been used in the creation of this work. No warranty may be created or extended by sales representatives, written sales materials or promotional statements for this work. The fact that an organization, website, or product is referred to in this work as a citation and/or potential source of further information does not mean that the publisher and authors endorse the information or services the organization, website, or product may provide or recommendations it may make. This work is sold with the understanding that the publisher is not engaged in rendering professional services. The advice and strategies contained herein may not be suitable for your situation. You should consult with a specialist where appropriate. Further, readers should be aware that websites listed in this work may have changed or disappeared between when this work was written and when it is read. Neither the publisher nor authors shall be liable for any loss of profit or any other commercial damages, including but not limited to special, incidental, consequential, or other damages.

Library of Congress Cataloging-in-Publication Data has been applied for:

Print: 9781394388134
ePub: 9781394388141
ePdf: 9781394388158

Cover Design: Wiley
Cover Image: Ron Dale/stock.adobe.com
Author Photo: Courtesy of Roxana Mohammadian-Molina

Set in 10/12pt SabonLTStd-Roman by Lumina Datamatics

Printed and bound by CPI Group (UK) Ltd, Croydon, CR0 4YY

C9781394388134_070826

Portions of this text were drafted with assistance from Claude 3.5 Sonnet by Anthropic. This AI tool helped organize my ideas, suggest alternative phrasing for complex concepts and improve clarity and conciseness throughout the writing process. All AI-generated content was carefully reviewed, edited and approved. The final analysis, conclusions and interpretations represent my views and expertise. I take full responsibility for the content and accuracy of this work.

Contents

Preface

The idea for this book began with a personal story on a damp day in Birmingham in 2012.

At the time, I was looking to buy an old factory in the city's historic Jewellery Quarter, which I wanted to turn into a modern co-living space for young professionals. Like many industrial buildings across Britain's former industrial heartlands, it had seen better days. Yet below the neglect, there was potential. The Jewellery Quarter has always been a place where craftsmanship and entrepreneurship meet, and the idea of giving the building a new lease of life was deeply appealing.

I had a capable contractor and a clear plan. What I did not have was a track record with a project of such scale, even though I had completed many smaller projects.

In theory, that shouldn't have been insurmountable. In practice, it proved exactly that. One by one, banks declined to finance the project. The reasons varied in detail but were consistent in essence: without a development track record, the risk simply didn't fit. The fundamentals were there, the contractor was highly experienced and the numbers broadly stacked up. But none of that was enough. The answer remained the same. No.

It was only after several months that a broker introduced me to a local lender I had never heard of before: a small, specialist firm operating outside the traditional banking system. It was what would later become known as a non-bank lender.

Unlike the banks, they were willing to look at the project itself instead of just my track record. They visited the site, spoke with the contractor and assessed the local market dynamics. Their underwriting process was thorough, but it was also pragmatic. They were prepared to structure a loan that recognised both the risks and the opportunity. That loan allowed the project to move forward.

At the time, I didn't realise that this experience would shape the direction of my professional interests for the next decade. But it was the first moment when I clearly saw how capital could come from outside the traditional banking system to enable projects that would otherwise remain on paper.

Over the following decade, my career increasingly intersected with the world of non-bank lending. Working within financial markets and later advising FinTech and credit platforms, I watched as private lenders, institutional investors and technology-enabled platforms began to fill the banks' shoes.

What I had first encountered as a niche corner of the market slowly revealed itself as something much larger.

Developers had started getting excited about new sources of funding that could move faster and structure more flexibly than traditional banks. Institutional investors began allocating capital to private credit strategies backed by real assets. FinTech platforms introduced new ways of originating and monitoring loans. In parallel, regulatory reforms reshaped bank balance sheets and reduced their appetite for certain forms of lending.

Taken together, these developments were quietly transforming the financial ecosystem surrounding real estate.

At first, the shift was easy to overlook. Private credit remained relatively small compared with traditional lending, and many observers assumed the change was short-lived. The prevailing narrative was that banks had retrenched in response to post-crisis regulation and that they would eventually resume their previous roles.

But over time it became increasingly clear that something deeper was happening. Across markets, private lenders were financing projects that banks no longer touched: development schemes in regional cities, refurbishment of historic buildings, bridge financing for complex projects and capital for small and medium-sized developers who struggled to access traditional credit.

Insurance companies, pension funds and sovereign wealth funds were allocating increasing amounts of capital to private credit strategies. Technology platforms were digitising parts of the lending process. Specialist funds were emerging to finance everything from logistics infrastructure to student accommodation.

Taken together, these forces began to redraw the map of real estate finance. What had once appeared marginal was steadily moving towards the centre of the market.

As my own exposure to the sector deepened—including becoming an equity investor in a non-bank development finance lender—I became increasingly fascinated by the broader forces behind this transformation. The story was not just about alternative lenders replacing banks. It was more nuanced. It was about how financial systems evolve when regulation, technology and investor behaviour change simultaneously.

Yet despite its growing importance, real estate private credit remains surprisingly under-explored. Discussions of private markets often focus on corporate lending or private equity, while the role of private debt in financing the built environment receives far less attention.

This book seeks to address that gap.

It examines the rise of real estate private credit from multiple angles: the regulatory shifts that altered bank lending after the financial crisis, the institutional investors seeking stable income in a low-yield world and the technological innovations reshaping how credit decisions are made. It also highlights the perspectives of practitioners—developers, lenders and investors—who are navigating this evolving landscape every day.

Throughout this book, I draw on conversations with those allocating capital, structuring deals and delivering projects who are actively shaping this market. Their perspectives reveal the practical realities behind the headlines: how deals come together, how risk is assessed and how capital flows through projects in practice.

The aim is not to present private credit as a flawless solution. Like any financial innovation, it carries risks and will inevitably face cycles that test the discipline of lenders and borrowers alike. But its rise offers a window into a broader transformation occurring across finance.

Looking back, the old factory in Birmingham's Jewellery Quarter now feels like an unlikely starting point for a book about the evolution of credit markets. Yet that early experience revealed something that would later become much clearer: the financial system is constantly adapting, often through small and practical decisions made far from the headlines.

Sometimes those decisions begin with a lender willing to say yes when everyone else says no. And sometimes they quietly reshape the way entire markets function.

Introduction

Beyond Banks: Lending, Power and the Long Arc of Real Estate Credit

The ascent of money has been essential to the ascent of man.
—Niall Ferguson, *The Ascent of Money*

Real estate lending—indeed, all types of lending—has never been just about money. It has always been about trust, power, influence and risk: who controls capital, who gains access to it and who ultimately bears the consequences when the tables turn.

From Renaissance Florence, where the Medici used the power of credit to shape politics and property ownership across Europe, to modern financial crises in which the sudden withdrawal of liquidity determines which borrowers survive and which do not, lending has always been as much a mechanism of control as a commercial transaction.

Every era has produced its own lenders and its own structures, yet property-backed lending has remained a constant anchor of the credit system through the ages. From ancient agricultural loans secured against harvests, to medieval pledges of land, to modern mortgages and institutional private credit funds, property has endured as collateral because it is tangible, visible, relatively stable and—unlike many esoteric financial products—it can be valued with a reasonable degree of certainty. Bricks and mortar may fluctuate in value, but they rarely vanish overnight.

And yet the same questions have echoed through the centuries: how should the risk of property-backed lending be assessed? What truly constitutes good collateral? And how far can leverage stretch before it snaps?

The tools used to answer those questions have evolved dramatically. Yet the underlying tensions have not. Today, sophisticated financial models, vast datasets and formidable computing power promise ever greater precision in underwriting risk and faster decision-making. But long before algorithms, dashboards and automated credit systems, lenders wrestled with the same uncertainties. Then, as now, lending decisions sat at the crossroad of risk and return.

This book is not a history of mortgages or real estate development finance. Instead, it is an attempt to understand where private real estate debt comes from, and why it has surged so forcefully over the past two decades.

Beyond Banks explores the growing influence of private credit in real estate finance through a practical, case study-driven lens. Drawing on real-world transactions across market cycles, institutional capital flows and conversations with practitioners, it provides a rare insight into how private lenders now operate alongside—and sometimes in place of—traditional banks.

To understand this shift, however, we must step back and recognise a pattern that repeats itself with remarkable consistency throughout financial history. Time and again, when traditional players struggle to adapt to changing economic realities and evolving demand, new forms of capital emerge to fill the void. That pattern is not new. It is as old as lending itself. The history of real estate finance is, in many ways, the history of what happens when established lenders retreat and new forms of capital take their place.

LAND AS THE FOUNDATION OF CREDIT

The idea of pledging land or property as collateral for credit is older than any bank on Earth.

In ancient Persia and Babylonia, people were already deeply engaged in the business of borrowing and lending. Farmers regularly secured loans by pledging fields, homes and future harvests. These arrangements were often informal and deeply personal, sometimes sealed just by a handshake or a word between parties who knew each other. Yet the underlying logic was already clear. Land was durable, visible and difficult to conceal. It made for a natural collateral.

But as trade evolved and society grew more complex, lending gradually moved from being a personal agreement into a structured system. The Romans brought a formal framework and legal sophistication to the centuries old business of lending. In their hands, lending became more than just a handshake, it became a legal contract. They developed mechanisms like the hypotheca, which separated ownership from possession, allowing borrowers to continue using land while it was pledged as security.

But Roman ingenuity didn't stop there. Ever the administrators, they developed different types of loans for different purposes, formalised creditor rights, codified rules governing collateral and even created early secondary markets by making debt transferable from one party to another. In other words, the Romans institutionalised lending.

CREDIT AND POWER

Throughout history, real estate lending has always reflected who controls surplus capital.

In today's world, credit feels impersonal, coming from institutions with balance sheets, regulatory frameworks, risk models and capital buffers.

But in the old days, lending was deeply personal. Even in the early sophistication brought by the Romans, one feature of credit stood out: capital flowed not from institutions, but from wealthy individuals. In antiquity, that meant royal households, aristocratic families and wealthy merchants. In medieval Europe, it meant landowners, the Church and feudal elites. Lending was an extension of power: economic, social and political, seen in how some lenders sought proximity to power, even bankrolling rulers and their wars. Those individual financiers, and later professional bankers, deployed their own capital and bore the risk personally.

Evidence of this dynamic appears vividly in the Persian Empire, where members of the royal household were active participants in credit markets, deploying personal wealth through agents and intermediaries, perhaps the early version of a personal wealth manager. Historical records from the Murashu Archives in Babylonia reveal a sophisticated system of property-backed lending in which land, crops and homes were regularly pledged as collateral centuries before the emergence of anything resembling institutional banking.

But as markets grew more complex, so too did the intermediaries. By the late medieval and early modern periods, legal reforms helped reshape mortgage law and rebalance relationships between lenders and borrowers. For example, legal principles such as the equity of redemption softened the harsh consequences of forfeiture, allowing borrowers greater protection against permanent loss of property.

Yet despite these developments, credit remained rare and expensive. Access to capital was limited to a relatively small portion of society.

The true transformation would arrive with the industrialisation.

THE DEMOCRATISATION OF PROPERTY CREDIT

The Industrial Revolution fundamentally transformed real estate finance by reshaping society itself. As populations moved from the countryside to the cities in search of work and opportunity, property ownership gradually shifted from aristocratic inheritance to middle-class aspiration. Urbanisation created a growing demand for housing and new financial tools to acquire it. New forms of employment created new cash flows—regular wages instead of seasonal harvests—and with them, the conditions for long-term amortised lending.

One of the most consequential innovations of this period came not from banks but from communities. Britain's building societies, founded by tradesmen pooling savings to finance homes, represented a profound revolution in credit. They institutionalised mutual trust. Capital was no longer the exclusive domain of elites; it was aggregated collectively, allowing individuals who lacked inherited wealth to access credit.

Over time, these structures enabled broader participation in property ownership. Mortgages became more standardised and scalable, gradually transforming homeownership from a privilege of the elite into an attainable goal for large segments of society. They were no longer confined to privileged few. Clerks, machinists, shopkeepers and teachers could now secure their place on the property ladder.

In the growing suburbs of London and along the smoke-darkened rows of factory towns, the mortgage took on a new meaning. It was no longer just a financial instrument or a legal contract. It became a quiet revolution, an instrument of progress, a tool that underpinned the dreams of a rising middle and working class in an increasingly urbanised Britain.

Banks eventually absorbed and expanded these models. By the twentieth century, real estate lending across most developed economies became dominated by institutional balance sheets and regulatory frameworks.

For decades, this system worked remarkably well.

CRISIS AND STRUCTURAL CHANGE

The stability of institutional lending has periodically been disrupted by financial crises.

In the United States, the collapse of the mortgage market during the Great Depression forced the government to rebuild housing finance through long-term fixed-rate mortgages, federal guarantees and the creation of secondary markets for mortgage securities.

Later episodes, including the Savings and Loan crisis of the 1980s and the Global Financial Crisis of 2008, exposed how quickly property markets can destabilise entire financial systems when leverage, optimism and weak oversight combine.

The 2008 crisis proved particularly consequential. As banks suffered huge losses and regulators responded with sweeping reforms, traditional lenders became more constrained by capital requirements, liquidity rules and regulatory scrutiny.

The reforms succeeded in strengthening the resilience of the banking system. But they also produced an unintended consequence. Banks became far less able—and therefore less willing—to finance many types of real estate projects.

Developers, promoters and operators still needed capital. But the institutions that had traditionally supplied it were retreating. Once again, a vacuum appeared. And, as history repeatedly shows, vacuums don't stay empty for long.

THE RETURN OF PRIVATE CAPITAL

Into that gap stepped private capital. Initially, non-bank lenders were viewed as opportunistic players: short-term replacements filling a void left by cautious banks. But over time they became something more durable. Institutional investors such as pension funds, insurance companies and sovereign wealth funds started allocating capital to private credit at scale.

Technology platforms improved loan origination and monitoring. Private credit funds started financing projects ranging from data centres to student housing. What had once been a fragmented corner of the market gradually institutionalised.

Private real estate debt did not appear in opposition to banks. Instead, it developed alongside them, addressing parts of the market where regulatory constraints made bank lending harder.

In many ways, this evolution represents a return to an older financial model, one in which private capital plays a central role in lending against real assets. History, in other words, had come full circle. Once again, lending adapted to economic reality.

This is the story of private real estate debt. This book explores that evolution in depth.

Chapter 1 begins where this introduction ends: in the aftermath of the Global Financial Crisis, when regulatory reforms reshaped the economics of bank lending and non-bank lenders moved from the margins towards the centre of the market.

The chapter examines this transformation from multiple perspectives. We start by analysing how the financial crisis and the sweeping regulatory reforms that followed—from Basel III to Dodd-Frank—fundamentally changed bank balance sheets and reduced the appetite of traditional lenders for certain types of real estate finance.

From there, the book moves from macro forces to market practice. We examine how private real estate debt deals are structured and executed in the real world, drawing on case studies that illustrate how alternative lenders finance projects that fall outside conventional banking templates.

The narrative then turns to the capital behind these loans. Institutional investors—including pension funds, insurers, sovereign wealth funds, family offices and asset managers—have become the quiet architects of this market, allocating capital to private real estate debt in search of stable income, diversification and long-term resilience.

Subsequent chapters explore how borrowers themselves have adapted to this new landscape, increasingly turning to private lenders for flexibility, speed and tailored capital structures. We also examine how financial technology, Artificial Intelligence (AI) and data are reshaping how loans are originated, underwritten and monitored.

Finally, the book looks ahead to the future of the market: the growing institutionalisation of private real estate debt, the evolving regulatory environment, more stringent Environmental, Social and Governance (ESG) requirements from institutional investors and the role that private capital is likely to play in financing the built environment in the decades to come.

Yet below the complexity lies a simple truth. Real estate lending has always been cyclical, adaptive and deeply intertwined with power. The institutions may change and the structures may evolve, but the underlying challenge remains the same: allocating capital against land in an increasingly uncertain world.

Private real estate debt is not an anomaly. It is the latest chapter in a very old story.

CHAPTER 1

After the Crisis: The Rise of Non-Bank Lending

STABILISING THE CORE, SHIFTING THE EDGES

> *The problems faced by banks during the financial crisis and the tougher bank regulation that followed have increased the scope for nonbank sources of credit, such as private lending. Properly managed, private lending could increase the efficiency and resilience of the financial system, but more visibility for regulators will be needed to ensure that private lending is not a destabilising force in periods of financial and economic stress.*
>
> —Dr. Ben Bernanke, Former Chair of the US Federal Reserve (2006–2014)

In the autumn of 2008, the world watched with mounting dread as headlines blared of collapsing banks and billions in investor wealth wiped out. It felt less like a correction and more like a creeping crisis that spilled from the financial pages to the breakfast tables of ordinary households, unsettling even those who'd never so much as glanced at the markets, from cautious pensioners to grannies clutching their savings. But the tremors turned into a full-blown rupture on Monday 15 September, when Lehman Brothers—a 158-year-old institution once thought untouchable—went under. Just like that, 25,000 jobs were gone. Confidence vanished overnight. And the financial world tilted on its axis. In the days and weeks that followed, credit markets seized up, interbank lending ground to a halt and the spectre of total financial collapse no longer felt hypothetical. It was uncomfortably close to home. Newspapers across the world carried apocalyptic headlines, likening the moment to 1929, or worse.

> Why did no one see it coming?
>
> —Queen Elizabeth II

The collapse set off a chain reaction that no regulator, no central bank and no global leader could fully contain. Financial giants—not just on Wall Street, but in the City of London, Frankfurt, Tokyo and beyond—buckled under the strain. Markets tumbled. Liquidity evaporated. And the engine of the global economy stalled, ushering in the deepest downturn since the Great Depression some 80 years earlier.

Figure 1.1 illustrates just how sharply the world's largest banks were repriced during the crisis. Financial giants once seen as unshakeable lost tens—and in some cases hundreds—of billions of dollars in market value within months, signalling a systemic shock that reverberated far beyond the financial sector.

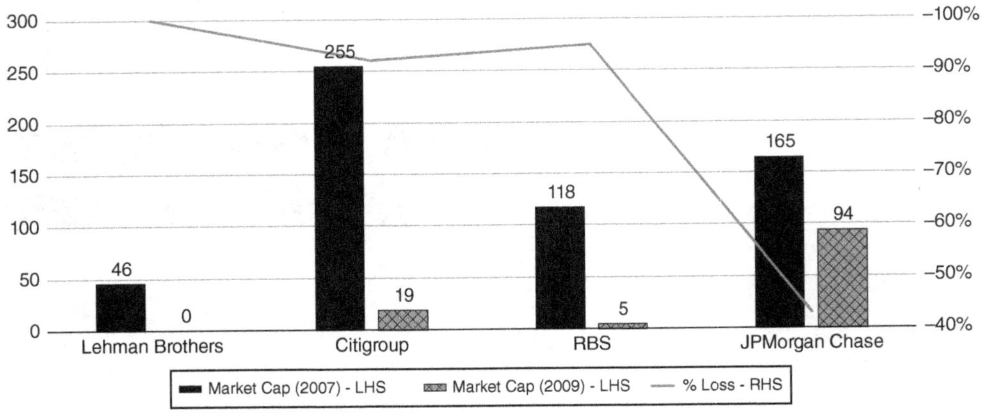

FIGURE 1.1 How the Crisis Wiped Out Bank Market Value

But the turmoil didn't stay confined to financial markets for long. The shock quickly spilled into the real economy, with the housing market among the first to unravel. House prices went into freefall. In the US alone, nearly nine million people would find themselves out of work over the next two years. Millions more across the globe faced the same grim reality. Governments scrambled to stem the bleeding, stepping in with eye-popping bailouts, pumping billions into tottering banks in a desperate bid to contain the chaos.

By the time the dust began to settle, the damage was staggering: an estimated USD 10 trillion in losses, the equivalent of more than one-sixth of global GDP in 2008. The financial system had been shaken to its very core. Figure 1.2 shows how the S&P 500's sudden slide marked the beginning of a wider, synchronised downturn that swept across global markets. Nothing would ever be quite the same again.

As the worst of the panic began to ebb, nearly 500 banks in America alone had collapsed. But perhaps the most profound damage wasn't visible in the immediate wreckage: it lay in what the crisis had laid bare: that the financial system, as it stood, was riddled with structural flaws. The rules that had governed lending and risk-taking were full of blind spots: some obvious in hindsight, others long ignored. And those blind spots made reform not only necessary, but sorely overdue.

When I discussed the structural roots of the crisis with Lord Adair Turner, former chair of the UK Financial Services Authority (FSA), he offered a characteristically clear diagnosis of the deeper problem.

> The fundamental problem is that modern financial systems, left to themselves, inevitably create debt in excessive quantities—particularly debt that funds the purchase of existing assets rather than productive new investment, above all in real estate. It is this pattern of debt creation that drives booms and financial busts. But the lesson of the past two decades is not simply that real estate debt is dangerous—it is that how debt is structured, governed and allocated matters profoundly.
>
> —Lord Adair Turner, Baron Turner of Ecchinswell, Former Chair of the UK Financial Services Authority (2008–2013)

FIGURE 1.2 When the S&P 500 Plunged During the Crisis

In the years that followed, policymakers around the globe set about picking up the pieces and rebuilding the system from the ground up. Regulators—from the Federal Reserve in the US to the European Commission, the UK's Prudential Regulation Authority and global standard-setters like the G20 and the Basel Committee—began rolling out a raft of new rules and recommendations designed to make banks safer, sounder and less prone to going bust. Capital buffers were beefed up, leverage rained in and rigorous stress tests introduced. It was, in many ways, a belt-and-braces approach, a wholesale re-engineering of the banking system aimed at avoiding another catastrophic collapse.

When I spoke with Professor Ben Bernanke, the man who helped steer the Federal Reserve through those defining years, one insight stood out: the post-crisis effort to shore up the financial system carried an unexpected twist. As he recounted during our discussion, in trying to make banking safer, regulators also set the stage for something entirely new: the ascent of private credit.

> The more you tighten your grip, Tarkin, the more star systems will slip through your fingers.
>
> —Princess Leia, Star Wars: A New Hope

As traditional banks came under tighter regulation and scrutiny, they also became markedly more cautious, particularly when it came to lending. Borrowers, especially

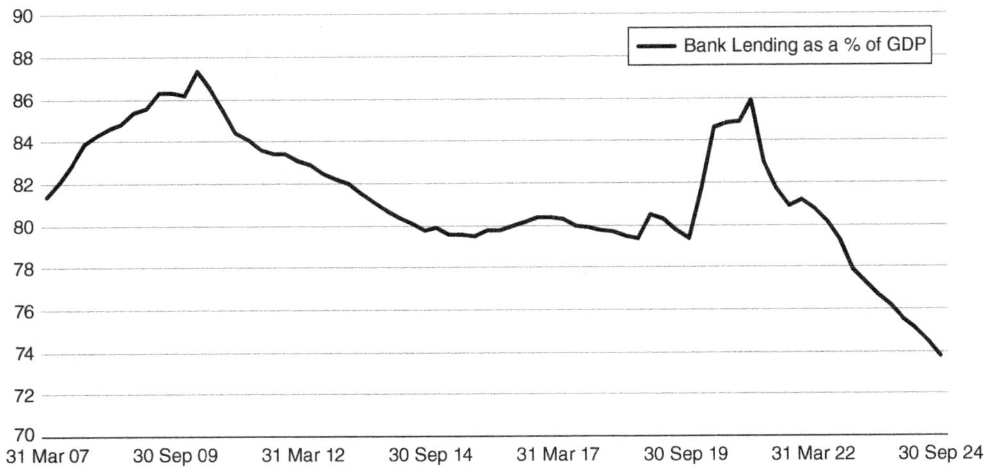

FIGURE 1.3 How Banks' Retreat Opened the Door for Private Credit

in the property sector, began to find that access to credit had narrowed dramatically. Deals that would once have breezed through credit committees before the crisis were now deemed too complex, too risky, too illiquid or simply more bother than it's worth for a banking system newly allergic to risk. Figure 1.3 shows that bank lending as a proportion of GDP has been on a steady downwards trajectory ever since.

That created an opening for a new breed of lender: private credit providers operating outside the regulatory paraphernalia of high street banks. What began as a temporary workaround for a gummed-up system soon morphed into a structural shift. Private credit was no longer just a stopgap; it became the backbone of a new lending ecosystem.

This chapter unpacks that transition: how a confluence of regulation, macroeconomic pressures and shifting investor appetite gave rise to a more fragmented and diverse landscape in real estate finance. We explore the rise of private credit providers, stepping into the breach left by the banks and helping to redraw the map of modern lending.

Through a series of global case studies and exclusive conversations with those who had a front-row seat in the process, we'll chart the arch of this transformation, from its early stirrings in post-crisis America to its spread across continental Europe, the UK and beyond. Along the way, we'll see how the motives of investors, borrowers and regulators intersected—and occasionally collided—to create the new normal in property finance.

But to understand how we got here, we must first rewind to the decisions made in the fog of the financial crisis because what escapes the spotlight often rewrites the script.

> You can't connect the dots looking forward; you can only connect them looking backwards.
>
> —Steve Jobs, Co-Founder and Former CEO, Apple Inc.

During my conversation with Professor Bernanke, he offered sharp insights into how early policy choices—meant to steady the ship—also ended up reshaping the financial landscape. His reflections help explain why, almost two decades on, the real estate lending market looks markedly different from the one that came crashing down in 2008.

This is the story of how capital slipped through the cracks of traditional finance, and where it ended up instead. It shows that what the system missed became the market's next move.

REBUILDING THE SYSTEM AFTER THE CRISIS

The collapse of the financial system in 2008 didn't just shake confidence in the markets, it shattered faith in the rules that were meant to keep those markets in check. Governments, regulators and global institutions quickly grasped that the crisis hadn't simply been the result of poor judgement, it had been made possible by a system fundamentally unfit for purpose.

In the scramble that followed, world leaders convened under the G20 umbrella, determined to ensure history wouldn't repeat itself. The task was urgent: mend the cracks in the global financial architecture and redraw the rulebook from scratch. They handed the brief to the Financial Stability Board (FSB)—a body made up of central bankers and regulators from across the globe—to coordinate a sweeping overhaul of financial regulation.

The ambition was bold but essential: to build a system that could serve the real economy—businesses, households, high streets and communities—without leaning on the kind of unchecked, short-term risk-taking that had come to define the pre-crisis era.

> Regulation should aim to be simple and robust ... and the authorities should maintain a clear focus on the issues that matter when the worst occurs—liquidity and leverage.
>
> —Mervyn King, Former Governor of the Bank of England (2003–2013)

What followed was nothing short of a regulatory overhaul, a shift as consequential as the New Deal-era reforms that reshaped the American financial system after the crash of 1929.

Across jurisdictions, lawmakers introduced a raft of tougher rules for banks: steeper capital requirements, tighter lending standards, stress testing as standard and firmer oversight of liquidity and leverage. These reforms, while trying to fix the roof after the rain, were meant to make banks more robust and better able to weather the next big shock. And in many respects, they did just that.

But there was a catch.

As banks became more tightly regulated, their capacity—and therefore their appetite—to lend began to wane. This was especially true in sectors like property and small-to-medium-sized enterprises (SMEs), where risks are trickier to price and returns much harder to pin down. The system had indeed been stabilised, but the gears had slowed.

The data in Figure 1.4 tells the tale: Commercial Real Estate (CRE) loans have steadily declined as a share of total bank deposits since 2007. What had once been a

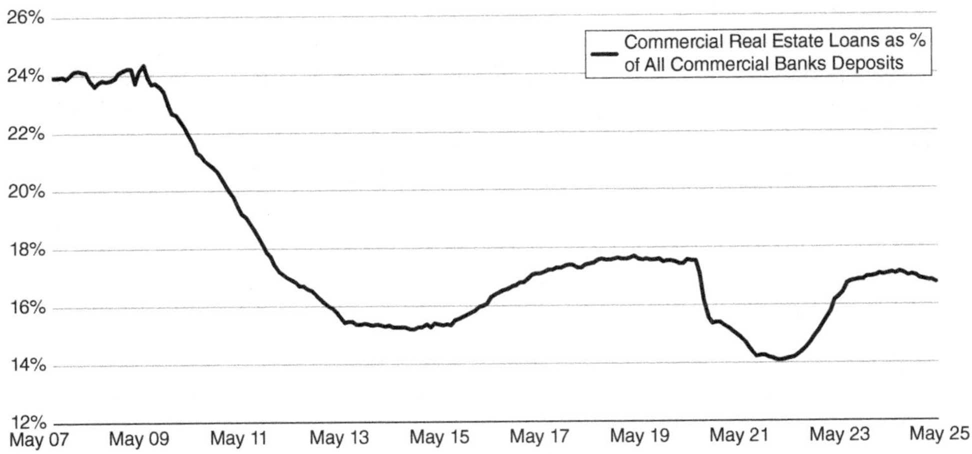

FIGURE 1.4 Tighter Rules and the Retreat of Bank CRE Lending
Source: Data from Federal Reserve Bank of St. Louis

natural pairing—deposits funding local developments—began to unravel and into that gap stepped a new generation of non-bank lenders.

That's where private credit stepped in.

Let's be clear, though: private credit wasn't dreamt up in the aftermath of the 2008 financial crisis—as explored in the introduction, private lending is as old as money itself—but the crisis gave it a shot in the arm. The post-crisis rulebook reshaped the risk-reward balance for high street banks and traditional lenders alike, leaving a gaping hole in the market. And where there's a gap, someone invariably steps in to fill it, often with a touch of ingenuity and a keen eye for opportunity.

> Nature abhors a vacuum.
>
> —Aristotle

This is the backdrop against which real estate private credit began to evolve. From niche, opportunistic plays into a global, institutional force. But to make sense of that evolution, we first need to look under the bonnet of the post-crisis reforms.

What precisely changed in the wake of the crash? Which new rules nudged banks to rein in their lending? And how did those shifts open the door for non-bank lenders to step into the breach, often more nimbly, more swiftly and with far fewer strings attached?

In the sections that follow, we unpack the regulatory reset that reshaped global finance, and in the process, redrew the boundaries of who lends, how and to whom.

DODD-FRANK, BASEL III AND THE NEW LENDING RULEBOOK

In the smouldering aftermath of the 2008 financial collapse, as public anger reached fever pitch and calls for reform echoed through Washington, Brussels and beyond, lawmakers responded with bold intervention and legislative thunderclap. On 21 July 2010, the Dodd-Frank Wall Street Reform and Consumer Protection Act—named after Senator Chris Dodd, then Chairman of the Senate Banking Committee and Representative Barney Frank, then Chairman of the House Financial Services Committee—was signed into law. Spanning over 2,300 pages of dense legislative intent aimed at ensuring such a catastrophe would never happen again, Dodd-Frank wasn't just a bill; it was a blueprint for a new financial order. For regulators, it was nothing short of a dream: sprawling, prescriptive and designed to leave no stone unturned in the banking system. For the industry, it was the beginning of a new era of oversight, red tape and constraint.

The thinking was clear, if not exactly straightforward: banks had become too powerful, too reckless and far too lightly policed. Dodd-Frank sought to rein them in. It expanded the state's role in financial regulation, imposed tighter capital and leverage requirements and made the business of lending—particularly the riskier kind—far more arduous. At its heart, the Act was a full-throated attempt to bolster the resilience of the banking system. But in doing so, it also quietly shifted the economics of credit. Lending became more costly, more regulated and far, far less profitable, especially for those parts of the market at the sharper end of the risk spectrum.

> For every action, there is an equal and opposite reaction.
>
> —Isaac Newton

Just a few months later, on 16 December 2010, the Basel Committee on Banking Supervision—made up of central bankers and regulators from across the globe—introduced its own set of sweeping reforms. Basel III, as the new framework came to be known, didn't appear out of thin air. It was the third instalment in a regulatory saga that had started decades earlier. Basel I, unveiled in 1988, was the first stab at global capital standards, a kind of regulatory safety net underneath the world's banks. Basel II followed in 2004, adding layers of risk sensitivity and new tools for supervision and market discipline. But when the financial crisis struck, those earlier rulebooks didn't hold up. They simply were no longer fit for purpose.

Then came Basel III: the global answer to Dodd-Frank. While Washington's response was loud, political and played out in the full glare of the media, Basel III was hashed out quietly behind closed doors, drafted by technocrats with spreadsheets instead of soapboxes. It didn't grab headlines, but it rewrote the rulebook, nonetheless, with beefed-up capital buffers, stricter liquidity ratios and sharper risk controls. Regulation, but with a clipboard instead of a stick: painstaking, dry as dust at times, but absolutely vital to stop the system getting derailed again.

The core issue both Dodd-Frank and Basel III aimed to tackle was straightforward: too many banks had entered the crisis with balance sheets that looked fine on paper, but were, in reality, as solid as a sandcastle at high tide.

WHEN CAPITAL RULES CHANGED THE GAME

Sometimes, the most consequential shifts in financial history don't come with brass bands or banner headlines, but from dense, easily overlooked clauses tucked away in the small print of sprawling legislation. Such was the case with Section 171 of the Dodd-Frank Act containing leverage and risk-based capital requirements, better known, at least among policy wonks, as the Collins Amendment. Named after Senator Susan Collins of Maine, this subtly powerful provision would go on to have an outsized impact on the business of real estate lending across the US financial system.

At first glance, the Collins Amendment seemed like common sense, a belt-and-braces rule meant to keep the banking giants on the straight and narrow. It required that large financial institutions—whether US bank holding companies or foreign banks operating stateside—all stick to the same capital requirements that applied to traditional banks, those insured by the Federal Deposit Insurance Corporation (FDIC). On the surface, it was about consistency, a level playing field and a bit of good old-fashioned prudence. But the devil, as ever, was in the detail.

> Small hinges swing big doors.
>
> —Anonymous

The Collins Amendment required top-tier financial institutions to calculate their capital requirements in two ways: once using their own fancy internal risk models called the Advanced Approach (AA) and again using a rule-based regulatory formula known as the Standardised Approach (SA). Whichever approach produced the higher number would become the one that counted. Sounds sensible enough and conservative in every way. But tucked away in this seemingly harmless rule was a subtle yet seismic shift that would quietly reshape the future of real estate development finance.

For years, banks had leaned heavily on internal risk models that drew on detailed, institution-specific data: tools designed to reflect the actual risk of their portfolios more accurately than the standardised formula. The result often was a more favourable, if not necessarily sunnier, picture of their balance sheets. Senior real estate loans, in particular, were frequently given low risk weights, based on past performance and internal assumptions. The upshot? These loans looked capital-light and commercially attractive, safe enough to justify large exposures without tying up too much precious regulatory capital.

But the SA told a very different story. It was based on one-size-fits-all formulas that assigned much higher risk weights to real estate exposures, especially those tied to development projects: assets notorious for their complexity, long timelines and sensitivity to economic cycles. Once the Collins Amendment kicked in, banks could no longer rely on their own models to justify lower capital charges. The regulator's more cautious, conservative view became binding, effectively stripping away the capital efficiency that had made development lending so appealing.

The impact was swift and decisive. Development finance, once a comfortable stomping ground for banks, suddenly became a weighted burden on their balance sheets. The lights went out overnight. Many chose to pull back, redirecting capital towards assets with friendlier capital treatment. Into the void stepped a new wave of lenders—private credit funds, insurance companies and non-bank institutions—ready to seize the moment and reshape the lay of the land in real estate finance.

To understand how the Collins Amendment worked in practice, let's imagine a fictional bank—Midland Commercial Bank (MCB)—navigating the post-Dodd-Frank and Basel III regime. MCB held USD 50 million in senior CRE loans on its balance sheet.

Under the SA, real estate loans typically carried a risk weight of 100%, meaning the entire exposure counted towards the bank's Risk-Weighted Asset (RWA) calculation. Under the AA, however, MCB wasn't relying on broad regulatory formulas. It had built bespoke, in-house risk models over many years, drawing on granular, loan-level data: borrower credit scores, Loan-To-Value (LTV) ratios, debt service coverage ratios, property types, geographic spread and historical performance metrics. For a portfolio of well-underwritten senior commercial property loans—particularly those secured by high-quality assets and backed by borrowers with strong credit profiles—the models often justified far lower risk weights.

In MCB's case, the portfolio was made up of low-risk, income-producing assets, with prudent LTVs and strong borrower profiles. Historical loss rates on similar exposures were minimal. As a result, let's assume that MCB's internal models assigned a risk weight of just 33% to its CRE loan portfolio, a reflection of what it saw as low probability of default and a high degree of collateral protection. From the bank's perspective, this wasn't aggressive modelling. It was simply risk-sensitive, data-driven lending. But under the Collins Amendment, even robust internal models like MCB's could be cast aside in favour of the regulator's one-size-fits-all approach.

Under the Collins Amendment, MCB could no longer just use the lower figure. It had to run both sets of calculations—and use whichever approach resulted in the higher RWA. Table 1.1 shows the impact on MCB's Return on Equity (ROE) under each scenario.

For MCB, the numbers told two very different tales. Under the AA, the bank's internal models painted a picture of efficiency: real estate loans looked like smart, low-risk bets with strong ROEs. It was the sort of lending that made commercial sense and kept shareholders happy. But the SA was less forgiving, to say the least. All of a sudden, the same portfolio appeared far more capital-intensive, dragging down returns and making the deal look far less appealing on paper. And thanks to the Collins

TABLE 1.1 Midland Commercial Bank Capital Requirement Comparison

	Standardised Approach (SA)	Advanced Approach (AA)
Notional Value of Loans (USDm)	50	50
Risk Weight (%)	100%	33%
Risk Weight (USDm)	50	16.5
CET1 Capital Requirement at 4.5% (USDm)	2.25	0.74
Cost of Bank Capital at 12% (USDm)	0.27	0.09
Post-Expense Net Spread at 0.75% (USDm)	0.38	0.38
Net Income After Cost of Capital (USDm)	0.11	0.29
Return on Equity (ROE)	4.7%	38.5%

Amendment, there was no room for manoeuvre: the regulator's more conservative view took precedence. MCB was suddenly forced to hold capital against the higher risk-weighted number, effectively penalising its development lending and pushing the bank to rethink where—and how—it deployed its balance sheet. The gloves were off.

BASEL III REDEFINES BANKING STRENGTH

Alongside the Collins Amendment to the Dodd-Frank Act, Basel III quietly tore up the old rulebook on what it meant to be a resilient bank. At its core were two powerful tools designed to prevent another global financial collapse: capital ratios, to measure the quality and quantity of a bank's shock-absorbing cushion and leverage ratios, a no-nonsense check on how far banks could stretch their balance sheets. Together, they marked a new era of discipline in global finance, one where strength wasn't just about profit but about staying power.

While capital ratios weren't new—they had existed in earlier Basel frameworks—Basel III transformed them from a box-ticking exercise into a true test of strength by tightening the definition of what counted as 'real' capital. It sharpened the definition of capital by placing a premium on so called Common Equity Tier 1 (CET1): the purest form of capital, made up of good old-fashioned ordinary shares, capable of absorbing losses without triggering broader panic. It also introduced harsher rules for what are known as Additional Tier 1 (AT1) instruments: perpetual bonds that could be written down or converted into equity if a bank ran into trouble.

But Basel III didn't just stop at tightening the rules for top-tier capital. It also turned its attention to what regulators call Tier 2 capital—the second line of defence in a bank's capital stack. This included things like subordinated debt, preference shares with loss-absorbing features, hybrid capital instruments and Loan-Loss Reserves (LLRs). Though not quite the gold standard like CET1, Tier 2 capital still played a vital role in helping banks weather a storm. Regulators wanted to ensure these instruments weren't just window dressing—they had to be genuinely loss-absorbing, and they had to work the same way across different countries. The goal was consistency, resilience and credibility. Whether a bank was based in Frankfurt or Johannesburg, the new Basel III rules applied right across the board: a global standard, regardless of geography.

These weren't just a few tweaks around the edges, they were a seismic shift. Before Basel III, banks needed just 4% of Tier 1 capital against their RWAs, and only half of that had to be CET1. Basel III raised the bar. The minimum Tier 1 capital was nudged up to 6%, with CET1 rising to 4.5%, while the remaining 1.5% could come from other instruments such as preferred shares. It was like someone flipped a switch, and everything stopped.

The Collins Amendment went even further in tightening the definitions of capital by eliminating hybrid capital instruments. Those once-handy, part-debt, part-equity securities were no longer welcome in the Tier 1 category. Only the purest forms of equity now counted towards a bank's core capital cushion.

But that was just the beginning. On top of this, regulators added a so-called Capital Conservation Buffer (CCB): an extra 2.5% of CET1 that every bank had to hold during the good times, like financial fat reserves to be dipped into in tougher periods. Then came the Countercyclical Capital Buffer (CCyB), an additional flexible layer of capital that national regulators could dial up or down depending on credit conditions in their own economies. Not every bank had to hold it, but those in fast-growing or overheating markets often did, and the CCyB could reach up to 2.5% of CET1 on top of the rest.

Add it all up and some of the world's largest, most systemically important banks faced capital requirements of 11% or more, a far cry from the measly 2% of CET1 they needed to have under earlier rules. But this wasn't just about more capital. It was about better capital too. Basel III aimed to build a tougher, more shock-resistant system, one where banks could take hits without toppling. It was nothing less than a full-scale rewiring of the global banking safety net.

Yet, as history so often reminds us, reforms can have ripple effects that go far beyond their original intent. In this case, the message to banks was crystal clear: hold more capital, lend more prudently and steer clear of risks that might land you in the regulator's bad books. And so they did.

> Every act of creation is first an act of destruction.
>
> —Pablo Picasso

To understand how the new risk-based capital requirements worked in practice, let's return to MCB—our fictional but representative mid-sized bank—navigating the post-Dodd-Frank and Basel III world. MCB held a mix of assets on its balance sheet: a tidy pot of AAA-rated sovereign bonds and cash, residential mortgages, CRE loans and unsecured personal loans. As Table 1.2 shows, these assets differed significantly in their underlying risk profiles.

Regulators now demanded that MCB assign a risk weight to each of the assets it held to calculate how much capital it needed to set aside, a kind of regulatory price tag that set how much capital the bank would have to keep in reserve. Cash and top-tier government bonds, rated AAA to AA-, were treated as the crown jewels of safety: risk weight zero. In banking terms, that's about as close to a free pass as you'll ever get.

Residential mortgages, however, were another story. These were split into two camps. The first covered owner-occupied mortgages, loans not materially dependent on the property's cash flow. The second included buy-to-let mortgages, where repayment relied squarely on rental income. For each, the capital burden would now hinge on the LTV ratio, the regulator's shorthand for how much skin the borrower had in the game.

TABLE 1.2 Midland Commercial Bank Balance Sheet

Cash and Government Bonds (USDm)	50	Very Low Risk
Residential Mortgages (USDm)	90	Medium Risk
Commercial Real Estate Loans (USDm)	50	Higher Risk
Unsecured Personal Loans (USDm)	20	High Risk

For owner-occupied mortgages, risk weights stepped up gradually: 20% for loans under 50% LTV, rising to 70% for those exceeding 100%. A typical 75% LTV home loan? About a 30% risk weight. Buy-to-let mortgages were treated with a bit more caution. Here, the same 75% LTV loan would attract a 45% risk weight and at the extremes—loans above 100% LTV—the figure could soar to 105%.

CRE lending fared even worse. These loans were generally slapped with the full 100% risk weight, sometimes even more—up to 150%—depending on the borrower's credit quality or the project's risk profile. And unsecured personal loans? They sat firmly at the bottom of the regulatory food chain, punished with a steep 150% risk weight, the price of volatility in its purest form.

The new regime stood in stark contrast with the pre-2008 framework. Before the 2008 crisis, banks had operated under simpler regimes. Basel I, for instance, applied a blunt instrument approach: 50% risk weights for residential mortgages, 100% for CRE, regardless of the LTV ratios, borrower profile or asset quality. Basel II tried to improve on this by allowing more sophisticated institutions to use internal ratings-based models, but it hadn't been widely adopted before the crisis struck in 2008.

Table 1.3 illustrates how this varying risk weights translated into the overall capital requirements for MCB's portfolio, showing the composition of the bank's risk-weighted assets under both typical and more conservative regulatory scenarios.

Let's assume that MCB has USD 15 million in Tier 1 capital (equity and retained earnings). When MCB ran the numbers, its USD 15 million in Tier 1 capital needed to support USD 178.5 million in RWAs, producing a Tier 1 capital ratio of 8.4%. On paper, the bank ticked all the right boxes: it met its Tier 1 regulatory requirements of 6% and comfortably cleared the 4.5% CET1 hurdle. But in practice, it was

TABLE 1.3 Midland Commercial Bank RWA Under Basel I and Basel III

Asset Type	Exposure (USDm)	Baseline Risk Weight (Basel I) RWA %	Baseline RWA (USDm)	Refined Risk Weight (Basel III/IV—Worst Case)	Refined RWA (USDm)
Cash and Government Bonds (AAA-AA-)	50	0%	0	0%	0
Residential Mortgages (Owner-Occupied, 75% LTV)	60	50%	30	30–70% (worst case 70%)	42
Buy-to-Let Mortgages (75% LTV)	30	50%	15	45–105% (worst case 105%)	31.5
Commercial Real Estate Loans	50	100%	50	100–150% (worst case 150%)	75
Unsecured Personal Loans	20	100%	20	150% (stricter calibration)	30
Total RWA (USDm)	210	-	115	-	178.5

beginning to understand a new reality: under the new rules, some lines of business were starting to look more trouble than they were worth.

Tier 1 capital ratio = Tier 1 capital/RWA = USDm 15/USDm 178.5 = 8.4%

Basel III's more granular risk weights under the SA were intended to fix the shortcomings of its predecessors. And yet, its broad-brush treatment of real estate—especially development and construction lending—rather missed the mark. Not all projects carried the same risk. Many posed far less risk than their assigned weightings suggested, but the new rules didn't make room for nuance. Banks were left holding far more capital than the actual risk warranted.

All of this created a clear and powerful incentive: either shrink RWAs or raise more capital. Most banks, quite understandably, chose the former. One lender I spoke with, who worked at a traditional bank during this transition, described the atmosphere as 'managed retreat'. The calculus had changed. Lending to real estate projects—particularly development—was no longer simply a question of credit quality or borrower strength. It became a question of capital efficiency. Deals that once made sense on their own merits now had to justify the regulatory capital they consumed. And increasingly, they couldn't.

He recalled how deals that would once have sailed through credit committee now began to stall under new capital hurdles. 'It wasn't that the projects were bad' he said, 'they just didn't stack up anymore: not for us'.

In that moment, the definition of a 'good loan' was quietly rewritten. It was no longer just about risk and return, but about how efficiently a loan used scarce balance sheet. And in that new equation, many real estate deals—especially those requiring time, flexibility and judgement—simply fell out of favour.

THE BLUNT EDGE OF SAFETY AND THE BANK RETREAT

Basel III didn't just tighten the screws. It hammered the message home. Alongside beefing up existing capital requirements, it introduced a new tool in the regulatory arsenal: the non-risk-based leverage ratio, with a minimum threshold of 3%. This was arguably the final straw that shifted bank's attitudes towards lending. For the business of lending, the leverage ratio was a game changer.

If risk-based capital ratios were designed with nuance and fine-tuning, the leverage ratio was their blunter cousin: less sophisticated, but no less influential. Unlike risk-weighted measures that could be massaged with complex models and rosy assumptions, the leverage ratio took a blunt but powerful approach, measuring the bank's capital against its total exposures, on and off the books. The ratio didn't care how safe or risky an asset looked on paper. It simply capped how far a bank could stretch its balance sheet, no matter the cleverness of its risk models.

Effectively, the leverage ratio was a simple test: how much core capital does a bank hold relative to the size of its entire asset base, regardless of how risky those assets might be. It was a safeguard, a floor underneath the safety net, ensuring that no amount of financial engineering could disguise an overstretched balance sheet. In other

TABLE 1.4 Midland Commercial Bank Total Assets

Cash and Government Bonds (USDm)	50	Very Low Risk
Residential Mortgages (USDm)	90	Medium Risk
Commercial Real Estate Loans (USDm)	50	Higher Risk
Unsecured Personal Loans (USDm)	20	High Risk
Total Assets (USDm)	210	

words, it didn't matter if a loan was made to a blue-chip company or a highly leveraged property developer: on the balance sheet, all assets were treated the same way.

In practice, this no-nonsense constraint made it far less appealing for banks to fund long-term, capital-intensive projects such as property development. Margins were tight, timelines lengthy and the leverage ratio made every pound lent feel heavier. For banks already feeling the pinch from stricter capital rules, it was a game changer.

To see it in action, let's go back to MCB, our fictional but familiar mid-sized lender. MCB had a diverse portfolio: USD 50 million in AAA-rated sovereign bonds, USD 90 million in residential mortgages (a mix of owner-occupied and buy-to-let), USD 50 million in CRE loans and USD 20 million in unsecured personal loans. That's USD 210 million in total assets. Table 1.4 sets out the composition of that balance sheet.

Now imagine MCB held USD 15 million in Tier 1 capital, its most solid form of equity and retained earnings. Its leverage ratio would be:

Leverage Ratio = Tier 1 Capital/Total Assets = USDm 15/USDm 210 = 7.1%

That would comfortably clear the Basel III minimum of 3%. But what mattered wasn't just the number. It was what it represented. For the first time, banks were being told, in no uncertain terms, to hold capital not just against risk, but against sheer scale. The leverage ratio, in effect, acted as a hard floor, a line in the sand. It didn't care about how diversified or prudently managed the bank's book was. It simply put a cap on how large a balance sheet could grow based on the capital behind it. A blunt instrument, to be sure, but regulators meant business.

THE VOLCKER RULE'S HIDDEN IMPACT

And then came another blow: the Volcker Rule. Part of the Dodd-Frank reforms and named after Paul Volcker, who served as the Chairman of the US Federal Reserve from 1979 to 1987, this rule aimed to prevent banks from making speculative investments with their own capital. This practice had spectacularly backfired in the lead-up to the 2008 crisis. While the Volcker Rule wasn't directly aimed at traditional lending activities such as real estate development finance, it had meaningful knock-on effects that shaped bank behaviour and strategy, particularly in how they thought about risk, return and regulatory scrutiny.

Paul Volcker's rule sought not only to restrict proprietary trading but to re-establish a moral firewall between insured banking and speculative activity. As he put it, 'If you are going to be a commercial bank, with all the protections that implies, you shouldn't be doing this stuff. If you are doing this stuff, you shouldn't be a commercial bank'.

He later lamented how critics claimed the regulation had become too heavy-handed, reflecting his belief that the original intent got lost in implementation: 'They got it wrong in any broad sense... They say it is too complicated we can't do it'.

In practise, the Volcker Rule added yet another layer of complexity and compliance risk to already tightly regulated activities. Although it didn't explicitly ban real estate lending, it certainly discouraged banks from dabbling in activities that looked speculative or illiquid, especially if it meant tying up significant amounts of capital on the books for long periods, as is often the case with development loans. These loans often involve long durations, delayed cash flows and market-cycle exposure, the sort of thing that might raise a few eyebrows post-Volcker.

The rule also marked a broader regulatory shift towards de-risking and tightening controls over how banks used their balance sheets. This fostered a culture of increased caution, where banks began to steer away from anything that remotely looked like proprietary risk-taking, including development finance, which can be seen as speculative, especially in early-stage or non-income-producing phases.

The message was clear as day: real estate risk no longer belonged on bank books. And so the great retreat began. Some banks exited real estate lending entirely. Others quietly shifted risky exposures off their books. Not long after the Volcker Rule was publicly endorsed by President Obama on 21 January 2010, Citigroup agreed to sell its real estate investment management arm, Citi Property Investors (CPI), to Apollo Global Management on 13 November 2010. The transaction was an early signal that a seismic shift was underway.

THE 150% PROBLEM: HVCRE

The regulatory shifts we have just described set the stage for what came next: by the early 2010s, banks had already begun quietly retrenching from the world of real estate development finance. The scars of the Global Financial Crisis were still fresh and risk appetite was waning. Still, it was only after 2015—when a new regulatory regime took effect—that the retreat became more pronounced.

The so called High Volatility CRE rule—or HVCRE, as it became known—might sound like a dry technical footnote in the sweeping post-crisis reforms, but for many banks, it was the final straw. Officially implemented in the US on 1 January 2015, the rule targeted a specific subset of loans: Acquisition, Development and Construction (ADC) financing, especially those that were considered speculative or under-capitalised. If a borrower hadn't put at least 15% equity in the deal, or if the project lacked stable cash flow from income-producing assets, the loan would be classified as HVCRE. And with that label came a harsh penalty—a whopping 150% risk weight, 50% higher than the standard treatment.

The impact was immediate. For banks already under pressure to optimise capital usage, the numbers no longer stacked up. Development loans—once a lucrative staple of commercial lending desks—were now capital-hungry liabilities. Even those institutions that had cautiously remained in the space began to exit. The business case had quietly unravelled.

To avoid the HVCRE designation, some banks tried to stay in the game by tightening credit terms. Borrowers were invited to bring more equity to the table, secure pre-lease agreements, or defer projects until they looked less speculative. But these tweaks did little to ease the capital burden. If anything, they pushed developers, famously asset-rich but cash-poor, further towards the outstretched arms of non-bank lenders. These alternative players weren't just willing to lend; they tailored their terms, moved faster and spoke the language of real estate developers. Slowly but surely, banks shifted their appetite elsewhere, towards safe assets that were easier to underwrite and friendlier from a capital perspective.

Meanwhile, the rules themselves caused no small amount of head-scratching. Lenders, lawyers and regulators spent years trying to interpret the fine print. What exactly qualified as 'substantial equity'? Did an income-producing component make a project exempt? In response to industry outcry, lawmakers passed reforms in 2018 under the Economic Growth, Regulatory Relief and Consumer Protection Act, narrowing the scope and rebranding the framework as HVCRE ADC. But by then, the market had already adapted and moved on.

The damage—or the opportunity, depending on your vantage point—had been done. A vacuum emerged where banks had once operated. And into that vacuum flowed a new class of lenders: private credit funds, insurance companies and alternative finance platforms, many of them backed by the very institutions that had once competed for mandates from banks.

In short, the HVCRE rule didn't just tweak the calculus of development lending. It reshaped the playing field. And in doing so, it helped catalyse one of the most significant power shifts in modern real estate finance.

THE ERA OF CHEAP CAPITAL

As we've already seen, the aftermath of the Global Financial Crisis ushered in a regulatory reckoning that fundamentally reshaped the way banks operated. Banks were hit with stricter capital requirements, heavier supervision and a tangle of new rules designed to rein in risky behaviour. For real estate finance, this meant banks increasingly shying away from anything outside plain vanilla deals that carried even the faintest trace of elevated risk: development loans, transitional assets, essentially anything non-core. In effect, the supply of bank credit shrank sharply.

But supply is only half the story.

> One hand cannot clap alone.
>
> —Middle Eastern proverb

Markets, of course, don't move on supply alone. There's always a demand element bubbling away in the background. And in the case of the rise of private real estate credit, that demand was driven—quite powerfully—by the interest rate environment that followed the crash. On the other side of supply sat the capital, still eager, still hungry, but now faced with a significantly reshaped playing field. And the real fuel behind the rise of private real estate credit wasn't just tighter banking rules. It was the monetary earthquake that followed the crisis, one that changed the financial landscape for over a generation.

When the global financial system teetered on the brink of collapse in 2008, central banks were swift to act by loosening monetary policy. Interest rates were slashed across the board at historic speed in a desperate bid to keep the economy from falling off a cliff. As showed in Figure 1.5, in the US, the Federal Reserve slashed rates to near zero. The Bank of England followed close behind. Across Europe and parts of Asia, policymakers went even further, with some countries tiptoeing into negative interest rate territory.

What was meant to be a temporary emergency measure to revive the economy became something far more permanent and turned into a defining feature of the post-crisis decade. In the UK, the Bank of England Bank Rate didn't rise above 0.75% until May 2022, an unprecedented stretch of monetary looseness in the Bank's three-century history. Globally, the 2010s became known as the decade of cheap money.

But interest rates can only be pushed so far. Once they hit rock bottom, they stopped working as a tool to boost the economy. Policymakers had to think outside the box, and cutting rates wasn't the only move central banks made. In the wake of the crisis, Large Scale Asset Purchases (LSAPs), or often simply referred to as Quantitative Easing (QE), quickly became part of policymakers' mainstream toolkit. Effectively, the programme meant central banks around the globe started printing fresh money to buy financial assets

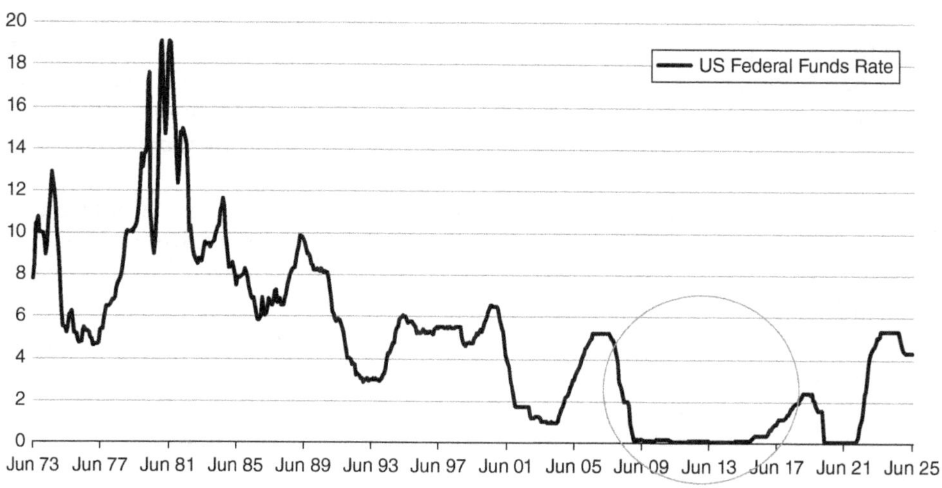

FIGURE 1.5 The Decade of Cheap Money

such as government and corporate bonds. This amounted to directly injecting liquidity into the financial system. Like low interest rates, QE was meant to be a short-term lifeline. Instead, it became a defining feature of the post-crisis decade.

The policy response to the Global Financial Crisis did what it was meant to do: it kept the economy afloat. But as is often the case with bold interventions, the medicine came with side effects. Asset prices soared. Equities, bonds, property, commodities, even currencies, all were swept up in a tidal wave of liquidity. In housing, demand surged while supply remained stubbornly constrained, fuelling sharp price increases and growing affordability concerns.

To understand why, let's take a step back and look at how QE works in practice. Imagine the European Central Bank (ECB) buys EUR 1 million in government bonds from an asset manager. In return, the asset manager now holds EUR 1 million in cash. Holding onto that cash isn't particularly appealing: it earns nothing. So, the asset manager tries to secure better returns elsewhere, perhaps in equities, credit, or even alternative assets. As more investors do the same, prices of these assets start to rise, pushing up valuations and creating a so-called 'wealth effect'. Households feel richer. Businesses can raise capital more easily. Spending ticks up. Investment follows.

But the sheer scale of the post-crisis QE was unlike anything the world had seen before. In November 2008, a mere two months after Lehman Brothers had collapsed, the Fed announced what would become known as QE1. It was a bold plan to flood the system by stepping in to buy hundreds of billions' worth of US home loans: the kind that had fuelled the housing boom in the first place. It was an extraordinary move, but the crisis demanded extraordinary measures.

Then, as the downturn deepened, the Fed doubled down. By the time QE1 wrapped up in March 2010, it had bought USD 1.25 trillion in home loans bundled into securities, USD 175 billion in federal agency debt and USD 300 billion in US Treasuries, sums that would have seemed unthinkable just a year earlier.

The experiment didn't stop there. In November 2010, the Fed launched QE2, this time committing USD 600 billion to long-term Treasuries. And when growth still faltered, it followed up with QE3 in 2012, a promise to keep buying, month after month, with no fixed end date. Forty billion dollars in agency Mortgage-Backed Securities (MBS) here, 45 billion in Treasuries there: the printing press was running at full speed. Together, these waves of QE rewrote the playbook of central banking and reshaped the global financial landscape for decades.

One of the most profound consequences of cheap capital was what happened to fixed income investments. With interest rates at historic lows, the traditional building blocks of fixed-income—government bonds, gilts, investment-grade credit—yielded next to nothing. The situation created a pronounced 'reach for yield'.

For pension funds, insurers and other institutional investors trying to hit long-term return targets or match liabilities decades into the future, this created a pressing challenge. The old, dependable sources of income had all but vanished as traditional fixed income no longer did the job. The old levers stopped moving the machine.

So, while economists dubbed the 2010s the 'lower for longer' era, for investors it was a nightmare. Almost overnight, these institutions found themselves in an impossible bind. They still needed to generate income, but the old playbook had run out of pages.

As we will explore in more detail in Chapter 3, investors were forced to cast the net wider, looking beyond the safety of mainstream assets. They had a choice: move up the risk curve—say, from gilts to high-yield bonds—or look further away altogether. That second option, the search for alternatives, began to gather pace.

And so began the great pivot, almost out of necessity. Gradually, capital started to shift, into private equity, infrastructure debt, private credit, real estate and frankly into anything that offered a sliver of extra return. These weren't just niche esoteric plays anymore. They started becoming essential components of institutional portfolios. In real estate, where the banks were pulling back, the timing was fortuitous. Private lenders were ready to meet the moment.

At the same time, demand for capital hadn't gone away. Developers still needed funding. Sponsors still wanted leverage for acquisitions or to revitalise tired properties. Yet the banks—now more cautious, constrained and compliance-heavy—were increasingly unwilling to lend.

That left a gap. And into that gap stepped a new kind of lender.

Private debt funds and alternative credit providers—nimble, lightly regulated and increasingly well capitalised—began to fill the void. They didn't face the same red tape as traditional banks. They could act quickly, tailor their underwriting to complex assets and price risk in a way banks could no longer afford to. For borrowers, they offered speed and flexibility. For investors, they offered something even more valuable: yield.

What followed was a more enduring trend, a structural shift. Over the course of the next decade, private credit—particularly in real estate—moved from the margins into the mainstream. Once the preserve of middle-market borrowers and opportunistic deals, it became a core allocation within the world's largest asset managers and private equity houses. No longer just a stopgap for broken bank markets, it evolved into a fundamental pillar of modern finance.

In Chapter 3, we will explore who the actual investors behind private debt are and how private credit fits into their broader investment portfolios. But for now, suffice it to say that the post-crisis world brought about a perfect alignment of conditions: traditional lenders pulling back, institutional capital searching desperately for yield and a new breed of lenders set to answer the call. Out of that, a multi-trillion-dollar private real estate credit market was born, not out of speculation, but out of necessity.

THE FIRST DOMINO

The story of private credit's rise is often told as a global shift, but in truth, it began with a sharp, early pivot in the United States. Long before European or Asian banks began reassessing their balance sheets, American lenders were already packing their bags and retreating from CRE lending. That head start was hardly a coincidence. It was regulation that lit the fuse.

In conversations with early private credit players, many pointed to the same catalyst: Dodd-Frank. Specifically, the Collins Amendment discussed earlier, buried deep within the post-crisis reforms. As we pointed out in earlier sections, this quiet clause effectively redefined what counted as capital, and did so on an unforgiving timeline.

Before the financial crisis, many US banks had leaned heavily on a tool called Trust-Preferred Securities (TrUPs), a hybrid instrument that blended characteristics of debt and equity. Initially developed as a mechanism to provide smaller banks access to capital markets by pooling the issuance of TrUPs into marketable Collateralised Debt Obligations (CDO), the market quickly grew to USD 60 billion of issuance from its inception in 2000 through its abrupt halt in 2007. From the banks' perspective, TrUPs were great: they were cheap, flexible and counted towards Tier 1 capital. But regulators viewed them as unreliable in a crisis. Under Basel III, their days were numbered. But global banks were given breathing room: a 10-year phase-out, stretching all the way to 2023.

In the US, things moved much faster. The Collins Amendment gave banks just three years, phasing TrUPs out of Tier 1 by January 2016. That tighter timeline had real consequences. Replacing those hybrid instruments with pure equity—a far more expensive form of capital—forced American banks to tighten their belts early. Events unfolded at speed: lending slowed and real estate, with its long durations and high capital charges, was one of the first sectors on the chopping board.

The pain was especially acute for smaller regional and mid-sized banks, many of whom had heavily relied on TrUPs to meet capital requirements. These weren't the well-capitalised Wall Street giants, they were the lenders embedded in local communities who financed development, construction and CRE projects. When TrUPs were stripped away, so too was their ability to extend credit to the sector they knew best and the communities they had been serving for generations.

ZIONS BANCORPORATION: WHEN CAPITAL RULES CHANGED OVERNIGHT

A RELATIONSHIP BANK BUILT ON LOCAL TRUST

Headquartered in Salt Lake City, Zions Bancorporation had spent decades carving out a stronghold in the American Southwest, becoming a trusted lender to contractors, mid-size homebuilders and small business owners from Nevada to Texas. The bank had built its business around SMEs and had become embedded in the fabric of local community, the kind of markets where lenders knew their borrowers by name and stood behind them when the going got tough, where on-the-ground relationships are key and banking still depends on trust, familiarity and a firm handshake.

WHEN CAPITAL STOPPED COUNTING

But in the years leading up to 2008, Zions, like many of its peers, had leaned heavily on TrUPs. At the time, TrUPs were seen as an innovative capital solution, allowing banks to raise capital in the form of subordinated debt while counting it as Tier 1 capital. For growing regional lenders like Zions, they were ideal: tax-efficient, cost-effective and regulator-approved. By the late 2000s, Zions had a substantial amount of TrUPs outstanding.

Then came the great reversal as the regulatory tide turned decisively. The Collins Amendment aimed to tighten capital standards by phasing out TrUPs as a qualifying component of Tier 1 capital for all but the smallest banks. The rules didn't bite immediately, but they had teeth, and a deadline. For banks with over USD 15 billion in assets—including Zions—the grace period ran out in 2016.

As TrUPs were phased out, Zions—like many other banks—found itself scrambling to rebuild its capital base with more expensive equity. That pressure filtered straight into the loan book.

THE SHOCK TO THE BALANCE SHEET

In December 2013, as Zions reviewed the final Volcker Rule—meant to curb banks' proprietary trading and ownership of certain investment vehicles—it suddenly found itself facing a capital shortfall, not because it was failing, but because the regulatory definition of capital had changed. What had been counted as sound, loss-absorbing capital yesterday, suddenly fell on the wrong side of regulation and was now seen as too risky, too complex and too flimsy for a post-crisis world.

On 16 December 2013, Zions announced a preliminary pre-tax charge of USD 629 million, triggered by its holdings of TrUPs CDOs, pools of TrUPs packaged into CDOs. These weren't toxic assets languishing on the balance sheet: far from it. Most were still investment-grade and fully performing. But the rulebook had changed. Overnight, the Volcker Rule banned banks from owning certain 'covered funds'—which included many CDOs backed by TrUPs—unless they met narrow exemptions. Under the new rules, banks such as Zions were told to clear them out by 21 July 2015, unless they could persuade the Federal Reserve to grant an extension until 2017.

In its statement at the time, Zions emphasised that the charge stemmed from a regulatory re-classification of formerly eligible securities instead of from deterioration in credit quality, a polite way of saying the rules of the game had changed overnight. The bank was forced to unwind positions, absorb the loss and reconfigure its balance sheet. Table 1.5 shows some of Zions' capital ratios changed as a result of applying the new accounting treatment resulting from the Volcker Rule to its financial statements on a pro forma basis.

The response was swift and sobering. In theory, Zions had until 2015 to offload its TrUPs CDO exposure from the balance sheet. In practice, it moved early, buying back portions of its outstanding TrUPs, issuing new preferred equity to replace instruments that no longer qualified as Tier 1 capital and steadily trimming risk. Development lending—once a core engine of growth—was scaled back. The bank de-leveraged, de-risked and, in effect, dismantled parts of its old playbook.

But even that wasn't quite enough. In 2014, Zions failed to meet the Federal Reserve's minimum capital requirements in the annual stress test, which included five regulatory ratios. It's minimum Tier 1 common ratio came in at 3.6%, below

(*Continued*)

(Continued)

TABLE 1.5 How the Volcker Rule Affected Zions Bank's Capital Ratios

	31 December 2012	30 September 2013	30 September 2013
	Actual	*Actual*	*Pro forma*
Common Equity Tier 1 Capital	9.80%	10.47%	9.74%
Tier 1 Risk-Based Capital	13.38%	13.10%	12.40%
Total Risk-Based Capital	15.05%	14.82%	14.13%
Tangible Common Equity Ratio	7.09%	7.90%	7.84%

the new regulatory threshold. The reasons weren't bad loans, but a low core capital ratio, collateral damage from the removal of TrUPs from the capital stack. Zions had, in effect, been penalised for a structure the regulators themselves had once endorsed.

RETREAT, REINVENTION AND RIPPLE EFFECTS

The implications rippled far beyond the boardroom. Developers who had long relied on Zions to fund land deals, housing starts and regeneration projects in cities like Phoenix, Albuquerque and Las Vegas suddenly found that lending appetite had waned. Some were offered smaller loans, tighter covenants, or more paperwork than they'd ever seen. Others were simply turned away. As one local builder put it, 'Zions used to approve a draw before you'd even hung up the phone. Now they needed a dossier and a six-week review'.

Zions did survive and even thrived in the years that followed. By 2015, its CET1 capital ratio had climbed back above 10%. The bank had reinvented itself as a more conservative, fee-oriented institution. But the legacy of the TrUPs phase-out lingers. For many observers, Zions became a case study in how well-intentioned regulation can accelerate structural change, not only within banks, but across the entire lending landscape.

The Collins Amendment was never designed to boost private credit, but that's precisely what it did. By forcing banks to retreat from certain forms of lending, it handed the baton to a new generation of non-bank lenders, reshaping how real estate and local development are financed.

For Zions, the lights never went out, but they certainly flickered. And in the space left behind, a different kind of capital quietly moved in.

But capital rules weren't the only reason the US was the first to see banks retrench, and set the process in motion elsewhere. Securitisation—once the tool that had supercharged bank lending—was also under new constraints. At the heart of the debate was a seemingly straightforward question. Should banks keep skin in the game?

Under Dodd-Frank, the answer was a resounding yes. Any lender selling a pool of loans—whether residential mortgages or CRE debt—was now asked to hold onto at least 5% of the credit risk. This 'risk retention' rule was meant to curb the excesses of the pre-crisis era, where originators could pass on risk by selling loans wholesale, often with limited ongoing exposure if those loans later deteriorated.

In theory, it was about aligning incentives. In practice, it tied up capital. Banks could no longer originate and distribute loans with the same ease, particularly in higher-risk categories. Each securitised deal now came with capital baggage.

Meanwhile, across the Atlantic and beyond, Basel III didn't impose the same leash. Banks outside the US could continue securitising with greater flexibility, selling off loans without retaining risk. That freedom allowed them to lend more aggressively for longer, even in real estate.

The contrast was stark. In the US, regulation triggered a sharp, early retrenchment. Banks stepped back. Credit lines dried up. Development deals stalled. But where traditional capital fled, private capital flowed in. As one senior lender at a large US bank told me, 'We weren't beaten by innovation. We were regulated out of the game'.

For private credit funds, this was the opening they had been waiting for. They didn't have to fight banks for deal flow, they simply filled the void the banks left behind.

> The banks stepping back created a vacuum—and for credit funds like ours, that wasn't just a challenge, it was a defining opportunity. We've been able to step in with flexible, intelligent capital precisely when and where the market needed it most.
>
> —Albane Poulin, Head of Private Credit, Gravis Capital

This wasn't a story of disruption in the classic sense. It was a transfer of risk, reshaped by legislation and accelerated by timing. The US pulled back first. Private credit stepped in, and the rest of the world would soon follow.

RETRENCHMENT GOES GLOBAL

As banks pulled back from lending in the wake of the financial crisis, the impact rippled far beyond the skyscrapers of global finance. It reached high streets, market town and backstreets, places where real businesses quietly got on with the business of creating jobs. For small and medium businesses, which make up the backbone of most economies, the retreat of bank credit wasn't just a nuisance, it was a major blow.

Nowhere was this more poignantly captured than in the story of Alexandre Callet, a young French restaurateur with big ambitions and a simmering sense of injustice. The frustration felt by many small business owners was memorably captured in the sign he placed outside his restaurant. In 2016, Callet, who ran the Michelin-recognised Les Écuries de Richelieu in the suburbs of Paris, made headlines not for his cuisine, but for an unusual protest. After being repeatedly denied a modest EUR 70,000 loan to open a second restaurant, he took matters into his own hands, with a touch of theatrical flair.

Outside his restaurant, he posted a sign that read:

> Dogs welcome, bankers forbidden (unless they pay an entry fee of EUR 70,000).

It was part satire, part statement, but wholly sincere. As Callet explained to reporters, the banks had treated him 'like a dog', and he decided to return the favour. It wasn't just personal. He spoke of a wider malaise affecting entrepreneurs across France, especially younger or first-generation business owners. Banks, he said, were no longer willing to back people with ambition, only those with assets. And he was hardly alone in that view.

Callet's protest might have been tongue-in-cheek, but it struck a chord across Europe. Across the continent and well beyond it, SMEs were finding that the doors of their banks—once open with coffee and handshakes—were now firmly shut. The new post-crisis reality, shaped by Basel III regulations and strict capital requirements, had turned even modest lending into a regulatory headache for banks. From their perspective, the economics no longer stacked up. Why extend credit to a small business, with limited collateral and patchy accounts, when capital charges made such lending prohibitively expensive?

The result was a quiet but relentless retreat from SME finance, not just in France, but across the UK, Germany, Spain, Italy and far beyond. What had once been the domain of local bank managers and relationship officers became a cold, centralised system of risk models and automated rejections. The flexibility and human judgment that once defined SME lending gave way to bureaucracy and box-ticking.

For entrepreneurs, the experience was not just frustrating, it was demoralising. Businesses with viable plans, solid cash flows and local roots were denied funding on technicalities. Promising ventures stalled. Expansion plans were shelved. And in too many cases, good businesses simply gave up. As the female founder of a small Spanish fashion scale-up recalled, 'It wasn't that our business didn't make sense: we had customers, revenues, momentum. But the bank wasn't really listening anymore. Everything had to fit a model, and if you didn't tick every box, the answer was no. It felt like the relationship had disappeared overnight'.

It's easy to forget, in the high-level discussion of monetary policy and regulatory reform, that the fallout from bank retrenchment was deeply personal. Behind every rejected loan application was a business owner like Callet—someone who had taken risks, created jobs, paid taxes—who now found themselves out in the cold. The irony, of course, was that banks had been bailed spectacularly out using taxpayer money to keep credit flowing. But by the time the dust had settled, it was the everyday businesses that found themselves locked out.

And so, in shopfronts and industrial parks across Europe, the stage was set for a new wave of lenders to step in, ones who didn't carry the same regulatory burdens or legacy issues as the banks. These were private debt funds, family offices, Peer-To-Peer (P2P) platforms and alternative credit providers. Where banks saw risk, they saw opportunity. And for SMEs, long overlooked and increasingly desperate for support, these newcomers were more than welcome.

REAL ESTATE LENDING IN THE CROSSFIRE

Although bank retrenchment rippled across the economy, one of the earliest and most tangible casualties of this new regime was real estate development lending, which suddenly became far more capital-intensive under the new rules. Long considered high-risk, high reward, this corner of the credit market began to wither under the weight of rising capital charges and increasingly conservative risk appetites. Projects involving land acquisition, development, or large commercial properties were deemed inherently risky, illiquid, slow-moving and often speculative. Regulators, still haunted by the housing crash, took a hardline stance. Capital requirements for these loans surged. Banks suddenly needed to hold significantly more capital for every dollar lent in this space. Banks, particularly the larger ones, found that the returns no longer justified the regulatory burdens.

To illustrate this further, consider if MCB held a USD 50 million real estate development loan portfolio. Under pre-crisis rules with CET1 of 2%, RWA of 100% and a Current Expected Credit Loss (CECL) charge of 1.5% of the loan amount, the required capital was USD 1.75 million when using the standardised approach. Post-crisis, with CET1 increasing to 4.5% and RWA increasing to 150%, the capital needed jumped to USD 4.125 million. The risk of the projects hadn't changed. The borrowers hadn't changed. But the cost of doing business had. The bank's return on equity plummeted-from 21% to 9%, as illustrated in Table 1.6. And that drop changed everything.

With the Volcker Rule limiting trading revenues and other high-return activities, banks such as MCB had to be more selective with how they used their capital. Real estate development lending, with its long lead times and chunky capital requirements, became harder to justify from a return-on-capital perspective, especially when compared with more capital-efficient products or off-balance-sheet lending structures.

Bank bosses simply did what they had to do: reassess. The numbers no longer stacked up. Lending to real estate—particularly to developers building speculative or large-scale projects—wasn't worth the capital commitment. The economics had shifted. This wasn't just about caution. It was about survival. Banks are businesses and capital is finite. If regulators require you to treat some loans as if they were highly risky, you eventually stop making those loans.

Faced with this new reality, banks had two options. They could raise more capital—dilutive and expensive—or they could shrink their RWAs. Most, understandably, chose the latter. They tightened credit standards, retrenched from certain asset classes and in many cases exited real estate lending altogether. Smaller developers and mid-market borrowers were hit the hardest.

TABLE 1.6 Midland Commercial Bank Return on Equity

Capital Requirement	Pre-Basel III	Post-Basel III
Notional Value (USDm)	50	50
RWA (%)	100%	150%
RWA (USDm)	50	75
CET1 Ratio Requirement (%)	2%	4.5%
Allowance for Credit Losses (USDm)	1.0	3.38
CECL (%)	1.5%	1.5%
Expected Loss (USDm)	0.75	0.75
Total Capital Required (USDm)	1.75	4.13
Cost of Bank Capital (%)	12%	12%
Cost of Bank Capital (USDm)	0.6	0.6
Notional Value (USDm)	50	50
Post-Expense Net Spread (%)	0.75%	0.75%
Implied Net Income (USDm)	0.38	0.38
Return On Equity (%)	21%	9%

This wasn't a theoretical exercise. It changed the way banks behaved. Entire credit portfolios were rebalanced. Internal discussions shifted from 'What's the credit risk?' to 'What's the capital cost?' Projects that might have made sense on a fundamental basis were shelved because they didn't make sense on a regulatory one.

Bank lending slowly started to become a shadow of its former self.

ANGLO IRISH BANK: THE BANK THAT BROKE THE BOOM

THE RISE OF THE CELTIC TIGER

For much of the 1990s, Ireland was hailed as a miracle economy. The 'Celtic Tiger' roaring with growth, foreign direct investment, EU convergence and tech-fuelled optimism. But as the new millennium dawned, the tiger lost some of its bite. Growth became increasingly dependent on domestic consumption and—more dangerously—on a booming property market. At the heart of that transformation was a banking system that grew too fast, took on too much risk and effectively overplayed its hand.

> What the gods wish to destroy, they first make proud.
>
> —Ancient proverb

THE BANK THAT RODE THE PROPERTY BOOM

Among the most aggressive players was Anglo Irish Bank, a small institution that started its journey in 1964 as a small commercial lender known as City of Dublin Bank but then reinvented itself as a CRE lending powerhouse.

TABLE 1.7 Fuelled by Property Driven by Debt

Bank	Customer Loans (2000) (EUR billion)	Customer Loans (2008) (EUR billion)	Growth (%)
Anglo Irish	8	72	800%
Allied Irish Banks	46	129	180%
Bank of Ireland	45	136	202%
Ulster Bank	4	39	875%

What began as a specialist lender soon turned into the poster child of Ireland's debt-fuelled property bubble. Few recognised the scale of the risks building beneath the surface. In fact, at the World Economic Forum in Davos in January 2007, the consultancy Oliver Wyman named Anglo the best bank in the world, based on its stellar performance over the previous five years. Just two years later the bank had to be rescued by the Irish government, which ultimately cost Irish taxpayers around EUR 30 billion.

Table 1.7 shows that between 2000 and 2008, Anglo's share of customer loans in Ireland ballooned by more than 800% and by the time the music stopped, some 70-80% of its loan book was tied to property development, often highly geared, thinly documented and extended to a close-knit circle of well-connected developers. The trouble was, almost the entire net worth of Anglo Irish's customers was based on their property portfolios. So, when the market crashed, all their equity vanished overnight. What once looked like a borrower with deep assets quickly turned into a house of cards. If all your collateral declines in value at the same time, there's nothing left to chase. There was no backup, no residual equity and no realistic route to recover the loans. Anglo suddenly found itself in a very sticky situation.

Other banks, Allied Irish Banks (AIB), Bank of Ireland, Ulster Bank and Bank of Scotland Ireland, were under pressure from their shareholders to keep up with Anglo. A significant portion of the loan book growth shown in Table 1.7 reflects increased property lending as they sought to match Anglo's expansion.

WHEN LENDING DISCIPLINE DISAPPEARED

One of those watching closely who lived through that pivotal period from the inside was Ajay Sharma, then a Senior Treasury Dealer at the bank based in Belfast, Northern Ireland.

As part of his role, Ajay was responsible for managing interest rate exposure on the bank's loans to its borrowers and he therefore had full visibility of the Northern Irish credit papers that the bank was writing. Reflecting on the frenzied years before the crash. he recalls:

(*Continued*)

(*Continued*)

> It became less about the borrower and more about the asset. You could almost feel the shift: deals were getting bigger, timelines tighter and the sense of caution had all but disappeared. Business appraisals for multi-million-pound property developments were being scribbled on fancy-white napkins in fine-dining restaurants and handed from property developer to senior banker. This then formed the basis for the credit paper being produced and rubber-stamped within a matter of days.

THE ILLUSION OF CONSERVATIVE LENDING

As became the case in other Southern European countries such as Spain, Ireland's adoption of the euro had brought in a tide of cheap, short-term international funding and Anglo was all too willing to ride the wave.

Like many Irish banks at the time, Anglo leaned heavily on wholesale funding markets to fuel rapid loan growth, while keeping only a modest deposit base. In Sharma's words:

> It wasn't just Anglo. Everyone was chasing yield. But we were probably the most aggressive; we went where others hesitated.

At the time, Anglo was lending at 70–75% Loan-To-Gross Development Value (LTGDV): on paper, a conservative ratio. But in practice, the bank was stretching far beyond that by cross-collateralising loans. A typical scenario involved a borrower who already owned an investment property that had been revalued upwards. When they sought to acquire a second property, Anglo would effectively lend them 100% of the purchase price, using both properties as security. On paper, the combined loan-to-value looked reasonable. But the entire structure depended on one crucial assumption: that values would keep rising. The moment the market turned and asset prices started falling, that illusion of prudence evaporated and loan to values vanished in a blink of an eye.

Lending standards gradually eroded. Risk management became reactive instead of proactive. And as Sharma recalls, internal alarm bells often rang too late:

> There were moments when we'd sit in credit committee and know deep down that the numbers didn't stack up. But the market was still climbing and no one wanted to be the first to blink.

Very quickly, lending became a race to the bottom and Anglo sprinted ahead.

THE FATAL FUNDING MODEL

There was also another issue. Unlike the traditional high street banks, which typically required borrowers to make both capital and interest repayments,

Anglo Irish Bank operated on a very different model. Its loans were almost entirely interest-only, with rolled-up interest often added to the outstanding balance. On paper, this approach supported strong profitability and rapid loan book expansion—the cornerstone of Anglo's high-growth strategy. But in practice, it meant that borrowers rarely reduced their debt and Anglo seldom saw real cash repayments. The model worked—so long as property values kept rising. But it also fostered a culture where clients became entirely unaccustomed to repaying principal. When the market turned, the flaw was exposed: there was no cushion, no paydown and no path to recovery.

> When the tide goes out, you find out who's been swimming naked.
>
> —Warren Buffett, Chairman and CEO, Berkshire Hathaway

Oversight from regulators remained light touch. Ireland's fiscal policies masked structural imbalances. Temporary transaction taxes padded revenues, rising asset prices lulled the system into complacency and a lenient regulatory regime allowed Irish banks to borrow heavily in the international money market and offered few speed bumps. The result: an overheated domestic economy, sky-high property prices and a banking sector built on sand. Anglo Irish Bank, emboldened by short-term success, pushed even harder, until the entire house of cards collapsed.

WHEN THE MUSIC STOPPED

Then came the shockwaves of the Global Financial Crisis. The run on Northern Rock in the UK in 2007 sent tremors across the Irish Sea. Bear Stearns collapsed in early 2008 and whispers about Irish Nationwide's solvency in September of that year turned into shouts. By the time Lehman Brothers collapsed, the crisis had become a full-blown storm, and Irish banks were dangerously exposed.

'That week after Lehman, everything changed', says Sharma. 'We weren't looking at profit anymore. We watched in horror as the Anglo share price seemed to halve in value on an almost daily basis'.

Funding markets froze and confidence evaporated. Anglo's access to liquidity vanished almost overnight. Despite a dramatic blanket guarantee of all Irish bank liabilities in late September 2008—an unprecedented, almost unthinkable move aimed at calming markets—it was too late for Anglo. Falling prices in the property market meant that Anglo's assets were now considerably lower than its liabilities, creating a full-blown banking crisis. On paper—and soon enough, in reality—the bank was insolvent, haemorrhaging funding and laden with bad loans. Underneath the surface lay an even deeper problem: concentration. Just twenty borrowers accounted for half of its entire Irish loan book while 51% of Irish Nationwide's book comprised loans to 25 individuals. When the property market crashed, so did they, taking Anglo down with them.

(*Continued*)

(*Continued*)

COLLAPSE AND CONSEQUENCES

By early 2009, the writing was on the wall. The bank was bleeding deposits, riddled with bad loans and no longer viable. Nationalisation wasn't a choice. It was an inevitability, the final act in one of Ireland's most spectacular financial implosions. Anglo Irish's collapse marked one of the darkest chapters in Ireland's financial history, and a turning point in the country's journey from boom to bailout.

'Almost overnight, development loans that had once been routine started triggering internal red flags: not because the projects were riskier, but because the capital treatment had changed', Ajay recalls now. His reflections on the internal recalibration of risk, pricing and balance sheet priorities offer a vivid account of how one line of legislation quietly redrew the boundaries of what banks could—and would—finance.

The fallout was severe and what followed was years of deleveraging. The National Asset Management Agency (NAMA) was created to manage toxic loans. Ireland faced a sovereign debt crisis and ultimately had to seek an EU-IMF bailout. For developers, the reckoning was brutal. In Northern Ireland, Taggart Holdings—once one of the region's largest builders—collapsed in late 2008. Ulster Bank and Bank of Ireland petitioned to have an administrator appointed to the Derry-based firm's Irish units, which included a holding company, as well as a Dublin-based subsidiary that had been effectively inactive for over a year. By 2011, more followed, including Thompson Developments and Lavelle & McAlinden. Anglo Irish Bank, now acting as enforcer instead of funder, aggressively pursued personal guarantees, including a GBP 90 million claim against Sam Thompson.

A BANKING FAILURE—AND SOMETHING DEEPER

Sharma offers a final, sobering reflection:

> It wasn't just a banking failure: it was a societal one. Credit became too easy, caution was seen as cowardice and when the music stopped, the silence was deafening.

At its core, the crisis exposed a deeper structural truth about modern finance.

The story of Anglo Irish Bank is a stark reminder of what happens when growth outpaces governance. A lender that once thrived on relationships and real assets lost sight of risk and in doing so, helped drag an entire economy into crisis.

The Irish banking crisis triggered years of institutional retrenchment, until a new cast of players began to emerge. In Sharma's words: 'The four to five years after the crash saw all lenders virtually disappear from the Northern Irish market'. But once the legacy loans began to land on banks' balance sheets, private equity funds entered the fray. Providers such as Cerberus and other so-called vulture funds were welcomed into Ireland and the UK and snapped up impaired loan books from institutions including AIB, Ulster Bank, Permanent TSB, NAMA and even Royal Bank of Scotland (RBS), acquiring dispossessed portfolios often at deep discounts. The respective governments at the time were so desperate to see more capital injections into their banking systems that they wilfully ignored the fact that they had already spent billions of taxpayers' euros & pounds on bailing out the banks. This effectively amounted to a second bailout for the banks. Borrowers never saw any benefit from these bailouts.

Over the next decade, Cerberus became one of the most active buyers of Irish distressed debt, purchasing over 2,200 loans from AIB alone in a EUR 1 billion deal as part of broader portfolios that once totalled over EUR 65 billion in loans across Europe. It was a shift that reshaped the financial landscape: banks shed their non-performing exposures and new investors assumed control, often processing repayments from borrowers over long run-off periods instead of expecting immediate value recovery.

Sharma reflects on the transition with concern: 'When those funds arrived on the scene, they were taking over debt no one else wanted. But they also had deep pockets and patience: something cash-strapped banks no longer possessed. The vulture funds made billions in profits: all of which left Ireland & the UK. They paid little or no tax on these gains. NAMA (the Irish bad bank vehicle) could have made these profits if it had been structured and managed correctly'.

But these funds—Cerberus, Lone Star, Apollo and others—were never set up to finance the small property developers and local housebuilders. Their capital was targeted at large-scale portfolios, trophy assets, or institutional restructurings. If you were a major developer with a headline scheme, there was a seat at the table. But if you were a small or mid-sized housebuilder, it was a different story altogether. If you were a small, distressed developer, you were told to pay up or go bankrupt.

'There were no options for SME developers at that point' recalls Sharma. 'Nothing was happening for them. The big guys got saved. The small guys had no choice but to go bankrupt or come up with extra equity from friends and family. It was a brutal time'.

What followed was a vacuum—particularly in regional markets—where small developers were left stranded, unable to access finance even as land values began to stabilise. It wasn't until around 2014–15, when the bottom of the market had effectively been reached, that alternative sources of finance slowly began to return. New lenders like Assetz Capital started entering the Irish and UK markets, offering targeted residential development finance to SMEs who had long been overlooked.

At the same time, a new generation of technology-led platforms emerged. Funding Circle, for instance, became one of the first P2P platforms to offer unsecured finance to small and medium-sized enterprises, often in sectors where banks still refused to engage. 'They played a big part in getting things moving again' says Sharma. 'Without them, I don't think many of the SMEs would've survived'.

But for all their innovation, the terms offered by non-bank lenders entering the market post-crisis weren't exactly generous. Structurally, their LTGDV ratios were often similar to those of the high-street banks before the crash, but that's where the similarities ended. Margins were significantly higher, hurdle rates steeper and arrangement fees more aggressive. For developers used to borrowing cheap bank debt in the Celtic Tiger years, the new environment was a rude awakening.

As Sharma puts it: 'You were getting 65-70% LTGDV, which was nothing new, but you were paying through the nose for it'.

In response, another layer of the capital stack began to emerge: wealthy individuals, often with deep local knowledge and a taste for yield, began putting their own capital to work. Some stepped in directly, others formed syndicates or invested via new lending platforms. This influx of entrepreneurial capital provided a bridge for SME developers who didn't have institutional backing but still had viable schemes. It wasn't cheap money, but it was accessible, and that made all the difference.

What emerged was a quiet revolution. A new ecosystem of non-bank lenders took over portfolios once held by traditional banks, bringing resource-heavy strategies and specialised servicing networks to bear on distressed loans. As the cheap funding of the Celtic Tiger era faded, this new capital structure became the backbone of Ireland's gradual financial recovery.

Even when traditional banks began to cautiously re-enter the market, many developers continued to favour non-bank lenders, not necessarily because they had no alternative, but because the terms were simply more workable. These lenders offered greater flexibility: they allowed interest to roll up, didn't insist on rigid pre-sale conditions and were often more pragmatic in their underwriting. For example, in the aftermath of the crisis, many borrowers had diversified or ring-fenced their assets, placing properties in the names of family members, trusts, pensions or siblings, in an effort to shield themselves from aggressive bank recoveries. When the dust began to settle and they were ready to build again, these ownership structures posed a problem. Banks, bound by rigid borrower requirements, would often refuse to lend unless every named owner was party to the loan. By contrast, private lenders were more accommodating: as long as the asset holder—say, a sister or a trust—was willing to grant a legal charge and recognise the lender's rights, the deal could proceed. This kind of creative problem-solving became a hallmark of early non-bank lending, and it's what enabled many developers to get back in the game. For developers trying to get projects off the ground in a still-fragile market, that kind of agility often outweighed the lower headline cost of bank finance.

BRAIDWATER GROUP: NAVIGATING THE POST-CRISIS VACUUM

> Northern Ireland's housing sector is at a critical juncture... without sufficient funding, the north risks failing to meet its affordable house-building targets. Social and affordable housing are essential tenures, ensuring everyone has access to a safe, secure home but with limited supply we are seeing an increasing number of families on waiting lists, rising homelessness and people living in temporary accommodation.
>
> —Justin Cartwright, National Director, Chartered Institute of Housing Northern Ireland

WHEN THE CRASH HIT NORTHERN IRELAND

When the Global Financial Crisis hit in 2008, few regions felt the aftershocks quite like Northern Ireland. For Joe McGinnis, the second-generation leader of Braidwater Group established by his father Patrick over 50 years ago, it wasn't just a banking crisis. It was an existential threat to everything his family had built.

'We had a substantial land bank—around GBP 40 million worth—and a few development sites that kept the lights on' Joe recalls. 'But we didn't have an investment arm to carry the interest costs. Once the market collapsed, we weren't selling land fast enough to cover the debt and everything started to unravel'.

SURVIVAL THROUGH RESTRUCTURING

Like many SME developers at the time, Braidwater had relied heavily on mainstream bank finance: in this case, Ulster Bank. When the crash came, so did the pressure. Asset values plummeted, investor appetite vanished overnight and projects that once looked watertight suddenly became impossible to finance or sell. Social housing contracts dried up as government spending was curtailed and demand for investor housing—once a key part of the group's strategy—disappeared.

Facing mounting pressure and evaporating cash flows, the McGinnises made a tough decision: they would restructure the business from the ground up. That meant shrinking the team, selling off non-performing assets and painstakingly renegotiating terms with their lender. 'We went through a structured workout plan with Ulster Bank' Joe explains. 'We didn't have the luxury of ring-fencing the development company from the land business. Everything was intertwined—and that made it even harder to restructure'. The crisis was being navigated not just by a company, but by a family business built across generations, as shown in Figure 1.6.

THE LONG ROAD BACK

The process was brutal. Some assets were sold at deep discounts. Others, like a hotel eventually leased to Travelodge, were traded off to generate liquidity. The goal was survival, not profit. 'There were weeks when my father and I sat down and seriously considered walking away' Joe admits. 'But we kept going, because we believed in the business and the people behind it'.

One of the turning points came with the support of David Clements from PwC, a well-respected restructuring expert who helped broker a credible recovery plan with the banks. That credibility mattered. 'Even though our debt wasn't huge in the grand scheme of things—GBP 40 million—it was everything to us. And having someone who understood the system made all the difference'.

(Continued)

(*Continued*)

FIGURE 1.6 Joe and Patrick McGinnis Behind Braidwater Group

TURNING TO ALTERNATIVE CAPITAL

By 2014, Braidwater had worked down nearly all its legacy land positions. What little remained was bought back to form the foundation of a new business: leaner, wiser and determined to avoid the pitfalls of the past.

As banks continued their post-crisis retreat, Braidwater turned to alternative funding. In 2015, they secured an equity investment from BGF (Business Growth Fund), which marked a significant turning point. 'We've also worked with private investors and structured deals on an asset-by-asset basis', Joe notes. 'But we've never returned to the kind of commercial bank financing we had before 2008: that door never really reopened'.

On his experience working with private investors, Joe notes: 'We had to kiss a lot of frogs in the early days in order to find the right partners and we've built a good relationship from that time, but it was very difficult to navigate at the time'. He continues 'We were fortunate enough to secure these relationships and the deal with BGF, many local house builders were not and left the industry. This has had a knock-on effect on the ability to deliver new homes. The number of housebuilders operating in Northern Ireland has greatly reduced given the challenges the industry faces alongside limited access to finance. As an example, revolving credit facilities for housebuilders do not exist in Northern Ireland whereas they are still available in England'.

A WIDER STORY FOR SME DEVELOPERS

Today, Braidwater is thriving again, but the experience left deep scars. 'The crash fundamentally changed how we think about risk, leverage and relationships with lenders. We're far more cautious now'.

Joe's story is emblematic of a wider truth: in the wake of 2008, it wasn't the big housebuilders that felt the ground fall from under them. It was the SMEs. And when the banks pulled away, it was private capital that stepped in to pick up the slack.

WHERE BANKS STEPPED BACK, OTHERS STEPPED IN

The retreat of traditional banks from SME property development finance has been both stark and sustained. Following the 2008 financial crisis, bank lending to smaller developers fell off a cliff, and it never truly recovered. The numbers speak volumes: according to specialist non-bank lender CapitalRise, lending to SME property developers declined by 49%, from GBP 9.7 billion in January 2017 to just GBP 4.9 billion by November 2024.

But this retreat was not evenly felt across the board. While smaller developers were left increasingly stranded, large-scale housebuilders and corporate developers saw the door held wide open. Bank lending to the largest property companies rose by 25% over the same period, growing from GBP 5.6 billion to GBP 7 billion. In short: capital didn't disappear. It simply flowed upward.

The 2008–09 financial crisis did more than just dent confidence in the banking system: it rewired the system itself. In its aftermath, banking regulations were significantly tightened, raising capital and liquidity requirements and heightening scrutiny. These reforms made it more costly and cumbersome for banks to lend, particularly to risk-weighted segments like SME developers. As a result, a material share of traditional intermediation began shifting into the hands of non-bank financial institutions (NBFIs).

Indeed, since 2009, core elements of lending and trading have migrated steadily outside the regulated banking sector. What began as a trickle has become a structural shift. According to the Financial Stability Board, the NBFI sector grew by 8.5% in 2023—more than twice the pace of the banking sector's 3.3% expansion—lifting its share of total global financial assets to nearly half, at 49.1%.

In that sense, the Global Financial Crisis didn't just disrupt bank lending; it lit the fuse for an entirely parallel financial system, one that has since grown into a defining force in global capital markets.

Into the vacuum left by banks stepped a new class of lenders. Private credit funds, direct lending platforms and debt-focused asset managers—many backed by global financial institutions and pension capital—began filling the lending gap with targeted, deal-specific capital. They brought underwriting discipline, greater flexibility and fewer regulatory constraints, making them nimbler and often better aligned with borrower realities.

> Private credit didn't emerge to reinvent the wheel: it emerged to keep the wheels turning when traditional finance pulled over. We weren't chasing disruption for its own sake. We were stepping into a space that desperately needed capital, discipline and a fresh perspective. Where banks saw red tape and regulatory headwinds, we saw underserved borrowers and long-term opportunity.
>
> —Albane Poulin

But what's striking is that this wasn't disruption in the Silicon Valley sense. There was no sleek app or overnight revolution. Private credit didn't rise because someone built a better engine—it rose because the old one broke down—and no one else had the inclination, or the regulatory clearance, to put it back. In the early days of the asset class, this was a disruption born of absence, a gap-filling exercise instead of a tech-fuelled revolution. As banks de-risked, private credit re-risked, but with selectivity, experience and intentionality.

Yet what was initially a substitute for retrenching bank capital soon evolved beyond that. Private credit soon was no longer just filling a void. It was flourishing. By the mid-2010s, it had evolved into a USD 1.5 trillion global market and was now firmly being labelled as its own asset class. But its real inflection point came after the COVID-19 pandemic.

In the years that followed the pandemic, central banks slashed interest rates to historic lows to keep the global economy afloat. At one point in the summer of 2021, more than USD 16 trillion worth of bonds offered negative yields. Even the once-dependable US 10-year Treasury offered less than 1%. Investors found themselves starved for yield in a world that had gone dry. Traditional sources of income—corporate bonds, government securities—offered only meagre trickles of return. BB-rated bonds hovered around 4.5%, B-rated perhaps nudged above 6%. Commercial Mortgage-Backed Securities (CMBS) did slightly better but still left many disappointed. And so, many investors—both institutional and private—began to look elsewhere. What they found was private real estate credit. For them, private credit's appeal lied in consistent yield, structural protections, low correlation to public credit markets and increasingly diverse strategies by geography, structure and sector. Figures 1.7 and 1.8 show that private credit strategies have delivered strong

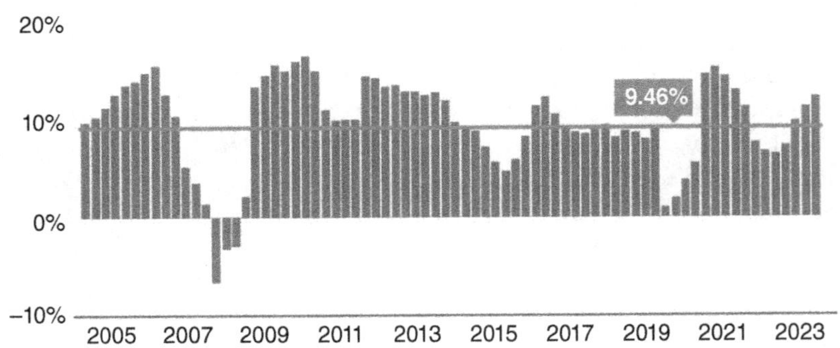

FIGURE 1.7 US Direct Lending Returns
Source: Data from Cliffwater Direct Lending Index (CDLI)

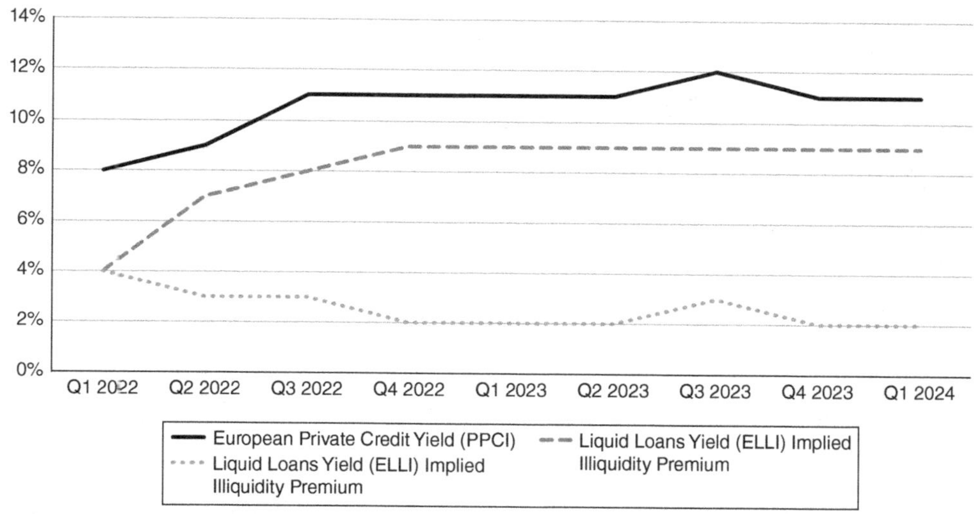

FIGURE 1.8 The Illiquidity Premium in European Private Credit
Source: Data from Morgan Stanley

and relatively stable returns, while also offering a measurable illiquidity premium compared with liquid loan markets.

Here was a corner of the market offering something substantial: first mortgages pricing at 5–8%, mezzanine and junior debt regularly reaching 9–12%. The returns were higher, yes, but so too was the substance. These weren't abstract financial instruments. They were loans secured against real buildings, real homes, real infrastructure. And they weren't speculative. They were helping developers build housing, redevelop neighbourhoods, or finance assets that banks no longer had the appetite to touch.

The reason this market could offer more wasn't alchemy, it was pure inefficiency. Private real estate credit lived in the cracks left behind by traditional finance: smaller borrowers, off-market deals, nuanced underwriting. The model rewarded those who could move quickly, think creatively and build real relationships. It favoured experience over bureaucracy. And it allowed lenders to back high-quality assets, often at a discount to where equity investors were entering the same projects.

One manager at a private credit fund I spoke with saw something deeper: a transformation in where capital comes from and how it moves. 'You're seeing a broadening of capital sources. Behind us, there are hundreds of capital sources that are changing and evolving over time, as opposed to a more concentrated system in the banks', he said.

For him, the rise of institutional investor's appetite for private debt wasn't just about chasing returns. It was about building a new architecture for real estate finance, one where long-term, relationship-driven and flexible capital was starting to replace the rigid, one-size-fits-all structures of the past. And if he's right, the next quarter-century in real estate debt won't just belong to the large asset managers of this world. It'll belong to those who understood that private credit wasn't simply a post-crisis patch, it was a reimagining. In the last chapter of this book, we will explore what comes next for private real estate debt.

FROM WALL STREET TO THE WORLD

What began as a uniquely American response to banking retreat didn't stay confined to Wall Street for long. Like a wave rolling out from the financial epicentre of New York, private credit soon found fertile ground overseas, most notably in the UK and Australia. These were not random choices. As Christian Faes, the Australian co-founder of LendInvest, would later recount, both countries had the ingredients that private lenders crave: financial maturity, openness to international capital and, perhaps most crucially, a legal framework characterised by certainty and the rule of law.

In London, the second largest financial centre in the world, the rise of private credit felt almost inevitable. The City's stature as a global financial centre made it a natural destination for funds eager to expand beyond US shores. But there was something even more foundational driving this shift: the strength and clarity of British common law.

Unlike in many continental European jurisdictions—where lenders could find themselves entangled in slow-moving courts or hobbled by borrower protections—the UK offered a lender-friendly environment and robust protection for creditors as well as those with security interests in assets. The UK legal system consistently enforces contracts and respects security rights, such as taking possession of collateral or selling it to recover outstanding debts. This offered a stable legal framework for business and individuals, which mattered deeply when the asset in question was a piece of real estate.

In the UK, when a lender holds a first charge over a property, they hold power. The Land Registry system ensures public, clear documentation of ownership and charges. If a borrower defaults, the lender doesn't have to navigate years of legal purgatory. They can appoint a receiver or move swiftly to repossession. That kind of enforceability gives investors confidence that their capital is protected, even in downturns. As one seasoned receivership agent, whose firm operates across multiple jurisdictions, put it:

> In the UK, the process is clear and well-trodden. Once a borrower defaults, a lender with a first charge can move quickly: appointing a receiver, taking control of the asset, and stabilising the situation before value deteriorates. You're not waiting on court timetables or navigating procedural uncertainty; the framework allows you to act. It's not without its steps, but they're defined, predictable and, crucially, enforceable.

Meanwhile, many lenders in Continental Europe quickly learned that the legal foundations underneath them told a different story. Unlike the UK's common law system—where lenders could draft bespoke contracts and rely on swift, predictable enforcement—civil law jurisdictions across Europe offered a more rigid, codified structure.

Here, contractual freedom was constrained and the toolbox for securing loans was notably limited. The concept of a floating charge—a flexible security over future property-related receivables—was either misunderstood or simply didn't exist in many countries. This posed challenges not just in structuring deals, but in anticipating how they might unravel.

But it was the enforcement process that truly set alarm bells ringing for lenders. In much of Continental Europe, recovering a distressed loan wasn't just about asserting your rights. It was about entering the labyrinth of the court system. Out-of-court settlements, common in the UK through mechanisms like receivership or power of sale, were virtually unheard of. Instead, lenders had to brace for formal judicial proceedings: slow, procedural and often mired in litigation.

For those financing property deals across borders, this meant one thing: when defaults happened, European law left them with slower, weaker and often more costly access to the very collateral meant to protect them. And in real estate, where time is money and asset values can shift quickly, that delay could mean the difference between recovery and ruin.

As the CEO of a pan-European private credit platform told me, 'In some jurisdictions, enforcement isn't a process—it's a negotiation with time. And time is rarely on the lender's side. What investors value most isn't just yield, but certainty—and that's precisely what fragmented legal systems struggle to provide'.

But there was also another catalyst that enabled the UK to leap ahead in the democratisation of private credit: the early and decisive regulation of crowdfunding. While common law offered legal certainty, it was the UK's open-door approach to financial innovation—underpinned by the Financial Conduct Authority (FCA)—that unlocked an entirely new investor base and helped build the infrastructure for modern alternative lending.

In 2014, the FCA became one of the first regulators in the world to introduce a comprehensive framework that regulated crowdfunding. By taking over consumer credit regulation from the Office of Fair Trading and introducing bespoke rules for P2P lending and equity crowdfunding, the FCA legitimised and structured what had previously been a grey market. Platforms like Zopa, Funding Circle and LendInvest were now operating in a regulated space, and that changed everything.

Retail investors, once shut out of real estate debt, could now participate under transparent and risk-adjusted terms. The new rules required investor categorisation (retail, sophisticated, high-net-worth), mandatory risk warnings, clear disclosures on default rates and platform performance and compliance with Treating Customers Fairly (TCF) principles. For platforms, this was a green light to grow.

Suddenly, private credit didn't just mean big institutions writing bespoke deals. It meant pensioners in Surrey, dentists in Devon and small family offices in London putting capital to work in bricks and mortar, often in places and projects that traditional banks had overlooked. This disintermediated model allowed investors to choose the projects they wanted exposure to, and, for the first time, back the UK's small and mid-sized housebuilders directly. And behind it all was a regulatory framework that struck a rare balance: protective but enabling; cautious, yet forward-looking.

This spirit of innovation wasn't limited to regulation. Just two years later, in 2016, the UK government introduced a world-leading open banking initiative, requiring the country's nine largest banks to securely share customer data (with their consent) with licensed third-party providers via standardised Application Programming Interface (APIs). The goal was clear: to unbundle financial services, break down monopolies and give rise to more competitive, transparent and consumer-driven markets.

The implications for private credit were enormous. Suddenly, new entrants had access to the data flows that were traditionally guarded by banks. As we will explore in more detail in Chapter 5, that meant smarter credit models, real-time affordability checks and better customer journeys. FinTech platforms could build leaner, faster lending businesses, targeted at underbanked segments that the traditional high street lenders had all but abandoned. In property finance, this translated into faster decision-making, sharper pricing and better borrower experience: all essential ingredients for SME developers and mid-market sponsors.

Taken together, the FCA's progressive stance on crowdfunding and the government's bold push into open banking laid the foundation for London's rise as a global FinTech capital. By the late 2010s, the city had become the testing ground for a new breed of non-bank lending platform: digital, data-rich and borrower-first. It was no coincidence that some of the world's most high-profile FinTech lenders—including LendInvest, Zopa and Funding Circle—were born not in Silicon Valley, but in London.

The combination of legal clarity, pioneering regulation and post-2008 bank retrenchment made the UK an ideal launching pad for real estate private credit. Pension funds, insurers, global asset managers and even retail investors began channelling capital into UK debt strategies. They weren't just seeking yield. They were seeking jurisdictions where the rules were clear, recoveries were realistic and the courts respected the structure of a deal.

As Christian Faes and others would help demonstrate, private credit wasn't just an American story. It was becoming a global one—reshaping markets across borders—and the UK was stepping firmly into the spotlight. As Faes recalls:

> There were also a number of other factors that contributed to the UK becoming a fast global leader in this new world of private lending. The Conservative government, post the *financial* crisis, led by David Cameron and his Chancellor George Osborne, were all in favour of this new breed of finance company that embraces technology. It seemed that the government and the regulator wasn't just wanting to make life difficult for the banks by increasing the amount of regulation and capital requirements that they had to deal with, they were also intent on ensuring that new startups could enter the financial services landscape and challenge the incumbent players. This new wave of FinTech companies were encouraged by the UK government's pioneering of the first crowdfunding and P2P legislation for investments and a new signalling of an open door for new bank applications at the Bank of England. This created an environment in London in the 2010s where innovation and financial services was all-encompassing, with full support from the government, the regulator and soon thereafter, the venture capitalists to fuel it. Naturally, this spawned a whole industry of new lending companies trying to take on different verticals from the incumbent banks.

As the former CFO of the GBP 9 billion Battersea Power Station urban renewal development in London and now a SME developer in Australia, Benn Zemek has experienced the impact of the bank retreat and subsequent private credit advance at both ends of the property development spectrum.

> As a very large and long-term mixed-use development, Battersea Power Station required substantial amounts of development debt (circa USD 5 billion) which would ordinarily require a large syndicate of traditional bank finance. However, the development commenced in the aftermath of the Global Financial Crisis in 2011 and therefore required some creative structuring in order procure the necessary development capital. The traditional non-recourse, interest capitalised development loan from the banking market was no longer possible. And the private credit market at that time also hadn't filled the void for projects on this scale and in any case was priced at a level that would not be feasible relative to the scale and timeframe of the project. Thus, we had to structure the facilities more like corporate debt with undertakings back to the institutional shareholders, in order to attract the necessary bank syndicate participants. We also explored and executed various other funding structures in the constant pursuit of well-priced capital to support the development, such as Murabaha financing (sharia finance) and forward purchase funding of specific commercial assets in the development (that could be suitably underwritten).
>
> At the other end of the development market, as a smaller private developer now in Australia, I have witnessed and benefited from the growth of the private lending market as it performs a crucial role enabling small to large scale property development; funding over a quarter of all residential construction in Australia and forecast to grow by a further 80% over the next five years. I personally think this level of private credit participation in the market is highly advantageous to the development sector as it generally offers an enhanced alignment of specialist expertise (vs banks) which improves underwriting, loan structuring/flexibility and risk management. That is, quality private credit funds tend to benefit from industry specialist teams who have a greater understanding of development risk and hence can provide better capital solutions for developers, who may otherwise not be able to procure feasible funding support and proceed with projects, which are critical in our current housing crisis.

CHAPTER 2

Anatomy of a Private Debt Deal

BRICKS, MORTAR AND THE BALANCE SHEET

When we launched LendInvest in 2013, the idea that private capital could directly fund property development was still novel—especially in a space long dominated by banks. But over the past decade, the story has evolved far beyond simply stepping in where banks pulled back. What's truly reshaped the market is the agility, speed and technological edge that private non-bank lenders bring to the table. For developers, it's no longer just about finding a lender when the bank says no—it's about finding a lender who can move quickly, structure deals creatively, offer flexible terms and leverage technology to deliver a seamless experience. Most importantly, it's about working with a lender who sees the deal through the same lens they do.

There's also the question of appetite: many of the projects our towns and cities genuinely need—affordable housing, care homes, community infrastructure—are developments traditional lenders often overlook or can't move fast enough to support. Private credit has shown it not only can but will.

—Christian Faes, Co-Founder & Chairman, LendInvest

In the previous chapter, we traced the fault lines that cracked the dominance of traditional bank-led real estate finance, giving rise to a more fragmented yet diversified lending landscape driven by private credit providers. But when we talk about real estate private credit, it's often described in abstract terms—mezzanine, unitranche, preferred equity, LTV, Loan-To-Cost (LTC) and LTGDV. Yet beneath the jargon lies something far more compelling and impactful: the human stories, real-world partnerships between housebuilders and lenders, structured to turn a simple vision into reality, strategic compromises done to bring those visions to life and most importantly, real-world outcomes we see across towns and cities. These are stories of collaboration: of housebuilders accessing capital that traditional banks no longer provide, of projects with deep social impact, like care homes and affordable housing, that would not have broken ground without private funding.

This chapter takes us beyond the theory and into the trenches. Over the next few pages, we follow the money as a catalyst: funding that turns vision on paper into lived-in homes, repurposes neglected Victorian buildings, enables the conversion of a derelict factory into New York Loft Style apartments and supports the creation of care homes that provide long-term security and dignity for older residents. The stories narrated over the next few pages bring private credit to life. These are deals that nearly fell through when banks backed away—or simply couldn't offer competitive terms—and yet were brought back to life through private credit. They reveal the shifting dynamics between capital and construction, between risk appetite and social impact.

What's striking about these stories is that each was developed by an SME housebuilder—the very lifeblood of the housebuilding sector not just in the UK, but around the world. These developers are the ones most acutely impacted by bank retrenchment, often lacking the scale, balance sheet strength, or political capital of national housebuilders. While large developers can still secure bank funding on reasonable terms, their smaller peers—often delivering the most creative and locally impactful schemes—find themselves frozen out.

In each example, we hear from the people behind the spreadsheets: developers under pressure to secure sites while navigating planning delays and unforgiving timelines; lenders eager to deploy capital, but only once risks are fully understood and priced; investment teams engineering capital stacks that can flex as projects evolve; and intermediaries brokering trust in a world where timing is often the difference between success and failure.

These key players reveal what happens behind the scenes. Their insights offer a window into the new DNA of real estate finance: complex, collaborative and increasingly bespoke. These conversations also reflect how in the early days of this shift, many borrowers were understandably hesitant. They were unsure whether these new lenders could really understand their needs or move with the urgency that property development demands. But as traditional lenders pulled back and non-bank capital proved itself to be faster, more flexible and agile, that hesitation gave way to partnership. What emerges is a new breed of lender-developer relationship, rooted not in red tape, but in trust, pace and commercial alignment.

What becomes increasingly clear as we explore these deals is this: the rise of real estate private credit isn't just a story of bank retreat. It's a story of how innovation in structuring, speed in execution and alignment of purpose have created space for private lenders to operate alongside—not in opposition to—traditional banks. Even in a world where banks hadn't retreated, they'd be hard pressed to match the agility and creativity private lenders bring to the table. Burdened by bureaucracy, regulation and legacy systems, traditional banks often can't accommodate the nuance and speed that today's developers need—especially in underwriting smaller, complex, or socially impactful projects which happen to have uncertain cashflows. Increasingly, the result is not displacement but partnership.

Through these stories, we peel back the layers of private debt, not as a financial instrument, but as an enabler of progress. These are the anatomy lessons of modern property finance: not taught in textbooks, but lived out, deal by deal.

GLOBAL CAPITAL, LOCAL IMPACT

It was a humid afternoon in the summer of 2018 when I found myself seated across from a sharply dressed American financier in a quiet corner of a members' club in London's Mayfair. A former investment banker, he'd recently launched a private credit platform to fund property developments across the UK.

As we spoke, his enthusiasm bubbled over as he shared details of several schemes he'd financed, including in Northern Ireland, which is often overlooked in mainstream development finance. At first glance, he seemed an unlikely match for Belfast or the rolling countryside of County Down: a former boss at a top-tier investment bank, more at home in glass-panelled City boardrooms than windswept roads across the Irish Sea. He'd only been to Belfast a handful of times, but each time—touring sites in and around the city—he'd seen something others had missed.

He told me he was actively deploying millions in property development loans across Northern Ireland. Affordable housing, small-scale regeneration, even community projects. These were not deals that made headlines, but they mattered deeply to the people who lived there. What struck me wasn't just the capital—though that, of course, was significant—it was the depth of effort he'd made to understand the market. He'd studied local planning rules, met with councils, spoken to developers and tracked comparable deals. In short, he'd approached Northern Ireland not as an afterthought for investors, but as a market worth understanding, and backing.

'Why Northern Ireland?' I asked? 'Because no one else is', he shrugged.

He was right. As we saw when we spoke with Joe McGinnis, after the 2008 financial crisis, most banks had quietly packed up and left the Northern Irish property market. Many had suffered heavy losses and simply didn't return. But it wasn't just the scars of the crisis that kept them away. The small scale of the Northern Irish market meant smaller sites, smaller loans and deals that were often too modest to justify the administrative overhead and regulatory complexity that came with traditional bank lending. For most lenders, it simply wasn't worth the effort.

And yet, bubbling below the surface, the Northern Irish market was alive with opportunity. A chronic housing shortage collided with the rise of a new generation of professionals, many working in emerging sectors like cybersecurity and tech the region had become known for. Belfast, in particular, was fast becoming a magnet for young talent and tech-driven job creation. First-time buyers were on the rise, demand was outpacing supply and local developers were keen to build: but they couldn't access capital.

Not long after, I sat down with the boss of a Northern Irish property development company. A quietly driven man with a clear vision, had founded the company with a mission to regenerate forgotten corners of Belfast and foster sustainable communities in their place. For him, development wasn't just about bricks and mortar, it was about renewal.

As a city once defined by its industrial might, Belfast's urban fabric was dotted with the remnants of a bygone era: crumbling warehouses, disused mills and empty factories. Where others saw dereliction, the developer saw opportunity. His approach was simple yet ambitious: breathe new life into old structures by turning them into high-quality homes, particularly aimed at the growing population of professionals choosing to stay, work and build lives in the city.

When I mentioned the financier's remarks about the lack of competition in the lending market, the developer nodded knowingly. 'He's right', he told me. 'The banks stopped lending and they never really came back. But the need didn't go away. We've had to look elsewhere, to partners who understand the local market, see the long-term value and are willing to get stuck in'.

Back to our Mayfair banker, what he saw was a market overlooked not because it lacked potential, but because it didn't fit the mould of institutional lending. And in that gap, he saw opportunity.

Both of these conversations stayed with me. They captured the essence of a broader shift I was starting to see everywhere: where banks once operated as the main arteries of local funding, today those arteries have narrowed. In their place, new channels have opened. Flexible. Fast. Global. As one developer told me, 'Before 2008, if I needed a loan, I'd walk into my local bank or building society branch and speak to someone I'd known for years. After the crisis, those people disappeared. Now, the names on the signs outside our sites are from London, New York, Zurich'.

Private credit, in this sense, is more than just an alternative funding source. It's a bridge. Capital raised in Manhattan boardrooms or Swiss family offices is financing local impact in places that banks have quietly exited and where those family offices would have never heard of.

DEALS IN THE REAL WORLD

What follows are stories that embody this shift. Behind every affordable housing scheme or care facility built through private debt, there's often a global thread: money that crossed borders to make something tangible happen on the ground. This is private credit as catalyst, where finance meets purpose and where a Mayfair meeting leads to homes in Northern Ireland. Our first case study explores the regeneration of a long-neglected industrial site and the role private credit played in breathing new life into the Hawkins Factory in Northampton.

OEH GROUP: REVIVING THE HAWKINS FACTORY

> Traditional banks saw too much risk—the heritage restrictions, the scale, the location. But where they saw hurdles, our non-bank lenders saw potential. Without that private funding, the Hawkins Factory would still be crumbling. They backed not just the numbers, but the vision.
>
> —Ermir Sefolli, Managing Director, OEH Group

A LANDMARK WAITING FOR A SECOND LIFE

Tucked into Northampton's historic Boot and Shoe Quarter stood the Hawkins Factory, a red-brick sentinel of Britain's once-mighty shoemaking industry. Built in the late nineteenth century, this Grade II-listed factory was no ordinary workplace. In 1855, it earned a Royal Warrant for supplying boots to Queen Victoria herself, outfitted climbers on the 1953 Everest expedition and produced military boots for British troops through two world wars. For generations, it was a cornerstone of local identity.

But time wasn't kind to the building. When it finally closed its doors in the 1990s, the once-bustling factory fell silent. Over the next two decades, it slipped into disrepair, becoming a ghost of its former self, as shown in Figure 2.1.

FIGURE 2.1 Hawkins Factory Before Regeneration
Source: With permission of OEH Group

(*Continued*)

(*Continued*)

The windows were shattered, the walls were weathered. What was once a proud symbol of British craftsmanship became a daily reminder of industrial decline.

TWO DECADES OF STALLED AMBITION

Its location—on the corner of St Michael's Road and Overstone Road—made it unmissable. For years, it stood there: prominent, central, but untouched. By the early 2000s, it had become one of Northampton's most visible undeveloped buildings. Despite being the subject of multiple planning applications attempts to kickstart its revival, progress was repeatedly thwarted.

Planning applications were submitted—some well-intentioned, others overly ambitious—but most stumbled at the first hurdle. Conservation concerns, listed building constraints and a near-impossible balance between modern use and historic preservation kept progress at bay. In 2016, it looked as though things might finally move forward when a renovation plan won approval. But disputes over window design and car parking allocations once again ground the project to a halt.

A DEVELOPER WILLING TO SEE THE POTENTIAL

By the time OEH stepped in, in 2022, the site had become something of a planning graveyard. A listed building filled with potential but weighed down by planning red tape and risk-averse lenders, a case full of promise but burdened by missed opportunities.

Still, OEH, a family-owned property development company specialising in the regeneration of Northamptonshire, saw what others hadn't: a chance to breathe new life into a building that once helped define the town.

'The plan for the building was to bring it back to the golden era it once had', said Sefolli.

> From the moment we first identified the opportunity, our focus was on aligning every stage of the process—from acquisition and planning, through to construction and final sale—with both the heritage of the site and the demands of today's market. This was about more than simply delivering apartments; it was about safeguarding the building's character while creating homes people genuinely wanted to live in. The success of this project lied in how we combined commercial discipline with respect for its history, ensuring that what we brought to market was not just property, but a lasting asset for the community.
>
> —Daniel Sutton, Operations Director, OEH Group

That vision became Hawkins Court: a carefully orchestrated regeneration project designed not just to deliver homes, but to reinvigorate Northampton's town centre.

OEH planned to convert the derelict factory into 89 stylish new homes; 17 studio apartments, 60 one-bedroom flats and 12 two-bedroom flats, all of which were designed as New York loft-style apartments, blending old-world craftsmanship with modern aspiration.

WHEN BANKS WALKED AWAY

Key features of the design paid homage to the building's industrial past: exposed timber beams, red-brick façades, iron-framed factory windows and vaulted interiors—all retained and restored, as shown in Figure 2.2. But this wasn't just a cosmetic upgrade. The project introduced energy-efficient infrastructure, delivering both architectural integrity and sustainability.

From the outset, OEH's ambitions went further than bricks and mortar. They sought to deliver affordable housing, support local jobs and create long-term economic value in an area often overlooked by institutional capital. Their goal wasn't just to restore a building: it was to re-anchor a community asset, one that had too long sat in limbo.

Despite the strength of OEH's vision, this regeneration project wasn't an easy sell. On paper, it ticked all the boxes of a difficult deal: a Grade II-listed building in a post-industrial town centre, complex in planning and deeply embedded in local context, heritage restrictions, legacy infrastructure and market comparables that couldn't match the project's ambition. Furthermore, the local market dynamics made the project unattractive to traditional lenders.

Mainstream institutions, with their rigid credit frameworks and risk-averse committees took one look, and walked away. It wasn't that they questioned the viability of the project. It was that they didn't know how to underwrite it. The building's quirks, its location in a regenerating area instead of a prime postcode and the careful balance of preservation and innovation made it hard to squeeze into a conventional banking model.

In the end, OEH didn't just need capital, they needed a financial partner that understood the nuance of regeneration and had the appetite to fund complexity. Private credit, not traditional banking, offered the solution. Indeed, OEH turned to non-bank capital to fund the deal, a decision that would align finance with local purpose.

PRIVATE CREDIT STEPS IN

Private lender Octopus Real Estate—an institution not only comfortable with complexity, but purpose-built for it—quickly got comfortable with the project. Where banks saw a crumbling factory and legacy risk, Octopus saw a heritage asset with regenerative value. Where traditional lenders hesitated over constraints, Octopus leaned in with bespoke structuring and human-led underwriting.

(*Continued*)

(*Continued*)

FIGURE 2.2 Interior of the Redeveloped Hawkins Factory
Source: With permission of OEH Group

Unlike a high-street bank operating from spreadsheets and centralised risk models, these lenders walk the site, sit in on planning consultations and work collaboratively to shape a financial solution tailored to the project's unique demands. Their approach is fast, flexible and informed by real understanding of regeneration finance.

> With a tight timescale to complete the loan and with a large redbrick conversion of an industrial building falling outside the appetite of most banks and many traditional lenders, we carefully selected Octopus as our partner of choice. They immediately understood the developer's

vision and what they were trying to achieve and acted as a sympathetic and flexible lender as the deal progressed.

Thanks to their empowered underwriters, efficient decision-making and skilled credit committee, we were able to complete on time—proving that bank lenders are not the only option to fund ambitious projects like this and giving the developer the financial means to deliver the conversion of this iconic building.

—Mason Ward—Head of Originations, Tiger Financial

STRUCTURING CAPITAL AROUND COMPLEXITY

The capital structure was designed to reflect the phased nature and layered sensitivity of the Hawkins regeneration. Structured as a GBP 9 million development loan facility with a 50% acquisition loan and a 100% development loan, it included multiple components that would have been extremely difficult to secure through traditional sources. The deal was completed within just 10 weeks, with the key terms summarised in Table 2.1.

The flexible drawdown model allowed OEH to align capital deployment with construction progress, reducing financing costs and supporting the careful restoration required for a listed building. Also, the ESG carve-out gave the developer room to prioritise retrofit and energy-efficiency measures, which would not only future-proof the building but also support other social and environmental outcomes.

This structure represented more than just financing—it was a vote of confidence in the scheme's social value. And crucially, it allowed OEH to stay true to the integrity of the building, instead of compromising to meet the rigid boxes of a bank's term sheet.

In every respect, private credit ended up being not just a lender of last resort—but a lender of right fit.

TABLE 2.1 Key Loan Terms for the Hawkins Factory Project

LTC	~75%—providing strong leverage while ensuring borrower alignment
Loan Amount (GBPm)	~6.5
Interest Rate	Competitive and reflective of the bespoke structure and listed-building complexity
Term	18–24 months with staged drawdowns aligned to build phases and planning milestones
ESG & Heritage Sub-Facility	Additional capital carved out for environmental upgrades and sensitive conservation works

(*Continued*)

(*Continued*)

PRIVATE CREDIT VERSUS BANK LENDING

The contrast between private credit and traditional bank finance was stark. While both provide capital for development projects, the way they assess risk, structure loans and work with borrowers can differ dramatically. Banks typically operate within rigid credit frameworks shaped by regulatory capital rules, standardised underwriting models and committee-driven approvals. Private credit lenders, by contrast, often adopt a more bespoke approach, structuring facilities around the specific realities of a project rather than forcing the project to fit predefined templates.

The practical implications of this difference are illustrated in Table 2.2, which compares the typical terms offered by private credit lenders with those commonly seen in traditional bank development finance.

TABLE 2.2 Private Credit Versus Traditional Bank Lending

Term	Private Credit Lender	Typical Traditional Bank
Loan Size (GBPm)	~9.0	Often lower or declined due to heritage risk and non-core location.
LTC	~75%	55–65% LTC, often capped lower for listed building conversions.
LTGDV	~65%	55–60%, depending on end-use and market absorption.
Term	18–24 months with phased drawdowns	12–18 months, rigid drawdown schedules.
Interest Rate	Variable reflective of complexity (e.g. 7–8% p.a.)	3.5–5.0% p.a. but rarely offered for heritage asset finance.
Arrangement Fee	1.0%	0.75–1.0%, sometimes waived for core clients.
Exit Fee	1.0–1.5%	Rare or nominal.
Broker Fee	1.0%	Usually not applicable (direct banking).
Speed of Execution	Fast (4–6 weeks), tailored process	Slow (10–16 weeks), credit and legal risk teams add delay
Underwriting Flexibility	High—heritage value, design-led adaptation considered	Low—difficult to assess adaptive reuse and listed constrains.
Risk Appetite	Strong for local regeneration, ESG retrofit sand placemaking	Weak—risk-averse to listed buildings and mixed-tenure design.

Term	Private Credit Lender	Typical Traditional Bank
Borrower Relationship	Hands-on, consultative, site visits included	Transactional and remote, limited post-approval flexibility.
Use of Personal Guarantee	Yes, capped	Yes, often higher or uncapped.
Covenants	Tailored to site (e.g. staged drawdowns, ESG retrofit KPIs)	Standard LTV/ICR covenants, little room for phased release or heritage factors.

FIGURE 2.3 Midlands Regeneration Project of the Year Award for Hawkins Court (2024)
Source: With permission of OEH Group

A FACTORY REBORN

By early 2024, the Hawkins redevelopment was complete, delivering 89 New-York Loft Style apartments and offering a blend of private sale, rental and affordable housing. Later that year, the project was awarded Regeneration Project of the Year at the prestigious National Property Awards (Figure 2.3) and praised for its sensitive architecture, impact-led investment and commitment to ESG goals.

(*Continued*)

(*Continued*)

> It felt like Northampton's biggest Christmas present this year—the long-neglected factory finally reborn.
>
> —Local resident quoted in the Northampton Chronicle, reflecting the anticipation surrounding the reopening.

Northampton gained more than housing stock. It gained a renewed sense of place. The project supported local trades, created jobs and reconnected residents to a site many had assumed would be lost forever.

WHY THIS CASE MATTERS

> Private credit didn't just back the build—it helped reboot the neighbourhood.
>
> —Ermir Sefolli

The story of the Hawkins Factory is more than a tale of bricks, beams and balance sheets. It's a case study in what happens when vision meets the right kind of capital, not just capital with depth, but capital with conviction.

At its heart, this was a regeneration effort rooted in community, not just commerce. OEH didn't set out to erase the past. They set out to preserve it, reimagine it and fold it into the future. The result? A striking transformation that kept the soul of the building intact, while opening the doors to modern, affordable homes in the heart of Northampton's historic Shoe Quarter.

But none of it would have happened without private credit stepping up where traditional finance stood back. Banks wouldn't touch the deal: too fiddly, too small, too niche. But private lenders looked past the spreadsheet and saw the substance. They understood the value of adaptive finance, of structuring capital around complexity, not in spite of it.

The outcome speaks for itself: economic uplift in a long-overlooked corner of town, renewed footfall in a once-forgotten area and homes that carry a story, not just a sales price. The regeneration of the Hawkins Factory is a reminder that the most powerful developments are often those that honour place, respond to need and are made possible by finance that dares to be flexible.

This wasn't just a funding story. It was a catalytic act of place-making—the kind that ripples far beyond the construction site and deep into the life of a community.

The Hawkins Factory revival offers more than a compelling regeneration story. It stands as a vivid reminder of the catalytic power of private credit in places where traditional finance fails. What began as a crumbling industrial relic, burdened by planning complications and decades of inertia, became a landmark example of what flexible capital, local commitment and development expertise can achieve when aligned.

What OEH achieved here was more than the rescue of a neglected structure; it was the repair of a gap in the town's social fabric. With the support of private credit, a long-abandoned factory was not only restored but reinterpreted for modern life, preserving Northampton's heritage while creating homes, economic activity and renewed civic pride.

But Hawkins is only one chapter in a broader story. Across Northamptonshire and beyond, sites that once powered local industry now sit in limbo and face uncertain futures, dismissed as too awkward, too risky, or too constrained for conventional lenders. Yet these very buildings are now being reshaped by developers who understand their communities, supported by credit providers prepared to back ambition over simplicity.

This shift is perhaps most clearly illustrated in OEH's next major undertaking: the regeneration of Higham Road in Rushden. While very different in scale, setting and history, this project shares the same essential DNA as Hawkins: a working past in need of rewriting, a local developer with a vision grounded in place and a financing environment where private lenders became the enablers of progress.

OEH GROUP: FROM BUS DEPOT TO HOMES

> This wasn't a flagship London scheme or a glossy headline-grabber. It was a local site with history, constraints and real demand. The challenge wasn't whether it could work—it was whether anyone was prepared to finance it.
>
> —Daniel Sutton

AN OLD DEPOT, NEW POSSIBILITIES

On Higham Road, just a short walk from Rushden town centre in the East Midlands of England, sat a site that most residents had learned to ignore. For decades, it had been home to Birch Bros, a local bus and coach operator whose roots dated back to the mid-nineteenth century, when it began running horse-drawn carriages in London. As the business expanded beyond the capital to Hertfordshire and Bedfordshire, Birch Bros eventually turned its attention to Rushden in the late 1930s.

In 1937, a new modern garage and coach station was built on High Street: a splendid Art Deco structure, designed to what contemporary newspapers described as cinema style, reflecting the optimism and mobility of the inter-war years. As shown in Figure 2.4, the depot quickly became a hub of daily life, with engines warming before dawn, drivers rotating shifts and buses threading together villages, factories and town centres across Northamptonshire.

(*Continued*)

(*Continued*)

FIGURE 2.4 Birch Bros Bus Depot on Higham Road
Source: With permission of OEH Group

But by the late 1960s, the economics of regional transport had shifted. In 1969, the depot ceased operations and by 1971 the business and remaining coaches were sold. Birch Bros quietly faded from the transport landscape, leaving behind buildings that no longer had a purpose.

A SITE LEFT IN LIMBO

For decades, the site lingered in limbo—fenced off, underused and slowly decaying—a reminder of Rushden's industrial past and its stalled transition into something new. Parts of the building were intermittently used for storage; others sat empty. Roofs deteriorated, hardstanding cracked and temporary fencing became permanent. What had once symbolised progress gradually became a reminder of stagnation: a centrally located brownfield site, too visible to ignore, yet too complicated to resolve easily.

REGENERATION WAITING TO HAPPEN

By the time OEH started exploring the Higham Road opportunity, the site had accumulated a familiar planning history: pre-application discussions, withdrawn proposals and a previous appeal. Structurally sound in parts, but constrained by legacy infrastructure and former industrial use, it had become a textbook example of latent regeneration, a site waiting for the right combination of patience, capital and local understanding.

As seen in the previous case study, OEH—the Northamptonshire-based, family-owned developer—had built its reputation on precisely these kinds of projects. Its focus was not transformational megastructures, but careful, repeatable regeneration in towns often overlooked by national capital.

Where others saw inconvenience, OEH saw familiarity. And where outsiders perceived risk, OEH recognised nuance.

OPPORTUNITY OTHERS MISSED

Rushden is not a market that features heavily in national development brochures. It does not boast the transport connectivity of London commuter towns, nor the branding appeal of university cities.

But that was precisely the point.

The town has a stable employment base, improving local amenities and strong demand for well-designed, attainable housing, particularly from first-time buyers, downsizers and local professionals. What it lacked was modern housing stock in walkable locations close to the town centre.

OEH's vision for Higham Road was therefore pragmatic instead of grand.

Marketed as Home Suite Home, the scheme would transform the former Birch Bros bus depot into a high-quality residential scheme that respected the site's industrial DNA while delivering contemporary homes designed for real people, not speculative yield.

The plan was to build 33 one- and two-bedroom flats, three townhouses and one small ground-floor commercial unit. In total, 37 residential units, blending retained structures with sensitively designed new-build elements. Industrial cues would be retained in materials and massing, but the emphasis was on light, efficiency and liveability instead of architectural theatrics.

'This wasn't about importing a concept', notes Sutton. 'It was about building homes that made sense for Rushden: in scale, pricing and design'.

OUTSIDE THE BANKING TEMPLATE

Despite its merits, Higham Road struggled to gain traction with traditional lenders.

'The feedback was consistent', recalls Sutton. 'The deal was too small to justify the work, but too complex to fit standard residential boxes. Former industrial use, part-conversion, secondary location: none of that plays well with automated credit models'.

Former industrial use raised environmental and planning considerations. The local market, while stable, did not fit neatly into national valuation models. And the adaptive reuse element—part refurbishment, part redevelopment—complicated underwriting assumptions.

(*Continued*)

(*Continued*)

For mainstream banks, the issue was not viability, but efficiency. Credit teams struggled to price the risk. Committees hesitated over resale comparables. And the administrative burden outweighed the perceived return.

What OEH needed was not cheap capital, but appropriate capital. A lender willing to underwrite the site as it was, not as a spreadsheet abstraction.

FUNDING WHERE BANKS WOULDN'T

That capital came eventually from Sancus, a Manchester-based non-bank lender specialising in development finance across the UK's regional markets. Built specifically to operate where banks retreat, Sancus combines relationship-led underwriting with local market fluency.

Unlike a traditional lender, Sancus approached Higham Road from the ground up. They walked the site with OEH, reviewed planning history in detail and assessed demand through local absorption instead of national averages.

The resulting facility was structured to reflect delivery realities instead of theoretical models, with the key financing terms summarised in Table 2.3.

CAPITAL ALIGNED WITH CONSTRUCTION

The facility combined acquisition finance and development funding into a single structure tailored to the scheme's needs.

Drawdowns were phased in line with build milestones, giving the developer flexibility while maintaining lender discipline.

At one stage, rising build-cost inflation threatened to compress contingency buffers. Instead of forcing a redesign, Sancus worked with OEH to re-profile drawdowns and extend timing flexibility: a small adjustment that preserved viability without compromising discipline.

TABLE 2.3 Higham Road Development Loan Terms

Total Facility Size (GBPm)	~4.8
Acquisition Loan (GBPm)	~2.1
Development Facility (GBPm)	~2.7
Term	24 months, plus a six-month extension at no additional cost
LTC	~70%
LTGDV	~62%
Interest Rate	Mid-to-high single digits, reflecting bespoke structuring
Drawdowns	Phased, aligned to build milestones

FROM DEPOT TO HOMES

Construction progressed steadily. The depot's industrial footprint was softened into residential scale. Old circulation routes were re-stitched into human ones. Where buses once queued, front doors now opened. The completed redevelopment is shown in Figure 2.5.

The scheme is expected to be completed by mid-2026. Once finished, the apartments will be brought to market through local agents and are likely to feature prominently in the *Northants Telegraph*. Pricing has been designed to remain within reach of local buyers, with demand expected to be driven by first-time purchasers, downsizers and local professionals.

Beyond the numbers, the scheme reactivated a dormant site, supported local contractors and improved the visual fabric of Higham Road. It proved that regeneration need not be spectacular to be successful.

FIGURE 2.5 Redeveloped Higham Road Residential Scheme
Source: With permission of OEH Group

(*Continued*)

(Continued)

FIGURE 2.5 (Continued)

THE CAPITAL STACK

Higham Road's financing illustrates a recurring pattern in regional regeneration. Projects that appear modest in scale can still require carefully structured capital, particularly when redevelopment involves brownfield land, adaptive reuse and local market dynamics. The key financial metrics for the scheme are summarised in Table 2.4.

TABLE 2.4 Higham Road Development Financing Overview

Metric	Higham Road
Total GDV (GBPm)	~7.7
Total facility (GBPm)	~4.8
LTC	~70%
LTGDV	~62%
Term	24 + 6 months
Structure	Acquisition + Development
Lender Type	Non-bank private credit

The structure balanced prudence with flexibility—protecting downside while enabling delivery.

THE REGIONAL FUNDING GAP

In many ways, Higham Road mirrors dozens of regeneration stories unfolding across Britain's secondary towns. Sites that are too small, too local, or too nuanced for institutional balance sheets, yet vital to their communities.

What differentiates successful outcomes from stalled ones is rarely planning policy or market demand alone. It is capital, and the type of capital willing to engage.

Private credit does not replace banks wholesale. But it fills the gaps banks leave behind. It funds the projects that matter locally but fall outside national templates. It underwrites complexity with judgment instead of avoidance.

For OEH, Higham Road was not an anomaly. It was a continuation of a strategy rooted in local knowledge, disciplined execution and aligned financing.

LESSONS FROM HIGHAM ROAD

Higham Road will never be a landmark listed in architectural textbooks. It will not win national regeneration awards. But its impact is no less real.

It returned a redundant industrial site to productive use. It delivered homes people can afford and want to live in. And it demonstrated—once again—that the future of British housing will not be built solely by mega-schemes or institutional giants.

Regeneration isn't always about transformation', reflects Sutton. 'Sometimes it's about restoration—restoring usefulness, relevance and confidence in places that quietly matter'.

Behind many such projects stands private credit, not chasing headlines but enabling outcomes.

What OEH's Higham Road deal ultimately illustrates is not just how private credit fills a financing gap, but how it reframes the narrative of risk. Where traditional lenders see complexity as something to be avoided, private capital can engage with context; where uncertainty deters, alignment and judgement can unlock progress.

In Rushden, private capital did more than finance a development. It enabled a project that needed patience, local understanding and a willingness to engage with history as much as with spreadsheets. The value of private credit here lay not in filling the void left by banks, but in underwriting a scheme that sat outside conventional templates.

That pattern is increasingly visible across other parts of the real estate market where demand is structural, delivery is constrained and traditional lenders struggle to reconcile operational complexity with standardised risk models. One such area is later-living and care homes.

Across the developed world, demographic forces are reshaping real estate demand. Populations are ageing rapidly; the cohort aged 65 and over is growing faster than any other age group, life expectancy continues to rise and this demographic often benefits from relatively strong and resilient purchasing power. The result has been sustained pressure on later-living infrastructure, from retirement housing to nursing and dementia care facilities.

Yet despite clear demand, delivery has lagged. Purpose-built care homes, designed to meet modern clinical, regulatory and accessibility standards, remain chronically undersupplied.

The reality is that traditionally, care homes have sat at an uncomfortable intersection for banks: operationally intensive, tightly regulated and reliant not only on asset value but on the operator's track record. For traditional lenders used to underwriting straightforward residential or commercial developments, that combination of construction risk, operational risk, staffing exposure, regulatory oversight and long-dated cashflow has often been enough to trigger conservative credit assumptions, higher discount rates or deter appetite altogether.

As one senior real estate lender put it to me: 'Banks are geared towards private-equity-grade assets or plain-vanilla residential delivery. Anything that criss-crosses with services and regulation tends to stall credit committees'.

If traditional lenders never had much of an appetite for the care sector, things deteriorated following the 2020 Covid pandemic when care homes quickly became one of the first sectors to face a credit crunch. Banks refused to lend money or provide new services for fear that the sector was about to crumble. In 2021, in the aftermath of the pandemic, a survey of care providers carried out by the Hampshire Care Association (HCA) found that 20% had been told their bank was concerned about their long-term viability.

Private credit lenders, by contrast, operate with fewer regulatory constraints and greater flexibility in how risk is assessed, structured and priced. Freed from rigid balance-sheet restrictions, they are able to underwrite based on asset-specific fundamentals: local supply and demand, operator quality and track record, cash-flow durability and long-term social relevance. In markets where care provision is both economically necessary and socially critical, that flexibility has translated into genuine appetite.

The next case study explores how private credit helped bridge the financing gap in later-living development. It examines why traditional banks continue to struggle with this asset class, how specialist lenders structure capital around operational risk and what it takes to align long-term financial returns with social impact.

MACC CARE GROUP: DELIVERING MODERN CARE INFRASTRUCTURE

> Over the last decade, care home lending in the United Kingdom has undergone a notable transformation. What was once viewed as a niche area of CRE is now widely recognised as a resilient and strategically important asset class.
>
> —Naz Nathani, Director, MACC Care Group

A DEVELOPMENT GROUNDED IN DEMOGRAPHIC REALITY

By the mid-2020s, MACC had become one of the UK's most experienced care-home developers and operators. Founded with a clear focus on delivering purpose-built residential and dementia care facilities, the group had built a reputation for combining development expertise with operational depth, a combination that lenders often say they value but rarely encounter in practice.

In Staffordshire, MACC had secured planning consent for a new-build care home in Codsall, a village on the western edge of Wolverhampton. The approved scheme proposed an 80-bed, purpose-built care home designed to accommodate residential, nursing and dementia care within a modern, high-specification environment, as illustrated in Figure 2.6.

The project reflects a broader shift within the UK care sector. As older, converted buildings become increasingly unsuitable for modern care standards, there is now an increased emphasis on the development of purpose-built facilities that provide greater accessibility, improved infection control, more efficient operational layouts and are generally future proof to both fulfil the rising demand and contribute to the phasing out of older accommodation.

The demographic context only reinforced the need. Across the country, the population aged over 75 has been growing significantly faster than the national average, placing sustained pressure on local care provision. Planning authorities and health bodies have repeatedly highlighted the shortage of modern care capacity, particularly for specialist dementia services.

FIGURE 2.6 Modern Care Home Development in Codsall
Source: With permission of MACC Care

(*Continued*)

(*Continued*)

On paper, the Codsall scheme appeared well aligned with those policy priorities. The design incorporated generous communal spaces, landscaped gardens and carefully planned operational facilities intended to support both residents and staff.

WHY CARE HOMES CHALLENGE CONVENTIONAL LENDING

Despite strong demand fundamentals, care-home development occupies an unusual position within real estate finance. Unlike standard commercial property, where income is typically derived from long leases to tenants, care homes generate revenue through operational performance, occupancy levels, staffing costs and regulatory compliance.

This hybrid nature—part real estate, part operating business—has historically made many traditional lenders cautious.

'Care-home lending has evolved enormously over the past decade', explains Nathani. 'What lenders increasingly focus on is not just profitability, but cash generation. Metrics like CFADS (Cash Flow Available for Debt Service) have become central to underwriting decisions because they reflect the operational realities of running a care home'.

That shift reflects the sector's growing maturity. While high-street banks once dominated care-home lending, the funding landscape has broadened considerably. Challenger banks, specialist healthcare lenders and private credit funds have entered the market, each applying different underwriting frameworks and risk appetites.

Traditional banks still tend to offer the lowest cost of capital, but they also typically require lower leverage and impose tighter covenants. Specialist lenders, by contrast, often operate at higher margins but provide greater flexibility, particularly for transitional assets or development projects.

WHEN CONVENTIONAL FINANCE FALLS SHORT

For many credit committees, lending on an 80-bed care home on a projection-led basis requires familiarity and confidence in the process and the developer. Income projections depended on future occupancy and operational performance rather than pre-leased rental contracts, and valuation comparables were relatively limited.

The hesitation reflected a structural reality of bank lending. Credit models built around standardised property assets often struggle to accommodate operationally intensive sectors such as healthcare.

'Even with planning permission secured and a strong operating track record', Nathani notes, 'many lenders simply don't have frameworks designed to assess the operational aspects of care homes as eventual value creation from mature trading defines the turnkey value of a completed development and tends to be the basis of development funding security assessment'.

A SPECIALIST DEVELOPMENT LENDER

In this case, MACC progressed discussions with Broadwood Capital, a specialist real estate lender focused on sectors where operational performance and real estate value are closely intertwined. Broadwood had existing relationship and familiarity with MACC having supported a previous development.

Founded to support mid-sized development projects across the UK, Broadwood has made later-living and healthcare assets one of the core focuses of its strategy. The firm's approach reflects a recognition that care homes require a different underwriting lens from conventional residential or commercial developments.

Instead of evaluating the project purely as property, Broadwood assessed the Codsall scheme as a combined real estate and operating business.

That meant examining not only construction costs and projected values, but also the operator's track record, local commissioning dynamics, staffing assumptions and the expected trajectory of occupancy growth once the facility opened.

A purpose-built asset paired with strong demographic fundamentals is key for an specialist lender and deeper analysis ultimately allowed Broadwood to become comfortable with the project.

In 2024, the lender agreed to provide a development finance facility of approximately GBP 14 million to fund the construction of the Codsall care home.

STRUCTURING FINANCE AROUND DELIVERY

Development financing for care homes must account for a sequence of distinct phases: land acquisition, construction, commissioning and operational ramp-up. Unlike many commercial buildings, care homes do not reach stable performance immediately after completion.

Broadwood's facility was therefore structured to reflect the project's practical delivery timeline.

The key financial metrics for the scheme are summarised in Table 2.5.

TABLE 2.5 Higham Road Development Financing Overview

Facility size (GBPm)	~14
Term	around 21 months, aligned with construction and commissioning timelines
Leverage	roughly 85% LTC
Structure	staged drawdowns tied to construction milestones
Funding source	Broadwood's Later Living Sustainable Construction Finance Fund

(*Continued*)

(*Continued*)

This structure provided MACC with sufficient capital to move from planning consent into construction while maintaining alignment between lender oversight and the realities of the build programme.

'What mattered most wasn't just access to funding', Nathani reflects. 'It was having a lender that understood how care homes are actually developed and operated and realistic timescales within which this can be achieved with confidence'.

UNDERWRITING BEYOND THE SPREADSHEET

Broadwood's due diligence extended well beyond construction budgets. The underwriting process examined MACC's operating portfolio, development track record and historical performance in successfully commissioning care homes and getting them to maturity.

In particular, the lender focused on the metrics that increasingly shape care-sector finance: occupancy trajectories, staffing stability and projected cash flows.

These indicators form the basis of the CFADS framework now widely used by specialist lenders in the sector which is an important variable for a development lender to stratify exit risk and timing to a senior lender at or following completion.

For mature homes with stable occupancy, lenders may ultimately extend leverage of 4.75 to 6.25 times EBITDA, depending on risk appetite and covenant structures. For assets which have proven trade and are on a trajectory to mature, some senior lenders are able to lend at a higher multiple with expected multiple settling within this range at maturity. Development lending, however, remains more conservative, reflecting construction risk and the time required for new homes to reach operational maturity.

Borrower contributions also remain central. Developers typically provide 15–20% of total project costs, often through land acquisition and planning expenditure.

MACC's long track record of delivering projects and refinancing completed homes helped reassure Broadwood that the Codsall scheme would ultimately transition into a stable operating asset.

NAVIGATING REAL-WORLD COMPLEXITY

Even well-structured development projects rarely proceed without challenges.

Pre-start matters, the discharge of planning conditions, and the discovery of design elements requiring minor amendments are common issues for developers, and they require a lender who understands and can accommodate these realities.

For traditional lenders, such changes can trigger covenant reviews or funding pauses.

'In regulated sectors like care, unknowns are inevitable', Nathani explains. 'What matters is how lenders respond when those unknowns arise'.

The issue was ultimately resolved without significant disruption, illustrating the value of lender flexibility, familiarity and confidence in complex development projects.

DELIVERING SOCIAL INFRASTRUCTURE

Once completed, the Codsall care home will provide 80 en-suite bedrooms designed for residential, nursing and dementia care, alongside landscaped outdoor areas within modern future-proof facilities.

Beyond the financial metrics, the project addresses a critical gap in regional care provision.

Across the UK, demand for later-living infrastructure continues to grow as the population ages and family-based care becomes increasingly difficult to sustain. Purpose-built care homes play a vital role in supporting both local communities and broader healthcare systems.

For investors, the attraction lies not only in yield but also in the resilience of the underlying demand drivers.

Demographic trends provide a relatively predictable foundation for long-term occupancy, while operational performance can generate stable cash flows once facilities reach maturity.

A CHANGING LENDING LANDSCAPE

The Codsall project reflects a broader transformation in care-home finance.

Over the past decade, the sector has shifted from a small, bank-dominated lending market to a more diversified ecosystem that includes challenger banks, specialist healthcare lenders and private credit funds.

Each plays a distinct role within the capital stack.

Traditional banks continue to offer the lowest pricing for stabilised assets. Specialist lenders, meanwhile, increasingly support development projects and transitional facilities where operational expertise and flexible structuring are essential.

For operators such as MACC, this evolving funding landscape has opened new strategic possibilities.

By building long-term relationships with multiple lenders, developers can align each project with the financing partner best suited to its risk profile and stage of maturity.

WHY THIS CASE MATTERS

The Staffordshire care-home development illustrates several broader themes shaping modern real estate credit markets.

(*Continued*)

(*Continued*)

First, specialisation matters. Sectors that combine real estate with operational complexity often require lenders with deep domain knowledge.

Second, flexible structuring reduces execution risk. Development finance aligned with real-world delivery timelines can prevent otherwise viable projects from stalling.

And third, private credit increasingly supports socially essential infrastructure. Care homes, hospitals and other healthcare assets represent areas where demographic demand intersects with long-term capital.

For MACC, the project ultimately demonstrated the importance of combined developer and lender expertise with asset complexity.

'Finance isn't just about cost', Nathani reflects. 'It's about finding partners who understand the sector and can support projects from planning through to operation'.

In sectors like care provision, that alignment can determine whether a project remains an approved plan on paper, or becomes a facility that serves communities for decades to come.

MACC's care home loan is a reminder that private credit's impact is often felt most keenly where capital is scarce and stakes are deeply human. By stepping into a sector that mainstream lenders had retreated from, it did more than finance bricks and mortar; it helped sustain continuity of care, dignity in later life and the delivery of essential social infrastructure.

THE CAPITAL BEHIND THE TRANSFORMATION

The stories we have seen reflect a pattern increasingly evident: when traditional finance hesitates, projects stall; but when specialist lenders step forward with the right structure and conviction, whole neighbourhoods begin to move again. In the case of the Hawkins Factory, the Higham Road project or the MACC care home, the outcomes speak to something larger than a single development. They show how private credit has become an active agent of renewal, funding schemes that mainstream lenders shun because they deem them too complex, too small, or too context-dependent. Yet capital alone does not explain the story. These projects succeeded because the financing aligned with vision and execution.

And that raises a fundamental question at the heart of today's real estate debt ecosystem: who is providing this capital and what motivates them to fund projects that banks no longer will?

These schemes are the visible expressions of deeper shifts in investor appetite, regulation and market structure. To understand why private credit has stepped so powerfully into this space—and why it is likely to remain a cornerstone of real estate finance—we need to follow the money and trace who is backing private debt.

CHAPTER 3

Follow the Money: Who Backs Private Real Estate Debt—and Why

THE SILENT ARCHITECTS OF CAPITAL

> *The way our investors think about private real estate credit today is fundamentally different from a decade ago. To them, it's no longer a peripheral strategy—it's a core building block in diversified portfolios. Investors want yield, they want downside protection and they want exposure to high-quality real assets without the volatility of equity. Private credit offers all of that. As the traditional lending landscape evolves, we believe this asset class is only going to grow in relevance and scale.*
>
> —Eugenio Sangermano, CEO, BF.capital GmbH

We began by tracing the rise of non-bank lenders in the aftermath of the Global Financial Crisis, and in the last chapter we saw how that shift plays out in practice through real-world deals funded by private credit. We've walked the ground with SME housebuilders, visited reimagined shoe factories and care homes and heard from those navigating the realities of construction finance in a post-bank era.

But there's one important question still lingering: who is actually making the payments?

Pull back the curtain and a quietly powerful line-up of actors emerges: layered, sophisticated, international and increasingly strategic. Behind the scenes of private real estate credit sits an eclectic cast of capital allocators, each playing a different role. From the cautious to the contrarian; from patient institutions—sometimes tucked away in a remote Swiss town—safeguarding pensions to fast-moving Wall Street funds chasing yield; from balance-sheet lenders to data-driven disruptors, all performing on the same stage and together reshaping the financial architecture of property development across the globe (Table 3.1).

Importantly, this ecosystem is far more diverse than meets the eye. At its core sit the pension funds, long-term stewards of capital whose primary goal is to meet future liabilities with steady, predictable cashflow. In a world of volatile markets, geopolitical uncertainties and lacklustre bond returns, private real estate credit has emerged as a compelling fit: secured, income-generating and backed by hard, tangible assets.

As one senior European pension fund allocator, with more than three decades of experience, put it, 'Fifteen years ago, real estate debt wasn't really on the radar for most

TABLE 3.1 Rising Allocations to Private Debt Across Institutional Investors

Year	Insurance Company	Private Pension Fund	Public Pension Fund	Foundation/ Endowment	Sovereign Wealth Fund	Average
2017		5.2%	4.7%			
2022		6.1%	3.6%			
2023	7.11%	6.18%	5.39%	4.12%		5.7%
2024	8.62%	7.12%	5.54%	4.48%		6.44%
H1 2025	6.6%	5.8%	5.4%	4.2%	6.9%	5.7%

pension funds. We were mainly equity investors. What's changed is the combination of regulation, dislocation and opportunity. Banks stepped back, spreads widened and suddenly you could access senior, asset-backed lending at returns that actually move the needle for a pension portfolio. For us, it's become a core allocation because it offers duration, income and capital preservation in a way few other asset classes can'.

Alongside pension funds sit the global insurance companies, many of them managing hundreds of billions tied to long-duration commitments like life and annuity portfolios. These institutions are also drawn to private debt's ability to generate structured, reliable yield, especially in a market where public instruments no longer offer a meaningful match for their long-term obligations.

Then there are the sovereign wealth funds—particularly those from resource-rich nations—looking to bullet-proof the future of their young populations by diversifying away from hydrocarbons and into tangible, income-generating assets with reliable cashflow. For these state-backed giants, real estate private credit offers a way to generate long-term, inflation-resilient returns while preserving downside protection through secured claims on property. It's more than just a yield play. It is a strategy rooted in intergenerational stability.

The institutional shift towards private debt is now unmistakable. According to Macfarlanes' 2024 Real Estate Debt Funds Report, private debt funds now account for over GBP 60 billion in deployed or committed real estate lending capital across the UK and continental Europe, a figure that has tripled in less than a decade. Nearly half of this capital comes from institutional investors—insurers, pension funds and sovereign wealth funds—while fund-of-funds and family offices make up a growing share of the balance.

For many institutions, part of the attraction lies in the blend of yield and security that asset-backed real estate loans offer. The same Macfarlanes report notes that the typical UK real estate debt fund today lends at LTV ratios between 55% and 70%, with net target returns ranging from 5% to 10%, depending on structure and seniority. That puts these funds firmly in the 'enhanced yield, controlled risk' camp, and helps explain their growing role as an institutional mainstay instead of an opportunistic niche.

To put it into context, the yield on the UK 10-year gilt currently hovers around 5.0%, while the US 10-year Treasury sits near 4.4%, only marginally above their

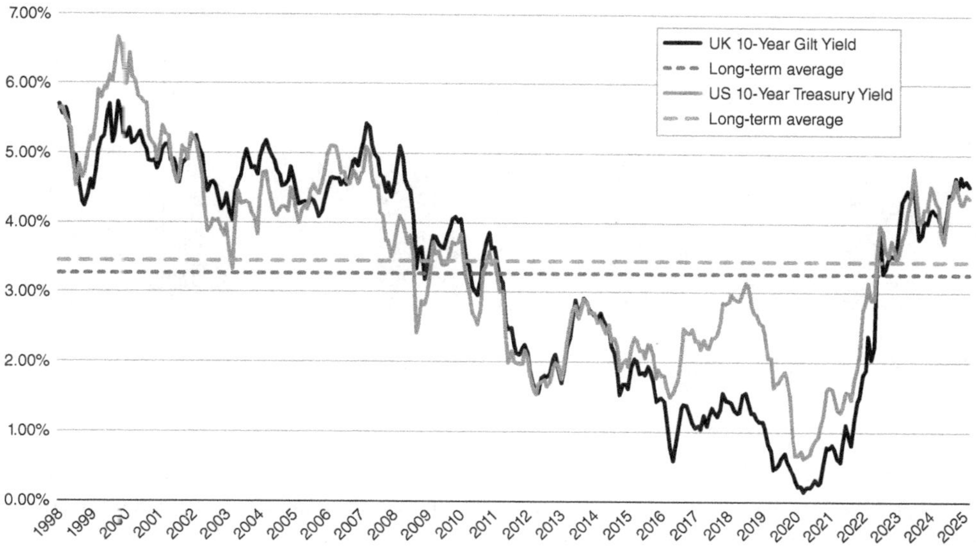

FIGURE 3.1 Sovereign Yields Relative to Long-Term Averages

long-term averages (Figure 3.1). For investors managing liabilities that stretch out for decades, such muted returns on supposedly 'safe' assets no longer cut it. Private real estate debt, by contrast, offers not only enhanced yield, but the added comfort of downside protection through secured claims, an increasingly rare combination in today's uncertain economic landscape.

But while institutions were first movers, the story didn't end there. Private wealth investors—high-net-worth individuals, family offices and boutique asset managers—have all followed suit, drawn by the same balance of yield and downside protection. The democratisation of access to lending opportunities through regulated platforms for smaller allocations has further opened the gates to retail investors.

Crucially, none of this capital deploys itself. Sitting at the centre of the system are the investment managers, the architects who structure, syndicate and guide this growing market. They range from global alternative giants such as Federated Hermes, Blackstone, Brookfield and Apollo—firms managing hundreds of billions, and in some cases more than a trillion dollars—to more niche and specialist private credit managers such as BF.capital in Germany, Alpinum Investment Management in Switzerland or Pemberton Asset Management across Europe. These firms combine deep local market expertise with institutional-grade governance and risk management. They source the opportunities, structure the funds, underwrite the deals and manage the risk and, crucially, know how to move quickly when traditional lenders stall.

And rising in tandem is a new generation of digital players, P2P lending platforms that are democratising access to real estate credit. What began as a fringe experiment has evolved into a regulated, technology-enabled infrastructure. These digital-first platforms now connect everyday investors—from retirees in Surrey to family offices in Singapore—directly with borrowers, offering transparency, speed and tailored risk

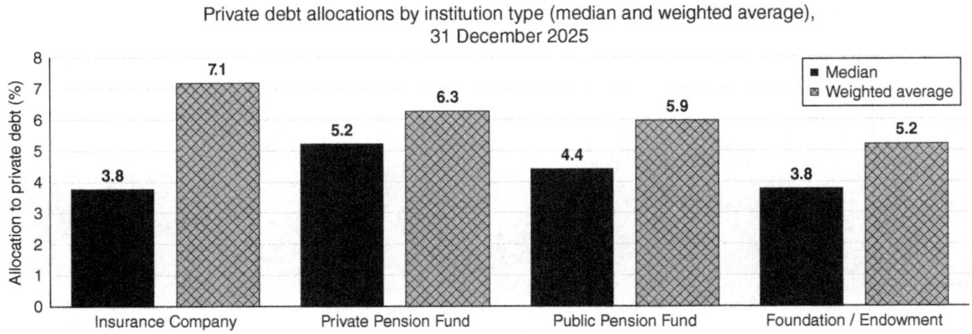

FIGURE 3.2 Private Credit as a Core Allocation

profiles. In doing so, they are opening up the asset class to investors who, a decade ago, would have never touched real estate debt, either because it was not on their radar or because those opportunities were simply inaccessible to them.

Together, this network forms the modern engine room of real estate finance. Private credit is no longer a niche or opportunistic play. It has become a core allocation in institutional portfolios across the globe, as Figure 3.2 shows. From North American pension funds to the sovereign wealth funds of the Gulf, from Australian superannuation funds to Swiss insurers, private credit is now woven into the way smart money thinks about real assets.

In this chapter, we go backstage. We hear from the CEOs, asset allocators and real estate heads who are actively shifting capital into private debt. What drives them? What return hurdles do they set? How do they decide which risks are worth taking?

These themes come to life through real case studies: a California pension fund backing an urban regeneration debt fund; a German specialist asset manager backing one of Berlin's largest and most prominent real estate projects; a German insurer channelling long-dated capital into senior loans for residential developments. Each example sheds light not just on investor preferences, but on the broader evolution of the capital stack, and how the architecture of real estate finance is being redrawn.

At a time when inflation remains stubborn—driven in part by geopolitical tensions disrupting supply chains and energy markets—and interest rates have been anything but steady, the appeal of private real estate credit is easy to grasp. But institutional appetite isn't static. This chapter also explores how allocation strategies are evolving in a post-zero interest rate environment, where the bar for illiquidity premiums is rising, due diligence is more rigorous than ever, and investors are increasingly attuned to political as well as financial risk.

HOW PENSION FUNDS BECAME LENDERS

Pension funds across the developed world have spent the past decades grappling with two long-term structural pressures. On one side: demographics. Longer life expectancy and falling birth rates mean ageing populations are drawing from the retirement pot for longer, while fewer active workers are replenishing it. In many advanced economies, roughly a quarter of the population is now aged 60 or over. On the other: markets. Public equity and government bond markets that used to be the backbone of pension investment portfolios have delivered increasingly meagre and volatile returns, putting further strain on long-term funding models.

These pressures are particularly acute in pay-as-you-go pension systems. As the ratio of contributors to beneficiaries drops, sustainability becomes harder to maintain. JP Morgan research shows the shift starkly: in France, the number of active contributors per pensioner has tumbled from around four in the 1960s to just 1.7 today. The trend is similar across other developed economies. In the UK, the number of working-age people supporting each pensioner is expected to fall sharply over the next 25 years, from 3.5 workers per pensioner in 2025 to just 2.2 by 2050.

In parallel, populist policy decisions in many countries to lower the effective retirement age have accelerated the draw on pension assets while narrowing the contribution base. The result has been a growing recognition that traditional pension models, conceived in the post-war welfare state era, are no longer sustainable over the long term. In other words, the traditional 20/80 pension portfolio is increasingly misaligned with today's economic and demographic realities.

In response, pension funds started to reposition their portfolios. Over the past decade, they have gradually shifted beyond the safety of listed stocks and bonds, emerging as some of the biggest backers of private debt. The move has been gradual, but profound. Private credit was initially viewed by pension trustees as a quirky, if not exotic, corner of the market: opaque, illiquid, operationally demanding and hard to mark-to-market. Today, many of the world's biggest retirement schemes treat it as a core portfolio building block, sitting alongside infrastructure debt, private placements and long-duration credit.

Legislative and regulatory changes have also supported this shift, allowing greater allocations to private assets in search of yield, diversification and income resilience. In France, the PACTE law (Plan d'Action pour la Croissance et la Transformation des Entreprises) marked a significant step forward by modernising savings frameworks and encouraging greater allocation to long-term assets, including private equity and private debt, within pension and insurance portfolios. At a pan-European level, the evolution of the European Long-Term Investment Fund regime—culminating in ELTIF 2.0—has also lowered structural barriers. By relaxing eligibility rules, broadening the range of permissible assets and opening access to a wider investor base, ELTIF 2.0 has made it easier for institutional allocators, including pension funds, to deploy capital into private markets. Together, these reforms reflect a broader policy shift: recognising private capital not as a peripheral allocation, but as a critical component in delivering yield, diversification and income resilience for long-term investors.

But as with the rise of private real estate credit more broadly, the trend has been led by the United States. US pension funds are now the single largest source of capital for private credit globally. Table 3.2 shows US pension funds with largest allocation in global private debt. According to Securities and Exchange Commission disclosures, public and private pension schemes accounted for roughly 30% of private credit fund assets as of June 2024.

TABLE 3.2 US Pension Funds Lead Private Credit Allocations

Pension Fund Name	Target Allocation in Private Debt	Actual Allocation in Private Debt
California Public Employees' Retirement System	42.07	16.36
Virginia Retirement System	15.72	16.12
Texas County & District Retirement System	12.13	13.10
Arizona State Retirement System	12.76	12.20
Tennessee Consolidated Retirement	6.50	7.28
Pennsylvania Public School Employees' Retirement System	4.49	5.99
Texas Municipal Retirement System	5.26	5.41
New Jersey Division of Investment	8.01	5.08
South Carolina Retirement System Investment Commission	3.30	3.39
Arizona Public Safety Personnel Retirement System	4.36	3.11

Data compiled 03 January 2025
Investor allocation data is provided by Preqin

The analysis includes the top 10 union, government or corporate pension plan sponsors with largest annual allocation in private debt as of 3 January 2025. It excludes pension funds with unavailable data on target and actual private debt allocation.

As another striking illustration of how central the asset class has become to modern pension portfolio construction, among the 200 largest defined benefit plans, allocations to private credit rose by more than 57% between 2023 and 2024.

Today, private credit is increasingly viewed not as an exotic, fringe alternative allocation for the most daring investors, but as a cost-efficient way to secure predictable income at scale for even the most conservative asset allocators. That shift is already visible in the allocation decisions of the world's largest public pension funds. The New York City Employees' Retirement System, which oversees approximately USD 264 billion in assets, has recently signalled a deliberate expansion into private credit, citing the asset class's relative affordability and the speed with which capital can be deployed compared to traditional private market strategies.

Equally, California's Public Employees Retirement System—the largest defined-benefit public pension fund in the United States, with roughly USD 503 billion under management—has taken a similarly decisive step. Over the past few years, it has increased its allocation to private credit from 5% to 8%, embedding the asset class more deeply into its long-term portfolio architecture instead of treating it as a peripheral source of yield.

Private credit's appeal to pension funds is easy to understand: asset-backed yield. Because unlike many other investors in the alternatives universe, pensions are not chasing quarterly performance or headline-grabbing returns. Their mandate is more elemental: to match predictable, long-dated liabilities with equally predictable, long-dated income. And in a world where public fixed income has struggled to deliver sufficient yield, private credit—particularly secured real estate debt—has become a natural destination for this patient capital that recognises that senior and whole-loan real estate credit behaves in ways pension funds value most, offering asset-backed security, contractual cash flows and resilience across cycles.

Put simply, pensions funds realised that real estate private debt allows them to earn a decent premium over bonds without having to take equity-like risk. And with banks retrenching from property lending, the opportunity set has grown just as the need for stable income has intensified.

Increasingly, access to private real estate credit is also filtering down to individual investors, with structures such as SIPPs and SSAS enabling private wealth to participate—albeit at a much smaller scale—in an asset class once reserved for institutions.

Across the US, Europe and Canada, allocations have expanded sharply. From the giant American retirement systems reshaping their fixed-income books, to Swiss regional schemes hunting for yield stability, to Canadian plans using private markets to future-proof their portfolios, pension capital is now one of the stabilising anchors of global real estate credit.

The following case study on the California Public Employees' Retirement System (CalPERS) illustrates how one of the world's largest pension funds has converged on a clear conclusion: private real estate debt is no longer niche, but a strategic response to a structural problem.

CALPERS: SCALE MEETS PRIVATE CREDIT

WHEN THE GIANTS MOVE

> Private credit, real estate and infrastructure are among the fastest-growing parts of our portfolio because they deliver the higher, more reliable yields long-term investors need. We're comfortable with longer lockups when the opportunity is right and today that includes a wave of demand around data centre and power infrastructure—areas where we're seeing significant interest and compelling ways to deploy capital.
>
> — Marcie Frost, CEO, CalPERS

In the often-opaque world of institutional capital, few moves carry the symbolic weight of a major pension fund allocation. With over USD 550 billion in Assets Under Management (AUM), CalPERS is not just a pension fund—it is a bellwether, a steady long-range thinker whose decisions often foreshadow where the most disciplined capital is heading next. So, when CalPERS shifts strategy, the market pays attention. Not just because of its sheer scale, but because when Sacramento's giant moves, it often signals a shrewd reading of the tectonic shifts reshaping the financial world beneath our feet.

(*Continued*)

(*Continued*)

And yet, for all its scale, CalPERS has always been more than a lumbering super tanker. It has built a reputation for something rarer: the courage to rethink long-held assumptions when the facts demand it and quietly rewriting its own playbook. So, when it committed an eye-catching USD 1.85 billion to real estate private credit in September 2023, it did so with the deliberateness of an institution that knows precisely what it is signalling.

The allocation—USD 1.5 billion to Blackstone Real Estate Debt Strategies V and USD 350 million to Mesa West Real Estate Income Fund V—wasn't just a large payment. It was a statement of intent: an endorsement of private real estate credit at a time when the asset class was coming of age. But what made the moment all the more significant wasn't just the sheer size of the allocation. It was the story it told.

THE YIELD DILEMMA FACING PENSION FUNDS

For the better part of the past decade, CalPERS, like most major pension funds, has been grappling with an uncomfortable reality: how to meet long-term obligations in a world of chronically low yields where traditional fixed income no longer pulls its weight. Bonds, once the steady workhorses of pension portfolios, have delivered anaemic returns in the face of ultra-low interest rates, macroeconomic shocks and shifting inflationary pressures.

WHY REAL ESTATE PRIVATE CREDIT FITS

Real estate private credit, by contrast, offers a compelling alternative. It provides portfolio characteristics that sit perfectly in a long-term investor's sweet spot: secured lending with conservative LTV ratios, tangible collateral, steady, contractual income, better yield than public fixed income and less volatility than equity. In a world still reeling from inflation shocks and banking retrenchment, the appeal is obvious. As CEO Marcie Frost put it bluntly in a recent conversation: 'private markets have become extremely important as we add active risk to build out the portfolio and get closer to our 6.8% return hurdle'.

CalPERS' growing enthusiasm for private credit—real estate in particular—also fits into a broader shift: a modernisation of how the fund approaches private markets full stop. Gone are the days when the primary lens was simply 'can it deliver alpha?' The new question being asked is far more nuanced: 'Can this asset class help us meet our promises, reliably, transparently and over very long horizons?'

Real estate private credit, with its combination of security, structure and scalability, increasingly answers 'Yes'. That conviction is reinforced by the performance of CalPERS' private debt portfolio, as shown in Table 3.3, where we see that the portfolio outpaced the policy benchmark over each time period shown.

TABLE 3.3 Private Debt Performance as of 31 December 2025

	FYTD (%)	1 Year (%)	3 Year (%)	Since Inception (%)
CalPERS Private Debt Portfolio	5.7	12.4	13.4	10.9
Policy Benchmark	5.5	9.2	11.7	8.2
Excess vs. Policy Benchmark	↑ 0.2	↑ 3.1	↑ 1.7	↑ 2.7

What's more, the portfolio's excess return relative to the policy benchmark increased over each time period compared to the prior quarter.

A SHIFT BORN OF PRAGMATISM, NOT FASHION

This strategic pivot was not the product of hype: quite the opposite. The shift reflected a deeper conversation across the organisation about resilience, long-term value and the structural changes shaping real assets in a post-zero interest rate world set against a backdrop of geopolitical uncertainty. In the boardrooms of CalPERS, a question was climbing steadily up the agenda: what kind of assets can generate dependable, inflation-resistant income over multi-decade horizons?

Real estate private credit—especially in sectors experiencing structural expansion—has emerged as a compelling answer. Frost has openly referenced the 'exuberance' around data centres, power infrastructure and other real-asset platforms where demand is accelerating faster than traditional financing channels can keep up. For an investor with obligations stretching decades into the future, such areas aren't speculative. They represent disciplined, long-range thinking and strategic clarity.

INSIDE THE ALLOCATION STRATEGY

At a portfolio level, CalPERS' approach expresses itself through a deliberate mix of private credit strategies, each serving a distinct role within the fund.

As shown in Figure 3.3 and Table 3.4, direct Lending strategies make up the majority of CalPERS' portfolio, accounting for 75% of commitments as of 31 March 2025, albeit down from 82% a year earlier. This reflects the historical reality that the bulk of private debt allocations were initially concentrated in corporate direct lending strategies.

These strategies have generated attractive returns overall and the strongest returns over the three-year and since inception time periods relative to the other

(Continued)

(*Continued*)

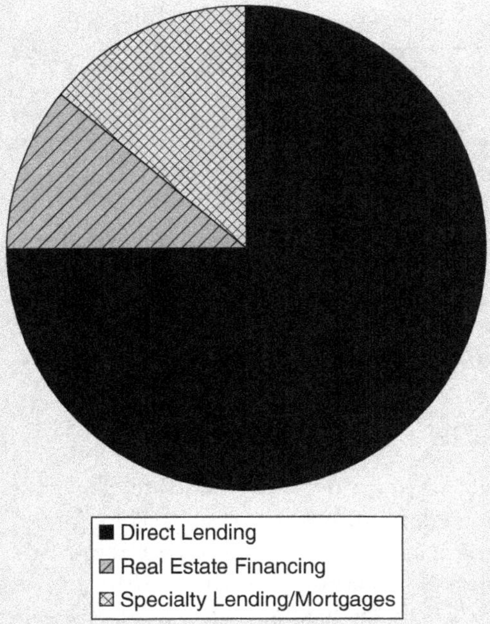

FIGURE 3.3 Commitment by Strategy (as of 31 March 2025)

TABLE 3.4 CalPERS Private Credit Performance by Strategy as of 31 December 2025

	NAV (USDm)	% of Total NAV (%)	FYTD (%)	1 Year (%)	3 Year (%)	Since Inception (%)
Direct Lending	19,685	81.3	5.7	12.5	14.1	11.7
Specialty Lending	3,344	13.8	5.1	10.0	10.0	9.0
Real Estate Financing	1,191	4.9	7.5	16.6	12.7	9.7
CalPERS Private Debt Portfolio	24,220	100.0	5.7	12.4	13.4	10.9

two strategies. But real estate financing has produced the highest absolute returns over the trailing one-year period.

However, the mix is beginning to broaden. As banks have retrenched and stepped back from more specialised forms of lending, areas such as real estate financing and specialty lending—long considered smaller and less accessible opportunity sets—are gaining traction. While still representing a minority of allocations today, these segments are expected to grow as institutional investors seek differentiated sources of yield and asset-backed exposure in a more constrained banking environment.

But higher yields alone don't explain the shift towards private debt. Instead, CalPERS is leaning into asset classes where secure income, collateral backing and long-term structural demand intersect. Private credit—especially when tied to real assets—offers something increasingly scarce in public markets: durable, inflation-resilient returns with measurable downside protection.

The fund's two chosen managers for its 2023 allocation illustrate its dual strategy as they serve slightly different but complementary purposes.

Blackstone's strategy is geared towards large-scale lending across major real estate markets, often in dislocated or transitional situations where liquidity is scarce, but asset quality remains strong.

Mesa West, by contrast, specialises in middle-market transitional loans—often value-add projects, multifamily developments or repositioning plays in gateway cities.

Together, they offer breadth and depth—two qualities CalPERS values when deploying capital at scale. 'We diversify not just across managers but across structures', Frost explains. 'Pooled vehicles give us scale and reach; separate accounts or club deals give us control and alignment. It's about balancing governance with opportunity'.

Return expectations are realistic and calibrated. Senior secured positions aim for steady, high single-digit returns, while mezzanine or structured credit is used selectively when collateral strength supports it.

'We're not chasing the highest number on the page', Frost notes. 'We're matching liabilities. That requires predictable income and strong underwriting—that's where real estate credit delivers'.

A SIGNAL THE MARKET CANNOT IGNORE

In many ways, this shift captured the fund's quiet power. It doesn't merely reallocate capital; it reframes the conversation about what long-term investing should look like in an uncertain age.

And for CalPERS, this shift wasn't a tactical play; it was part of a reimagining of what long-term, steady capital should look like in today's risk landscape. The fund increasingly views private credit as a core allocation—not a side dish—a view reinforced by consistently resilient private debt performance across cycles as shown in Tables 3.3 and 3.4.

And when the largest public pension fund in the United States says that secured, income-generating real estate credit is now part of its long-term backbone, others tend to follow.

'We're living through a regime shift', Frost observes. 'Inflation's resurgence, rate volatility, banking dislocation—the landscape has changed. Private credit sits at the intersection of those forces'.

(*Continued*)

(*Continued*)

As she puts it: '...we still have a lot of conviction in the private markets, private debt in particular ... We are in a very strong liquidity position, which allows the allocation to private equity and private debt to tick up ... to capture those outsized returns that we've seen certainly over those longer periods of time'.

THE RIPPLE EFFECT ACROSS GLOBAL CAPITAL

CalPERS is not alone. The reallocation reflects a wider trend. Pension funds around the world—from Canadian plans to European insurers to sovereign funds in the Gulf—are reallocating towards private credit and away from traditional public markets. But CalPERS' move carries outsized weight: it doesn't merely reflect the trend; it accelerates it.

CalPERS' USD 1.85 billion bet is more than a portfolio adjustment, and it signals more than confidence in individual managers. It speaks to a conviction in real estate private credit as a long-term, core allocation—not a niche or opportunistic play, but a structural pillar of the future pension fund toolkit. It is a quiet but unmistakable statement: the giants are moving, and this time, they're backing debt.

Perhaps most significantly, it sets a precedent. Pension funds, once wedded to the 60/40 traditional portfolio and wary of anything perceived as illiquid or complex, are increasingly emerging as key funders of the built environment, not through equity, but through debt. And when the largest public pension fund in the United States leads the way, it's hard to imagine others not taking notice.

'We're living through a regime shift in capital markets', Frost notes. 'Inflation's resurgence, interest rate volatility and banking dislocation have all reshaped the playing field. Private credit sits at the intersection of those forces, and we're positioning accordingly'. 'We're not just chasing yield anymore', another CalPERS insider said off the record. 'We're looking for resilience—and real estate credit gives us both'. In that sense, CalPERS' USD 1.85 billion bet wasn't just a deployment of capital. It was a market signal: a flare in the sky. The giants are moving. And this time, they're backing debt.

CalPERS' move into real estate private credit matters not because of its size alone, but because of what it represents. When a fund of this scale embeds private credit into its long-term portfolio architecture, it signals a broader redefinition of what defensive and income-generating now mean for institutional capital. Real estate private credit is no longer a workaround for a low-rate world, nor a tactical substitute for bonds. In the hands of investors such as CalPERS, it has become a core instrument of portfolio resilience, quietly reshaping how the world's largest pools of capital finance the built environment.

But not all shifts in institutional capital come from the world's largest pension giants. Some of the clearest signals emerge from funds better known for caution than for boldness. Across continental Europe—in Switzerland, Germany, France, Spain and other countries with deeply rooter pension tradition—home to some of the world's most conservatively governed systems, funds have also started to rethink how they generate income and manage long-term risk. Their move into private markets is measured instead of dramatic, but no less indicative of a broader shift.

Many of these pension funds have long embodied continental prudence: disciplined, methodical and risk aware. Yet in recent years, they have ventured into private credit, often stepping in to fund landmark real estate regeneration projects. For institutions known for their conservatism, this has not been a tactical adjustment but a structural repositioning.

The rationale is straightforward. Traditional fixed income has struggled to deliver real returns, while public markets have become more volatile and less predictable. Private credit, by contrast, offers contractual income, seniority in the capital structure and tangible downside protection—attributes that align naturally with long-dated pension liabilities. In effect, it can help stabilise portfolios by partially decoupling performance from economic cycles. In Europe's tightly regulated pension system, where capital preservation and governance are paramount, that combination of resilience and control carries particular weight.

The shift among European pension funds reflects a wider trend across the continent and beyond, with allocations to private markets rising steadily over the past decade. What was once peripheral is becoming core: in Switzerland alone, around a quarter of pension funds now allocate to private debt, up from roughly 8% ten years ago.

Importantly, this evolution is not simply about returns. Pension capital flowing into private debt and real assets is helping finance housing, infrastructure and economic activity in areas increasingly underserved by banks. For funds rooted in the real economy, that alignment matters.

If these examples illustrate how conservative European pension capital is cautiously broadening its toolkit, Canada's largest plans show what happens when that evolution is taken further. At Ontario Teachers' Pension Plan (OTPP), private markets are not an allocation at the margins but a core part of the investment model.

With over CAD 250 billion under management, OTPP has increasingly used private credit—including real estate-backed lending—as a way to generate stable, contractual income aligned with its long-dated liabilities. As banks have retreated, it has stepped into lending markets with scale and discipline, treating credit not as a tactical substitute for bonds, but as a structural component of portfolio resilience.

This approach reflects a broader shift among Canada's leading pension funds, where private markets are embedded at the heart of portfolio construction instead of layered on top of it.

THE RISE OF INSURER-LED PROPERTY LENDING

Insurance companies have always played the long game. With billions tied up in long-duration liabilities, such as life insurance policies and annuities, they are intuitively wired to think in terms of decades, not quarters. This long-term view gives them a unique edge: unlike banks or short-term funds they aren't under pressure to chase quick liquidity or protect themselves against sudden redemption demands. That means they can easily invest in illiquid assets like real estate private debt, the kind of slow-burning, high-security investments that align perfectly with their liabilities.

This balance-sheet longevity allows insurers to lend differently. They don't need the steep liquidity premiums other lenders demand, so they can offer lower interest rates or stretch out maturities without compromising their return objectives. And in a market where borrowers are under intense pressure to shave a few basis points off their funding costs, insurers have quietly become some of the most competitive and sought after lenders in the game. Their focus on downside protection, regulatory capital efficiency and predictable income means they are particularly well suited to senior, asset-backed lending, where risk can be tightly controlled and cash flows are stable over long horizons. This positioning has helped insurers scale their presence in real estate debt across core European markets.

Playing the Long Game in Property Debt

In the years following the Global Financial Crisis, while Europe's banks grappled with legacy loan books and regulatory burdens, a quieter but no less consequential shift was taking place. As traditional lenders retrenched, a handful of insurers began to see real estate debt not just as a niche opportunity, but as a strategic extension of their core business models.

One of the earliest movers in the UK was Aviva, a name better known for pensions and life insurance than for property finance. But underpinning Aviva's legacy of annuity promises was a powerful structural advantage: a long-dated liability profile naturally matched to long-term, income-generating assets. This was reinforced by Aviva's relatively low weighted average cost of capital, reflecting the stability and predictability of its insurance cashflows and its diversified funding base. By contrast, many banks face a higher all-in cost of capital, driven by short-term funding dependencies, tighter regulatory capital requirements and ROE constraints.

That differential gave insurers like Aviva greater flexibility to underwrite real estate loans at competitive pricing while still achieving attractive risk-adjusted returns. Illustratively, on a GBP 100 million real estate development loan, assuming a 2% target lending margin, Aviva would need a minimum required loan yield of 10.5% while a bank would need 12.2%. This means Aviva can, in theory, price the same loan 150–200 basis points cheaper than a bank and still meet its internal return hurdles. In a market where margins matter and discipline is paramount, this structural cost advantage has enabled Aviva to lend across parts of the real estate debt spectrum that might otherwise have been the preserve of specialist non-bank lenders.

But despite being uniquely suited to asset-backed lending, Aviva's evolution into a lender was not an overnight pivot. It began with modest steps under the banner of Aviva Commercial Finance, which had previously financed infrastructure and logistics portfolios. But as the lending landscape shifted, so too did the ambition. In what became one of its earlier large-scale real estate loans, Aviva made headlines in 2010 when it extended GBP 205 million of long-term debt to Peel Group, secured against 53 income-producing industrial, logistics and office properties mostly in the North West region of the UK and in Scotland. The deal was structured over a 20-year horizon, an alignment of liability and return that few banks could offer and few borrowers could resist.

The fit between Aviva's capital base and borrowers' needs ran both ways. Developers were drawn to Aviva's ability to offer long-dated, competitively priced funding, while for Aviva the rationale for real estate lending was clear: a chronic housing shortage in the UK, combined with banks' retreat from development finance, especially beyond prime city centres. By stepping in to fund senior construction loans for residential and industrial developments, Aviva was both meeting its internal yield requirements and solving a market problem that had become increasingly urgent.

Aviva's entry into real estate debt also reflected a broader macro trend. Inspired in part by its American peers like MetLife and Prudential—who had long played a dominant role in US commercial mortgage markets—European insurers were rethinking how their capital could be deployed more effectively. In the US, insurers had long accounted for nearly one-fifth of all CRE finance. In Europe, they were still the exception, not the rule.

But change was brewing. The looming implementation of Solvency II, the EU-wide regulatory framework for insurers, on 1 January 2016 brought both challenges and incentives. Under Solvency II, senior secured real estate loans—particularly those with low loan-to-value ratios—attracted relatively favourable capital treatment compared with other private assets. As one investment director remarked at the time, 'Solvency II is having a profound effect on how insurance companies decide to invest. There's now an actual incentive to lend'.

Aviva was not alone. AXA, Allianz, Legal & General and Canada Life would each explore debt strategies of their own. Yet Aviva's approach was distinctly pragmatic and UK-focused. While others looked across borders, Aviva doubled down on residential-led regeneration, logistics developments and other real assets with stable income potential and strong collateral value.

In time, Aviva's lending platform would grow more sophisticated, capable of underwriting not just vanilla loans but complex deal structures, sometimes participating alongside banks, sometimes leading transactions outright. In many cases, insurer capital complemented bank balance sheets instead of replacing them, with insurers providing long-dated tranches that banks were no longer able to hold. Yet the DNA of the business remained the same: a long-term mindset, a deep understanding of liability matching and a willingness to step in where others had pulled back.

Today, Aviva is not just an insurer but a material player in the UK's real estate debt market: a lender of record for projects that might otherwise have stalled. Its capital has become part of the scaffolding behind Britain's post-crisis recovery, reshaping the funding ecosystem for a new era. In 2025, Aviva Investors' Multi-Sector Private Debt Long-Term Asset Fund committed over GBP 37 million in green loan financing for the redevelopment of 95 New Cavendish Street in Fitzrovia, Central London, supporting a sustainable office refurbishment targeting high environmental and connectivity standards: a deal that underscores how insurer-backed capital is increasingly funding high-quality, long-duration real estate projects that align with both investor mandates and broader policy goals.

Aviva's journey illustrates how insurance capital, when paired with long-dated liabilities and a disciplined cost of capital, can fundamentally reshape domestic real estate lending markets. But this insurer-led transformation is not uniquely British. Across continental Europe, similar dynamics are playing out at even greater scale. If Aviva shows how an insurer can become a cornerstone lender within a single national market, the next case study looks at how Allianz has taken the same structural advantages and deployed them across borders, building one of Europe's most significant private real estate lending platforms in the process.

ALLIANZ: SCALING THE LONG GAME ACROSS EUROPE

Headquartered in Munich, Allianz is one of the world's largest insurance and asset management groups. Through its asset management arm, Allianz Global Investors and PIMCO, the group manages north of EUR 1.7 trillion in assets, giving it both the scale and the institutional depth to shape markets instead of merely responding to them.

Within Europe, Allianz's footprint runs deep. The group has insurance operations across almost every major European country and long-standing relationships with corporate borrowers, developers and public-sector counterparties. This geographic breadth, along with a vast pool of long-dated insurance liabilities, made Allianz a natural long-term lender. But when its Real Estate arm first ventured into debt in 2011, it was with the cautious footing typical of a German corporate giant. That was the time when bank retrenchment from property finance was starting in the aftermath of the crisis and Allianz did not need to reinvent itself to step in. It just extended an existing philosophy—liability-driven investing, capital preservation and disciplined underwriting—into European real estate debt.

In the early days, Allianz's lending capacity came from a handful of the group's German insurance companies: well-capitalised, long-term focused and naturally aligned with the slow and steady nature of senior real estate credit. It was a classic insurer play, matching long-dated liabilities with high-quality, income-producing assets.

But the years since have seen a quiet transformation.

Fast forward to today and Allianz's real estate debt platform has blossomed into a pan-European machine, fuelled by over 20 in-house Allianz Group organisations across the continent. No longer confined by country-specific balance sheets or fragmented mandates, the group made a strategic pivot in 2018: it created a centralised Luxembourg-based debt platform that pools capital across its European operations. This operational shift—more than administrative housekeeping—marked a turning point.

That ambition quickly materialised in a string of deals that signalled a new phase. In August 2018, Allianz participated in a GBP 300 million senior-plus-mezzanine financing package for Blackstone's St Katharine Docks in London, a waterside mixed-use redevelopment brimming with development risk and letting uncertainty. The loan was notable not just for its size, but for its structure.

It included a capex tranche and was co-lent alongside mezzanine capital from Brookfield, reflecting Allianz's willingness to move up the risk curve.

Shortly before that, Allianz had financed a EUR 281 million loan to McArthurGlen to refinance the Noventa di Piave Designer Outlet near Venice, pushing its Italian loan portfolio to nearly EUR 400 million and extending its reach into southern Europe.

But perhaps the most telling moment came with the launch of Allianz's enhanced debt programme, a strategy to blend higher-return loans into its traditionally conservative book. The inaugural deal? A GBP 50 million development financing package for 80 Fenchurch Street in the City of London, sponsored by Partners Group.

Under the enhanced strategy, Allianz began considering stretched senior and junior loans up to 75% loan-to-value and construction loans between 50% and 65% loan-to-cost-metrics traditionally more associated with debt funds than insurers.

London, too, became a central part of the strategy. Having only entered the UK market in 2017, Allianz saw in Brexit uncertainty a long-term opportunity. 'We are not loan traders, we are loan investors', Fuchs affirmed. 'London is a global gateway city and, as such, will remain of interest to us over the long term'.

Still, Allianz hasn't abandoned its insurance roots. In parallel with its value-add ventures, the firm continued to anchor long-term, conservative loans-such as the 20-year senior debt facility to Austria's Signa Group to refinance Berlin's Upper West tower, a gleaming mixed-use icon in the heart of the German capital.

By the end of 2018, Allianz Real Estate had originated around EUR 1.2 billion in real estate loans, with a robust pipeline expected to push that figure past EUR 2 billion, well ahead of the EUR 1.9 billion it closed in 2017. Its European loan book now sits just shy of EUR 7 billion, a figure that underscores the growing ambition—and influence—of this insurance giant turned credit heavyweight.

From a German insurance outpost to a pan-European real estate lender, Allianz's story is a microcosm of a broader shift. As banks retreat and institutional appetite for private debt surges, insurance groups like Allianz are stepping in: not just with capital, but with strategic intent and a vision for long-term investing in a rapidly changing world.

NATION-BACKED CAPITAL AND REAL ESTATE CREDIT

Sovereign wealth funds are uniquely positioned in private real estate credit's capital stack. Backed by mighty state balance sheets instead of the constraints of bank funding cycles or liability-driven pension fund models, they are among the most patient and strategic investors. Their mandates—typically shaped by intergenerational capital preservation, macro-stability and national development goals—aligns well with long-duration, asset-backed debt strategies.

Despite this natural pairing, sovereign wealth funds historically approached real estate primarily through equity: by snapping up landmark buildings, trophy assets and large-scale development partnerships in prime cities.

But things have slowly evolved over the past decade. As public markets have become more volatile and bank lending has retreated, sovereign investors have increasingly turned to real estate debt for yield that is both anchored in hard assets and protected by robust collateral.

Funds such as GIC, Abu Dhabi Investment Authority (ADIA), Mubadala and Norges Bank Investment Management have all expanded their use of private credit strategies across real assets, including property. ADIA, for example, has increased its allocation to real estate debt through partnerships with global asset managers, including mandates focused on senior secured lending in developed markets.

For them, real estate private credit offers a compelling mix of characteristics. Senior secured lending provides predictable income streams, strong collateral backing and structural protection in stressed scenarios: features that align well with sovereign objectives of capital preservation and portfolio stability. At the same time, private credit allows sovereigns to deploy capital at scale, often through club deals, co-investments or bespoke mandates alongside specialist managers, without competing in crowded equity auctions.

There is no single playbook for how sovereign capital enters real estate credit. In some cases, it is deployed through direct lending platforms or joint ventures with established credit managers; in others, it has involved large-scale allocations to private debt funds with global reach. However it is structured, the underlying instinct is consistent: a preference for control, transparency and alignment. Sovereigns are rarely passive capital providers. Their sheer scale, governance frameworks and public accountability demand clear oversight of risk, the ability to influence outcomes and structures that align capital deployment with long-term economic and strategic objectives.

One example of sovereign wealth funds' growing appetite for real estate private credit can be seen in ADIA, which in 2024 committed capital to Cheyne Capital's European real estate debt strategy. Through its investment in the Cheyne Real Estate Credit Holdings (CRECH) programme, ADIA gained exposure to senior and subordinated lending across European property markets, including residential, student housing and senior living assets. The prior year, it had already begun allocating to real estate debt strategies targeting transitional and income-producing assets, signalling a clear shift: sovereign capital increasingly flowing into structured lending instead of direct ownership. These allocations are typically long-dated, conservatively underwritten and designed to generate stable income across cycles.

A similar logic underpins Mubadala's partnership with Apollo Global Management. By deploying capital across large-scale credit platforms, including asset-backed and real estate-linked lending strategies, Mubadala is not only diversifying its portfolio; it is building scalable exposure to income-generating assets with embedded structural protection. The partnership reflects a broader sovereign preference for credit strategies that offer both yield and resilience, without the execution risk associated with direct development or competitive equity holding.

Singapore's GIC offers yet another variation of this theme. Instead of relying on a single channel, it has invested alongside major global managers such as Blackstone while also backing real estate platforms that incorporate both equity and structured financing. This hybrid approach allows GIC to participate across the capital stack, capturing opportunities where pricing is most attractive while maintaining a strong bias towards downside protection. The emphasis, once again, is not on ownership for its own sake, but on disciplined deployment of capital into diversified, asset-backed income streams.

Taken together, these examples point to a broader evolution. Sovereign wealth funds are no longer confined to the role of long-term property owners. They are increasingly acting as providers of credit, shaping how real estate is financed as much as what is ultimately built.

Crucially, sovereign capital also brings a stabilising influence on the market. With less sensitivity to short-term mark-to-market volatility and fewer liquidity constraints than many institutional peers, these large state actors can remain active lenders through market cycles. In periods of dislocation, this allows them to act as counter-cyclical providers of credit—stepping in when banks pull back and pricing discipline returns.

In that sense, sovereign wealth funds are not just another source of capital in real estate private debt. They are long-term anchors: investors whose timeframes stretch beyond cycles, whose capital can absorb complexity and whose growing presence reflects the maturity of private credit from an opportunistic play into a strategic, state-backed allocation.

INVESTMENT MANAGERS AS CAPITAL ARCHITECTS

> A decade ago, private real estate credit was seen as a niche—a tactical play for those willing to take on complexity in search of yield. Today, it's a strategic allocation. Institutional investors aren't chasing opportunity; they're building resilience. They want transparency, structure and control—a predictable bridge between long-term liabilities and real assets that actually serve the economy.
>
> —Eugenio Sangermano

In earlier sections of this chapter, we lifted the lid on who are the institutions bankrolling the rise of private real estate debt: pension funds hunting for long-duration stability, insurers trying to match their liabilities with something sturdier than government bonds and sovereign wealth funds seeking resilient, asset-backed returns they can hold for a generation or more. But none of that capital deploys itself.

At the heart of today's real estate private credit markets sit the investment managers, the quiet conductors of capital who translate institutional ambition into real-world impact. Through their structuring, underwriting and governance, they transform these vast pools of institutional money into investable, measurable and scalable debt strategies. These capital architects don't just lend, they build the frameworks through which private credit operates, ensuring that institutional money doesn't simply chase yield but builds lasting value across the real economy.

BF.CAPITAL: ENGINEERING INSTITUTIONAL REAL ESTATE DEBT

FILLING THE GAP LEFT BY BANKS

Among the new generation of private debt specialists, Stuttgart-based BF.capital stands out. Its story mirrors the broader reinvention of continental Europe's private debt landscape. Founded as a subsidiary of BF.direkt AG, a specialist in real estate financing advisory, BF.capital began as a small specialist lender with a clear conviction: that disciplined, transparent debt investing could restore confidence where traditional lending had faltered. Less than a decade later, it manages not only real estate credit but also a substantial private debt fund portfolio—with more than EUR 1.5 billion in institutional AUM—and has become one of Germany's most respected independent managers of real estate private debt. Sangermano, the steady hand and strategic mind behind BF.capital's ascent in Europe's private-debt landscape, says:

> We see ourselves as architects of long-term value, not just providers of capital. The evolution of private debt and especially real estate debt in Europe is about more than yield: it's about discipline, transparency and partnership. Institutional investors today want predictability, but they also want purpose: the ability to finance real assets that support economic growth while maintaining robust risk control. Our role is to translate those expectations into structures that align incentives, protect downside and create sustainable performance across cycles.

BF.capital's emergence in 2017 is emblematic of the wider transformation we've traced so far: the rise of non-bank lenders reshaping real estate finance. At a time when traditional banks were retreating from property lending in the wake of Basel III and Germany's own tightening supervisory frameworks, BF.capital moved in to fill the void, not as a high-yield opportunist, but as a long-term institutional partner.

'BF.capital was founded on a simple insight', explains the quietly formidable Sangermano. 'Real estate remains a core pillar of the European economy, but institutional investors needed a modern, transparent and risk-controlled channel to access it through debt instead of equity. We provide that bridge'.

INVESTOR BASE AND RETURN PHILOSOPHY

> Our investors aren't chasing double-digit numbers. Their focus isn't on maximising yield, but on securing the most dependable income stream. They're looking for consistent, risk-controlled income that behaves like a true institutional asset. That changes everything about how you underwrite, monitor and communicate risk. In our world, stability is alpha.
>
> Our typical investors are insurance companies, pension funds, regional banks and foundations, all seeking stable, collateralised returns at a time

when government bonds offered little in the way of yield. Their mandate isn't to outperform every quarter; it's to meet liabilities thirty years from now. That naturally shapes both the way they think about risk and the way we structure our products.

In terms of return expectations, BF.capital targets net yields in the 5–7% range for senior and whole-loan strategies, rising to 8–10% for select mezzanine tranches or bespoke development finance mandates. 'Our focus has always been on risk-adjusted return, not absolute yield', Sangermano notes. 'If a deal promises an extra hundred basis points but adds a layer of structural uncertainty, we walk away'.

STRUCTURING CAPITAL THROUGH MANDATES AND FUNDS

Most of the capital is deployed through bespoke segregated mandates and closed-ended funds, each with defined investment horizons of five to seven years. 'We build long-term relationships with our investors. Many prefer customised mandates aligned to their liability structures, duration targets and internal reporting frameworks. The German insurance landscape in particular values this managed account model: it offers transparency, governance and control'.

BF.capital has also developed pooled vehicles for mid-sized institutions seeking diversification without the overhead of direct mandate management. 'These vehicles tend to be semi-open structures with quarterly liquidity windows', says Sangermano, 'but we never compromise on alignment: capital in, capital out and governance shared'.

RISK DISCIPLINE AND CAPITAL STACK POSITIONING

On the risk spectrum, BF.capital's allocations sit primarily in the senior secured and whole-loan space, with selective exposure to mezzanine debt in markets or sectors where it can maintain strict collateral discipline:

> We rarely, if ever, underwrite first-loss positions. That's not our mandate. Our investors want downside protection, collateral transparency and predictable cash flow. We deliver that by staying at the safer end of the capital stack, but structuring smartly enough to still capture yield.

Risk management is woven into BF.capital's DNA, with its structuring approach grounded in an institutional framework, a discipline Sangermano credits to his team's unique blend of real estate underwriting and capital-markets expertise. The firm applies a three-dimensional lens to risk: Market risk, including macroeconomic and rate volatility; Credit risk, focused on tenant and developer resilience; Structural risk, related to collateral, covenant and jurisdictional enforcement.

(*Continued*)

(*Continued*)

> Every fund or mandate starts with three design questions: What risk can we quantify? What risk can we mitigate? And what risk must we simply avoid? That discipline is what our investors value most. They don't just buy yield; they buy process, governance and trust.

FROM CAPITAL TO REAL ASSETS

He pauses before adding, with quiet conviction:

> At the end of the day, we see ourselves as translators between two worlds: the capital markets and the real economy. We take long-term capital and turn it into productive, collateralised lending that builds homes, offices and infrastructure. We sit between banks, insurers and developers and operate as a transmission mechanism, channelling institutional demand for yield into granular, asset-backed loans that support everything from value-add refurbishments to mid-sized residential developments in Germany and Austria. That's the real story of private credit—not leverage, but translation.

PRODUCT DESIGN AND PORTFOLIO CONSTRUCTION

Yet the real innovation lies in the structuring. BF.capital's funds are often tailored around specific risk-return corridors—senior, whole-loan and mezzanine tranches—lent against income-generating assets—typically office, logistics and residential portfolios—as well as high quality development projects. This approach enables institutions to participate selectively in the capital stack while preserving transparency and governance standards that mirror traditional fixed-income portfolios. The firm also takes a portfolio-level approach to credit risk, combining local real estate expertise with institutional-grade risk analytics. Loans are often structured as whole loans or senior tranches with conservative loan-to-value ratios, typically in the 60–70% range and strong covenants.

As Sangermano puts it: 'We're not replacing banks; we're complementing them, stepping in where regulation limits flexibility but demand remains strong'.

SCALING ACROSS ASSET CLASSES

This positioning underscores a broader shift: private debt managers like BF.capital are redesigning the way risk is distributed, not by taking extreme positions, but by engineering access, creating products that institutional investors can understand, measure and hold at scale.

BF.capital's expansion into infrastructure and corporate debt further demonstrates how private real-estate credit managers are diversifying, moving from project-specific lending towards multi-asset, multi-duration strategies that blend the characteristics of traditional credit funds with the asset-backing of real estate.

At a time when European insurers face Solvency II constraints and negative duration mismatches, such strategies offer a pragmatic solution: long-term, secured exposure with tangible collateral, and a story investors can defend to their boards.

A SECOND GENERATION MANAGER

In many ways, BF Capital exemplifies the second generation of private debt managers: those who have built credibility not by marketing yield, but by designing trust into the structure itself. Their ascent reminds us that the future of real-estate finance is not simply about who lends, but about who designs the framework through which lending becomes investable again.

The firm's approach has also evolved in response to the new rate environment. Rising yields have redefined the appeal of private real estate credit, especially in Germany, where institutional investors long accustomed to negative rates are now rebalancing their portfolios. BF.capital has leaned into this shift, offering tailored mandates and bespoke fund structures that align with each investor's liability profile, particularly insurers balancing long-dated obligations.

This layered approach has allowed BF.capital to maintain stable performance through cycles, including during the recent volatility in European commercial property markets.

In many ways, BF.capital epitomises the institutionalisation of private real estate debt in Europe. Its model reflects a broader investor mindset shift, away from chasing yield at any cost, towards building resilient, risk-graded income streams that integrate seamlessly into long-term portfolios.

'Private credit is not an opportunistic trade', Sangermano concludes. 'It's becoming a strategic allocation. Our job is to make sure that allocation behaves like a true institutional asset: predictable, transparent and durable'.

BF.capital's story illustrates how Europe's new generation of private debt managers is professionalising non-bank lending from the inside out, not by chasing yield, but by engineering structures that institutional capital can trust. Yet as private real estate debt matures, the landscape is no longer defined solely by agile, specialist players. It is increasingly shaped by the coexistence—and, in many cases, convergence—of two distinct models: the focused, entrepreneurial specialist and the global, multi-asset platform.

Firms like BF.capital represent the former. They operate with precision, deep local knowledge and a highly specialised lens, often rooted in a single asset class or geography. Their edge lies in origination, structuring and the ability to move decisively in fragmented markets where nuance matters and relationships drive deal flow. They are, in many ways, the craftsmen of private credit, building portfolios loan by loan, mandate by mandate, with a strong emphasis on alignment and control.

By contrast, global asset managers bring a different kind of strength. Scale, institutional infrastructure and portfolio construction capabilities allow them to integrate real estate debt into broader multi-asset strategies. Their focus is not just on originating loans, but on how those loans interact with the rest of a portfolio: how they diversify risk, match liabilities and behave across cycles. Where specialists excel in depth, large platforms bring breadth.

Importantly, these models are not in opposition. They are complementary. The growth of private real estate debt has created space for both: specialists to source and structure opportunities with granularity, and global managers to aggregate, scale and institutionalise those exposures within diversified portfolios. Together, they form two sides of the same ecosystem, one rooted in execution, the other in portfolio architecture.

Nowhere is this evolution more visible than at firms where credit discipline meets active ownership, ESG integration and engagement-led investing, a model exemplified by Federated Hermes.

FEDERATED HERMES: MANAGING RISK, NOT CHASING YIELD

A STRATEGIC ENTRY INTO REAL ESTATE DEBT

> Real estate debt is often misunderstood as a yield trade. In reality, it's a risk-management tool, one that, when structured properly, delivers income, resilience and diversification across market cycles.
>
> —Vincent Nobel, Head of Asset-Based Lending, Federated Hermes

As a large global asset manager—overseeing roughly USD 870 billion in AUM—Federated Hermes has consistently leaned towards a stewardship-driven and long-term approach to capital. When it decided to dip its toes in real estate debt back in 2015, it did so at the same time many managers were beginning to explore the space. But where some managers approached private credit as a tactical yield enhancer, Federated Hermes positioned it as a strategic income allocation, seeking to deliver predictable cash flows while retaining control, transparency and a level of downside protection.

When I spoke with Vincent Nobel, Head of Asset-Based Lending, he was unequivocal: Federated Hermes approaches real estate debt not as a short-term trade, but as part of a broader portfolio architecture, one seeking to deliver stability, diversification and a level of resilient capital preservation across market cycles. Vincent joined Federated Hermes in 2015 to launch the firm's real estate debt business. 'We understood very early on that real estate debt's main appeal should be the potential for stable income from rents, along with seeking capital protection against downward movements in the value of the underlying assets', he explains. 'The asset class fits naturally into institutional portfolios precisely because it behaves like a fixed-income asset, but with better structural protection', he continues. 'Our investors are not seeking opportunism. They want stable cash flows, conservative leverage and confidence that risks are understood, managed and actively monitored'.

FROM NICHE STRATEGY TO PORTFOLIO BUILDING BLOCK

Federated Hermes' entry into real estate debt reflects a wider shift in how institutions think about private credit. A decade ago, the asset class was often viewed as a deeply specialist corner of alternatives—attractive in theory, but difficult to scale, benchmark and manage from a governance perspective—in short, not a natural fit for every institution. Today, it is increasingly treated as a core income allocation, sitting alongside infrastructure debt, private placements and long-duration credit strategies. 'When I began building the real estate debt business at Federated Hermes ten years ago, the idea of a dedicated private debt conference was rare. Today, I'm invited to speak at several a year. If you want a measure of how sentiment has shifted, that tells the story', says Vincent.

What changed was not simply the opportunity set, but the framework around it. As banks retreated from property lending under post-crisis regulation, private managers were forced to rethink how real estate debt should be structured, diversified and communicated to institutional investors operating under tight governance constraints.

Federated Hermes responded by anchoring its real estate debt strategies in the language institutions understand best: diversification, risk control and predictability of outcome.

Those principles aligned directly with one of real estate debt's strongest selling points: its low correlation to other asset classes, including real estate itself. The past few years have made this clearer than ever; while real estate equity weathered sharp repricing, senior real estate debt delivered steadily rising income with far less volatility. 'Real estate debt is a powerful diversifier in institutional portfolios', Vincent says. 'It's both a defensive real estate position and an illiquid form of credit, and the low correlation to other asset classes has real potential to reduce total portfolio volatility'.

That philosophy is central to how Federated Hermes constructs and manages its real estate debt strategies.

RETHINKING DIVERSIFICATION IN PRIVATE MARKETS

One of the Federated Hermes' most distinctive contributions to the debate around the role of private credit in a portfolio is its reframing of diversification in private real estate debt. As outlined in its 2024 paper on portfolio diversification, traditional portfolio theory—built around liquid securities, daily pricing and volatility metrics—offers limited guidance for illiquid, bilateral loans held to maturity.

(*Continued*)

(*Continued*)

'Private real estate debt doesn't behave like public credit, and it shouldn't be forced into that mould', notes Vincent. 'Loans are typically held at par, they don't mark-to-market daily and there is no meaningful benchmark. So, the challenge isn't outperforming an index, it's managing specific risk intelligently across a portfolio'.

Instead, diversification in real estate debt is about reducing idiosyncratic risk: spreading exposure across borrowers, asset types, geographies and income drivers; avoiding concentration in any single tenant, sponsor or market dynamic; and building portfolios that can absorb stress without impairing capital.

'In private debt, the risk cannot be defined as daily price movement. Risk is the fact that future outcomes may differ from expectations and with that an impairment of the position', Vincent argues. 'Diversification in portfolios of illiquid assets is not about correlation coefficients. It's about ensuring no single loan, borrower or market shock can materially damage the portfolio'.

This approach has resonated strongly with insurers and pension funds, particularly in Europe, where capital charges, liability matching and internal risk committees demand clarity over downside exposure instead of headline yield.

INCOME, RESILIENCE AND CYCLE BEHAVIOUR

Another pillar of the Federated Hermes approach is the role of real estate debt as a stabilising force within broader portfolios. Properly structured senior and whole-loan strategies, the firm argues, can deliver relatively stable income even during periods of heightened market volatility—precisely when traditional assets such as equities and listed real estate can suffer sharp drawdowns.

Real estate debt's defensive characteristics—contractual cash flows, asset-backed security and seniority in the capital stack—mean it can perform a fundamentally different role to equity or opportunistic credit. Instead of amplifying cycles, it can help smooth them.

'For many of our investors, the appeal is not maximising returns in good years', explains Vincent. 'It's protecting income and capital in bad ones. Real estate debt can act as ballast, delivering resilience when other parts of the portfolio are under pressure. We see it as an indispensable component of any real assets barbell strategy'.

This emphasis on cycle behaviour has become especially salient in the post-2022 rate environment, as volatility returned to both equity and fixed-income markets. For allocators accustomed to negative rates and compressed spreads, private real estate debt now offers a rare combination: income, security and visibility.

STRUCTURE OVER SPECULATION

At the portfolio level, Federated Hermes' strategies are typically focused on senior and whole-loan exposures, secured against high-quality commercial and residential assets across core European markets, with selective exposure to development or transitional assets where risk is appropriately structured and priced. Loan-to-value ratios are conservative, covenants are robust and underwriting places particular emphasis on downside scenarios instead of base-case projections.

Capital is deployed through carefully constructed portfolios instead of one-off transactions, with diversification engineered deliberately instead of incidentally. Asset types, locations, sponsor profiles and maturity profiles are balanced to avoid hidden concentrations—a process that becomes more important as portfolios scale.

Instead of offering a one-size-fits-all product, the firm favours tailored solutions aligned with investor objectives, regulatory constraints and liability profiles. In this sense, the manager acts less like a lender chasing deal flow and more like a portfolio architect, designing credit exposure to behave predictably over time.

Crucially, these strategies are designed to integrate seamlessly into institutional balance sheets to present investors with lending opportunities with strong potential for consistent, uncorrelated returns. Capital is often deployed through segregated mandates and bespoke vehicles, tailored to each investor's liability profile, regulatory framework and reporting requirements. Duration, cash-flow visibility and capital treatment matter as much as headline yield.

RESPONSIBILITY AND GOVERNANCE AS DIFFERENTIATORS

Federated Hermes' long-standing commitment to responsible investing also informs its real estate debt strategy. ESG considerations are not treated as an overlay, but as part of credit analysis itself, affecting asset quality, liquidity, refinancing risk and long-term value. Climate resilience, energy efficiency and regulatory transition risk are analysed not as abstract ideals, but as factors that directly affect asset value, cash-flow durability and exit optionality. In markets where environmental standards are tightening and capital allocation is increasingly scrutinised, this has become a core differentiator.

'For a long-term lender, ESG factors are credit factors', Vincent notes. 'Energy efficiency, obsolescence risk, regulatory standards—these directly influence cash flow durability and collateral value'.

That perspective aligns closely with the expectations of modern institutional investors, for whom governance, transparency and stewardship are no longer optional.

TRANSLATING CAPITAL INTO RESILIENCE

In many ways, Federated Hermes exemplifies the institutionalisation of private real estate debt. It does not frame the asset class as a yield substitute for equities, nor as a tactical response to temporary dislocation. Instead, it positions real estate

(*Continued*)

(*Continued*)

debt as a structural component of institutional portfolios, designed to deliver income, mitigate risk and behave defensibly across cycles.

The firm's contribution lies not in reinvention, but in translation: translating the complexity of real estate lending into a form that pension funds and insurers can understand, govern and hold at scale.

As private credit continues to replace bank balance sheets in property finance, that role—designing trust into the structure itself—may prove just as important as the capital deployed.

All of this can sound rather theoretical: portfolio architecture, downside protection, diversification across borrowers and markets. But institutional discipline only earns its keep when it proves itself in practice.

For Federated Hermes, positioning real estate debt as a risk-management tool does not imply an aversion to complexity. It implies selectivity. It means backing transactions where the underlying fundamentals are strong, the structure is defensible and the capital stack is aligned, even when circumstances are less than straightforward.

The firm's approach is perhaps best understood not in the abstract, but in a specific moment: when a borrower, facing a sudden withdrawal of bank funding and an immovable completion deadline, required certainty instead of than optimism.

The acquisition of Atlantic House by Thomas London Day Schools offers a clear example of how institutional capital, when structured with discipline, can step in where traditional lenders hesitate—and do so without compromising on risk.

THOMAS LONDON DAY SCHOOLS: A JOURNEY TO SECURING ALTERNATIVE FUNDING

BACKGROUND AND CONTEXT

In late 2021, Thomas London Day Schools set out to acquire Atlantic House in Kensington, aiming to consolidate their activities within a purpose-built educational facility. Atlantic House and the adjacent Lytham House, originally erected in 1860, boasts a distinguished history, becoming Kensington High School in 1897 and, more recently, serving as student accommodation for Richmond University (Figure 3.4).

Although the property is not listed and has undergone numerous twentieth century extensions (diminishing its architectural significance) Lytham House remains an excellent example of Victorian London design. The building makes a positive contribution to the local streetscape and enhances the character of the surrounding conservation area. However, by the time it went on the market, the premises had fallen into disrepair, with some later additions in particularly poor condition (Figure 3.5). Initial assessments indicated that a carefully designed new

FIGURE 3.4 Atlantic House and Lytham House, Kensington (Pre-Acquisition)
Source: With permission of Thomas London Day Schools

FIGURE 3.5 Property Condition at Acquisition (Pre-Refurbishment)
Source: With permission of Thomas London Day Schools

link building could enhance its appearance and help it integrate more seamlessly into the neighbourhood.

RATIONALE FOR ACQUISITION

Before the proposed purchase, Thomas London Day School's Kensington branch operated from two converted townhouses in the vicinity. The school had outgrown these properties, now featuring cramped classrooms, outdated amenities, and the inconvenience of students having to walk between locations for physical education, dance and outdoor sports. The acquisition of Atlantic House offered the opportunity to provide a contemporary, purpose-built environment tailored to modern educational needs.

FINANCING CHALLENGES

The school's initial financing plan hinged on selling its existing properties and supplementing the proceeds with a bank loan. Arrangements were made with their long-standing banking partner, receiving initial approval. However, as the completion deadline loomed, the bank unexpectedly withdrew its offer due to internal restructuring, leaving the school without the required capital. With just three weeks remaining, Thomas London Day School's legal advisers reached out to Federated Hermes seeking urgent assistance in sourcing alternative funding.

NON-BANK FINANCING SOLUTION

Acting swiftly, Federated Hermes undertook a rapid evaluation of the property and agreed to underwrite the acquisition, bridging the funding gap left by the

(*Continued*)

(*Continued*)

FIGURE 3.6 Refurbishment Works Underway at Atlantic House (Construction Phase)
Source: With permission of Thomas London Day Schools

FIGURE 3.7 Atlantic House Approaching Completion (Final Stages of Refurbishment)
Source: With permission of Thomas London Day Schools

bank's withdrawal. This non-bank loan enabled Thomas London Day Schools to complete the purchase within the now challenging timeframe. The loan was repaid once refurbishment commenced, at which point construction finance replaced the bridging facility (Figures 3.6 and 3.7).

OUTCOME AND IMPACT

This successful intervention enabled Thomas London Day Schools to relocate to a state-of-the-art, modernised Victorian building, now operating on a net-zero carbon basis. The transformation is best understood visually (Figure 3.8).

The new facility features exceptional amenities, including an indoor PE and assembly hall, dance studio, music room with soundproofed practice booths, computer suite, science laboratories and a library (Figure 3.9). The Federated Hermes loan represented more than just a financial commitment.

The built environment continually requires investment to reduce its environmental footprint. This transaction facilitated the comprehensive refurbishment of a 160-year-old building, transforming it into a contemporary school while

FIGURE 3.8 Completed Thomas London Day School, Kensington (Post-Refurbishment)
Source: With permission of Thomas London Day Schools

FIGURE 3.9 Redeveloped Thomas London Day School, Kensington (Post-Refurbishment)
Source: With permission of Thomas London Day Schools

FIGURE 3.10 Opening of Thomas London Day School, Kensington
Source: With permission of Thomas London Day Schools

preserving and enhancing the local streetscape and conservation area. This case demonstrates the crucial role non-bank financing can play in enabling educational institutions to overcome unforeseen funding obstacles and achieve their development goals (Figure 3.10).

TURNING LOANS INTO LENDING DRY POWER

As we've already seen, pension funds and insurance companies benefit from some of the lowest Weighted Average Costs of Capital (WACC) in the market. That structural advantage allows them to lend relatively cheaply. So, it's no wonder that their capital is among the most attractive and sought after sources of funding for borrowers.

For alternative asset managers and private credit funds, the picture looks different. Their equity is typically more expensive, and competing head-on with insurer and pension balance sheets is rarely straightforward. To bridge that gap, many funds make use of what is known in the market as back leverage.

Back leverage is, in essence, borrowing at the fund level against an existing portfolio of loans. Instead of raising fresh equity, the fund uses its already-originated loans as collateral to secure additional financing: typically from banks or large institutional lenders. The aim is not to change the underlying credit risk, but to extend the reach of the capital: to deploy more, scale faster and enhance returns without diluting investors.

To see how back leverage works in practice, consider a fictional real estate credit fund: NorthBridge Capital.

In 2022, NorthBridge closed a GBP 500 million portfolio of senior loans to mid-sized residential developers across the UK. The mandate was clear: finance shovel-ready, income-producing schemes that traditional lenders were either too slow or too risk-averse to support. The portfolio was conservatively structured: first-ranking security, strong covenants, diversified borrowers and assets concentrated in prime suburban and commuter-belt locations.

The question then became a familiar one for successful credit funds: how do you do more without repeatedly returning to investors for fresh equity? This is where back leverage came into play—the quiet engine behind many of the largest private credit platforms.

Instead of allowing the GBP 500 million portfolio to amortise over time, NorthBridge transferred the loans into a Special Purpose Vehicle (SPV) and arranged a GBP 300 million back-leverage facility with a global investment bank. From the bank's perspective, the collateral was compelling: a diversified pool of performing loans, secured against real assets, with predictable cash flows and robust reporting.

Crucially, the facility sat behind the fund's equity instead of replacing it. But its impact was transformative. With an additional GBP 300 million of capital unlocked, NorthBridge could originate new loans, deepen relationships with developers and increase portfolio turnover, without altering its credit standards or investment thesis.

From the outside, nothing seemed to change. Borrowers still dealt with the same fund, on the same terms, with the same underwriting discipline. But underneath the surface, back leverage had turned a static loan book into a scalable lending engine.

The strategy, of course, comes with constraints. Back-leverage facilities typically impose portfolio-level covenants, concentration limits and restrictions on loan modifications or early sales. Funds need to maintain performance thresholds and accept a degree of oversight from their financing counterparties. But for managers confident in their underwriting and portfolio construction, the trade-off is often worth it.

As one partner at NorthBridge put it: 'Back leverage doesn't change your investment thesis: it accelerates it. If you trust your underwriting, it's the ultimate force multiplier'.

In a market where insurers and pension funds enjoy structurally cheaper capital, back leverage has become one of the key tools allowing private credit managers to compete at scale, amplifying equity, increasing velocity and quietly reshaping the economics of non-bank lending.

INSIDE THE MECHANICS OF PRIVATE CREDIT'S QUIET ENGINE

The previous sections have explored who funds private real estate debt: the pension funds rethinking fixed income, the insurers matching long-dated liabilities, the sovereigns diversifying for the next generation and the investment managers bringing these capital pools together into working deployable investment strategies. But understanding who writes the cheques only tells half the story. The real question—the one that ultimately decides whether this capital finds its way into actual real estate lending—is how it is deployed.

What really happens beneath that 'how' rarely makes it into the spotlight. It sits in the operational engine rooms: the platforms, underwriting systems, servicing teams and data frameworks that turn board-level asset-allocation decisions into real loans backing real assets. In today's market, much of that operational lift is being carried not by the institutional investors themselves, but by specialist platforms that have quietly become the connective tissue of private credit.

Some evolved from FinTech beginnings. Others grew out of niche lending expertise. And a select few manage to bridge both worlds, combining the agility of their P2P origins with the governance and sophistication needed by institutional capital. Which brings us to one of the clearest illustrations of how modern private credit actually works in practice.

LANDBAY: PLUG-AND-PLAY MORTGAGE LENDING

A PLATFORM BUILT FOR SCALE

Stepping into Landbay's offices in the heart of London reveals a business that still buzzes with the energy of its startup days, but now carries itself with the confidence and precision of a seasoned institution: a purpose-built engine for mortgage origination that speaks to both brokers and balance sheets. It still remembers its grassroots—the P2P roots that taught it how to move fast and keep borrowers front of mind—but today its heartbeat is institutional.

Julian Cork, Landbay's quietly formidable Chief Operating Officer, summed up the shift with disarming clarity. Institutions want the economics of lending without the headache of building and running an entire lending operation, and as we explored earlier, many banks now find themselves in the same boat, squeezed by higher capital charges and ever-tightening regulatory hurdles that make it

(*Continued*)

(*Continued*)

harder for them to lend at the scale or speed the market demands. Landbay's response was simple and pragmatic: build the engine, tune it and let others plug into it.

> Banks, institutional investors and asset managers come to us having made a clear choice: they can either build a lending platform from scratch—which costs time, money and a lot of headaches—or they partner with a specialist that already has the origination, underwriting and servicing capability in place. That's what Landbay is: the plug-and-play option for organisations that want exposure to mortgage lending but without the three-year build plan.

THE PROBLEM LANDBAY SOLVES

As we've already explored, for many institutional investors—pension funds, insurers, asset managers and banks—the logic of lending is fairly straightforward: secured, yield-bearing real estate loans can sit neatly alongside long-dated liabilities. The practicalities, however, are far more complex. Building a lending origination stack requires retail and broker relationships, underwriting teams, servicing infrastructure, compliance frameworks, brand trust and regulatory know-how. It's expensive, slow and operationally risky.

Landbay's journey shows how platforms can become the industrial solution to that problem. The company packaged years of specialist lending experience into an institutional offering: Mortgage-as-a-Service. It underwrites, originates and services buy-to-let loans on behalf of capital providers, delivering a reliable pipeline of assets that meet institutional underwriting expectations.

> If your DNA isn't originations, let the specialists do what they do best. We bring the brokers, the tech and the risk framework; you bring the balance sheet.

Landbay's institutional appeal comes down to one word: discipline. Its average Loan-To-Value sits conservatively; covenants are practical and enforceable; and the broker network filters for professional landlords instead of speculative amateurs. Importantly, the platform has invested heavily in its core underwriting platform and data architecture: the parts of the chain that most visibly protect investors.

> Forward flow investment partners like certainty—institutional mandates value a consistent track record and performance data that they can rely on.

THREE WAYS TO ACCESS MORTGAGE LENDING

Over a cold November morning in Landbay's Victoria offices—stealing a few minutes before addressing his company's weekly town hall—Julian laid out the three practical options facing any institution looking to build exposure to mortgage debt: 'There are really three paths', he said. 'And none of them are simple'.

The first path is to build it all yourself. It's easy to see the appeal: total control, brand ownership and the freedom to set underwriting standards that echo your own strategy. But in practice, that means putting together a full credit team, setting up a broker distribution network, building a regulatory and IT backbone from scratch and running all the operational plumbing. You then need to build your brand, track record and reputation in the market. It is expensive, slow and plagued by execution risk. As Julian puts it, 'You're signing up for a three-year deal and a very large cheque, and that's before you've even written your first loan'.

The second path is to buy loan books. Fast, clean and at first glance efficient: you get exposure without the operational burden. But what you gain in speed, you lose in certainty. You're effectively inheriting someone else's origination quality, someone else's underwriting assumptions and someone else's data gaps. 'It's fine', Julian shrugged, 'if you can live with asymmetric information and the risk that you're buying history, not capability'.

WHY THE PLATFORM MODEL WINS

And then there is the third path: partnering with a platform: lending-as-a-service. This has become the Goldilocks option for many institutions. Instead of building an entire lending infrastructure or buying someone else's past decisions, they plug into a platform like Landbay's origination engine, set bespoke credit criteria and deploy capital at speed with full transparency. They get institutional-grade underwriting without carrying the operational burden, and without the blind spots that come with secondary purchases.

Julian summed it up with the clarity of someone who has seen all three models up close: 'Buying originated paper is fine, if you can stomach the unknowns. Building it up from scratch is fine, if you've got the time, capital and appetite for complexity. But using a platform blends the best of both: speed, quality control and operational simplicity'.

In a world where banks are constrained by capital rules and institutions are hungry for the economics of lending without the weight of building a lending operation, the platform model isn't just a convenience. It is—quietly but decisively—becoming the new operating system of real estate lending.

FROM RETAIL ROOTS TO INSTITUTIONAL PLATFORM

Landbay's beginnings as a P2P platform left it with a rare advantage: deep experience of the distribution side of real estate lending. Those early days—dealing with thousands of retail investors, iterating products at speed and learning to earn trust in real time—helped it build a muscle memory that most institutional lenders never develop.

(*Continued*)

(*Continued*)

But as retail regulatory overhead and institutional appetite both increased, the business evolved its model. Landbay closed its P2P retail funding arm in 2019 and doubled down on the infrastructure that would define its next chapter: technology, broker distribution and a disciplined underwriting engine for institutional funding partners.

This evolution was shaped, in no small part, by Julian himself. Despite having held senior roles at major investment banks, he didn't approach real estate lending like a traditional banker. His tech roots and computer science background gave him a different lens entirely: he thought like an engineer. For Julian, systems, processes and scalability weren't back-office chores to be delegated; they were the product. Infrastructure wasn't a cost centre; it was the engine of the business.

'Julian brought a tech mindset to an industry that historically relied on paper and gut feel', one colleague told me. 'He thinks in terms of platforms, not pipelines. That's why institutions trust us: the plumbing and the data actually works'.

The pivot was a natural evolution. The early P2P days taught Landbay customer-centric underwriting and rapid iteration. The institutional era demanded something different: process discipline, audit trails, extensive data provisions and a governance framework that could withstand institutional-grade scrutiny.

Landbay managed to marry both worlds.

As Julian puts it, 'Starting life with retail investors taught us one thing above all: we had to earn trust every day. That discipline translated naturally when we moved to work with institutional partners: they want data, not slogans'.

HOW INSTITUTIONAL PARTNERSHIPS WORK

When Julian describes how Landbay works with institutional investors, it's less a clinical process map and more a choreography: a sequence of quiet, carefully engineered steps designed to give large pools of capital both speed and control.

'It starts with intent', he said. 'Every institution arrives with a view of risk, return and responsibility. Our job is to translate that into something operational'.

The process begins with the investor setting out its compass: the risk appetite, target yield (margin over swap), preferred geographies, LTV boundaries and product set. At any stage, Landbay has circa 150 mortgage products in the market. Each funder funds one or many products and each product is funded by one or many funders.

Whole-loan exposure in a forward-flow model, he explained, is the purest form funders 'wet fund' a loan at origination. 'Investors value the simplicity: what we underwrite is what they own. No tranching, no structural nuance. Just clean credit exposure and simple full economics of the loan'.

These forward-flow agreements are effectively a standing commitment to buy a steady, pre-defined pipeline of new loans to the funders' specification. 'It's the workhorse structure', Julian said. 'Perfect for capital that wants scale mortgage exposure without evaluating each loan individually. They set the credit box; we originate into it'.

And once a funder has built their portfolio of loans there are many options available to them. Many banks simply buy and hold, but those funds that have originated into warehouse lines will want to facilitate a securitisation exit transforming their pool of mortgages into bonds to sell in the market and crystallise returns.

Whichever structure is used, Landbay does the heavy lifting: sourcing through its broker network, underwriting to the institution's specifications and funding in the structure the investor has chosen. Governance—dashboards, audit trails, covenant monitoring, monthly servicing and detailed data reporting—sits at the heart of the relationship.

'Our data feeds, dashboards, audit trails and covenant monitoring are designed to give an institutional investor the exact same level of comfort they'd expect from an in-house team—only often far quicker to market', Julian said.

The outcome is simple but powerful: institutions get speed, precision and credit discipline; Landbay gets lending scale in a balance sheet light construct. And in a world where institutions need deployment and banks are constrained by capital and regulation, that is exactly the kind of machinery the market has been missing.

NATWEST AS A PROOF POINT

If there was a moment that signalled Landbay had truly crossed the threshold from ambitious specialist to institutional partner of consequence, it was the NatWest retail bank funding deal to fund Landbay's buy-to-let loans. In the world of mortgage lending, partnerships with high-street banks aren't handed out lightly; they are earned: slowly, quietly and through the kind of operational discipline that only becomes visible under scrutiny.

Julian recalls that phase with a kind of understated pride. The collaboration wasn't a glitzy announcement but a confirmation that Landbay's machinery—its tech, its underwriting discipline, its people and its data and governance spine—could stand shoulder-to-shoulder with one of the country's major lenders.

Working with NatWest to deliver professional landlord mortgages did more than expand Landbay's reach. It demonstrated something bigger: that platforms could sit in the same arena as the incumbents in terms of lending, not as fringe challengers, but as complementary partners providing speed, granularity and specialist expertise banks cannot always justify building in-house.

'That partnership proved two things at once', Julian said. 'First, that platforms can be credible lending partners to the large incumbent banks. And second, that banks increasingly recognise a pragmatic truth: they don't need to build every capability themselves'.

For NatWest, the attraction was efficiency and specialism. For Landbay, it was validation: the kind that only arrives when a major high-street institution entrusts you with its balance-sheet ambitions. In a sector where caution is the

(*Continued*)

(*Continued*)
default setting, this was Landbay's quiet proof of concept: not a statement, but a milestone.

TECHNOLOGY AS INFRASTRUCTURE

If there is a single thread running through every part of Landbay's model, it is the quiet but unmistakable presence of technology: not as window-dressing, but as the machinery that keeps the whole operation running. Julian spoke about it with the steady confidence of someone who has spent a career in tech, not property finance, and it shows. At Landbay, the platform isn't an accessory to the business; it is the business.

In the glass meeting rooms overlooking Victoria's morning rush, he described how Landbay's systems pull in loan-level data, reconcile it and push it back out through investor dashboards with almost clinical precision. For institutions accustomed to quarterly spreadsheets and retrospective updates, that level of visibility is not just helpful, it is transformative.

'Investors tell us they don't want surprises', Julian said. 'They want to know exactly what they own, what stage each loan is at, where the risks sit. So we built the tech to make that data available: clean, audited and in real time'.

The platform's architecture is designed with institutional scepticism in mind: automated audit trails, servicing oversight, covenant monitoring and reporting packs designed to meet the strictest due-diligence checklists. And below all that sits something rarer: a system that lets investors monitor originator risk, not months later, but as it evolves.

From Julian's perspective, this isn't about bells and whistles. It's about replacing uncertainty with clarity, the kind of clarity that makes a bank, a fund or an insurer comfortable deploying hundreds of millions through an external origination partner. In a sector where opacity once reigned, Landbay's technology offers the opposite: illumination.

WHAT THIS MEANS FOR THE MARKET

Landbay's trajectory illustrates a broader structural shift: lending is being unbundled. Origination, underwriting, funding and servicing can now be modularised. Institutions can pick and choose their exposure, mixing bespoke mandates with pooled products and securitisations. For the real-estate-finance ecosystem, platforms like Landbay are the connective tissue that make that modular architecture possible. 'If you think of modern real-estate finance as an assembly line, platforms are the new factories. They let capital flow efficiently from investor to borrower, without the historical frictions'.

LOOKING AHEAD

Julian sees the next phase as one where platforms and capital become closer collaborators. For Landbay, the priority remains the same: deliver consistent, secured returns while maintaining the underwriting standards and transparency that institutional partners demand.

When I asked him about the future of real estate private debt, he didn't hesitate. 'Over the next five years I expect to see more capital flowing via platform partnerships. The world wants asset-backed, predictable income and institutions increasingly understand that they don't have to build everything themselves to get it', he said.

FAMILY OFFICES IN REAL ESTATE CREDIT

In quiet corners of Geneva, Singapore, New York and Dubai, a shift has been taking place in the investment playbooks of the world's ultra-wealthy. Private investment firms of wealthy families—the discreet financial engines behind dynasties and entrepreneurial legacies—have been investing more in alternatives and increasingly backing private real estate credit.

It's a far cry from the days when these offices focused largely on equities, trophy real estate or early-stage venture bets. Now, they're acting more like specialist credit investors, and for good reason.

According to BlackRock's 2025 Global Family Office Survey, alternative assets are more important than ever to family offices, making up 42% of their portfolios, up from 39% in the 2022–2023 survey. Furthermore, the forward-looking questions in the survey suggested that private credit and infrastructure are the most-favoured alternative assets among this category of investors, with nearly one-third planning to increase their allocations: the strongest appetite shown for any alternative asset class, including private equity or hedge funds. In some portfolios, private credit now accounts for 15–30% of total exposure.

So what's behind this shift?

> At IQ-EQ, we've seen family offices increase allocations to private real estate debt because it delivers what many are prioritising today: predictable income, disciplined downside protection and access to high quality transactions that traditional lenders are no longer servicing. Within their portfolios, family offices typically view the asset class as a stable income anchor that also helps preserve capital through different market cycles. What resonates most is the level of control and transparency they can achieve, from bespoke structuring to clearer visibility on risk and recovery paths. Looking ahead, we expect family office participation to deepen and further professionalise, but without losing the relationship driven approach that defines this segment. Family offices will continue to favour managers who demonstrate alignment, clarity, transparency and a consistent ability to protect capital.
>
> —Peter Unwin, Head of Private Wealth & Family Office, Middle East, IQ-EQ

This evolution is driven by pragmatism as much as optimism. After several years of underwhelming returns and liquidity challenges in private equity—where IPO markets have stalled and capital is often locked up for longer than expected—many family offices are questioning whether high fees are worth it. According to the same BlackRock survey, nearly three-quarters, a full 72%, now cite fees as the biggest challenge in private markets, up dramatically from 40% just two years ago.

In contrast, private credit offers a compelling value proposition: contractual income, downside protection via secured lending and yield premiums relative to public debt markets. For family offices—many of which have longer time horizons, lower liquidity needs and direct access to origination partners—this is a perfect match.

There's also a psychological and operational alignment. Family offices, often built on entrepreneurial instincts, prefer to back real assets, real businesses and tangible value, not abstract financial engineering. In private real estate credit, they find something deeply familiar: secured cash flows, physical collateral and the ability to get close to the deal.

That's why high-profile families—from Asia's Andre Koo Jr. to the UK's David and Simon Reuben—have turned to private credit as a pillar of their investment strategy. Even Vulcan Capital, originally tied to Microsoft co-founder Paul Allen, has increased its exposure.

And they're not alone. Again, according to BlackRock, while private equity still plays a dominant role in family office portfolios, sentiment there is increasingly mixed, with only 30% of family offices expressing a bullish view.

Private real estate credit, by contrast, is on a quiet winning streak. An asset class once seen as niche that now stands as a new frontier for generational wealth. It combines everything family offices crave: visibility, yield, control and resilience. And as the dislocation in bank lending continues, more families are stepping into the void.

As one European family office principal put it:

> Private real estate debt has moved from opportunistic to essential for us. It gives us something increasingly rare: visibility. We know where our capital sits, we understand the collateral and we can structure around risk in a way that simply isn't possible in public markets. In an environment where liquidity can be deceptive and valuations uncertain, we would rather lend against real assets than rely on market sentiment. It's not about stretching for return. It's about protecting capital while still making it work.

They are not just preserving wealth. They are lending into the future, and reshaping the very structure of real estate finance in the process.

FROM WALL STREET TO YOUR STREET: DEBT GOES RETAIL

As we saw in the introduction, private credit is as old as money itself. Long before banks and structured finance, lending was deeply personal: a wealthy individual or merchant extending capital to a landowner, builder or trader, often within a tightly knit community. In that sense, the rise of P2P lending in the 2010s was less a revolution than a return to roots: a full-circle moment in the history of credit, and a tool that once again enabled everyday investors to access real estate private debt.

As we have already discussed at length, in the aftermath of the Global Financial Crisis, two powerful forces reshaped the investment landscape. Ultra-low interest rates slowly erode the returns of traditional fixed-income products, while banks—still nursing their wounds from the crisis—had started to pull back sharply from sectors like real estate development finance. That retreat left a gap and institutional capital rushed in to fill it. Private credit was suddenly in demand, offering yield, security and an understandable asset: loans secured against brick-and-mortar real estate.

But while institutions were quick to seize the opportunity, retail investors remained largely excluded. In those early years, real estate credit was a private club, dominated by banks, pension funds, insurer, specialist lenders and ultra-wealthy individuals. If you weren't operating at scale, access was effectively off-limits. Development finance remained opaque and high-barrier, with multi-million-pound loans arranged quietly behind closed doors. For everyday investors, participation wasn't just difficult, it was structurally out of reach.

That began to change in the early 2010s with the rise of P2P lending, driven both by technological advances and by regulatory changes that enabled retail participation. Suddenly, a new generation of FinTech entrepreneurs started asking a deceptively simple question: why should access to property-backed lending be reserved for the few? Why couldn't technology open the door to many?

And slowly, the walls began to crack.

As Christian Faes, Co-Founder and Chairman of LendInvest, recalled in Chapter 1, the post-crisis UK environment proved particularly fertile ground for this shift. Under the Conservative government led by David Cameron and Chancellor George Osborne, policymakers were not only tightening regulation on banks but actively encouraging a new breed of technology-enabled finance companies. Rather than simply constraining incumbents, the aim was to open the financial system to competition.

The UK became a global pioneer in crowdfunding and P2P regulation, signalling a clear willingness to support innovation while maintaining oversight. At the same time, the Bank of England opened the door to new banking licences, and venture capital began to flow into emerging FinTech platforms. The result was a uniquely supportive ecosystem in London during the 2010s, one where government, regulators and investors were broadly aligned in fostering disruption within financial services.

This combination of regulatory openness and technological innovation catalysed the emergence of an entirely new segment of lenders. A wave of platforms began to target niches underserved by traditional banks, including real estate development finance, gradually building a parallel credit ecosystem alongside the incumbents.

Enabled by this FinTech wave—online platforms, automated underwriting and data-driven credit analytics—P2P lending offered something genuinely new: the ability for everyday investors to access secured, yield-generating real estate loans once dominated by banks and institutions. Minimum investments fell dramatically. Lock-up periods shortened. With just a few clicks, investors could gain exposure to property-backed lending opportunities that had previously been inaccessible.

In the UK, that idea of democratising private credit crystallised in 2013, with the launch of LendInvest, a startup that would become one of the most influential pioneers of P2P property lending. Its ambition was bold but straightforward: use technology to connect everyday savers directly with property developers in need of short-term, secured finance. For the first time, individuals could fund deals that had previously sat squarely in the domain of merchant banks and specialist credit funds.

As Rod Lockhart, CEO of LendInvest, told me:

> We set out to address a structural gap in UK property finance. Regulation and rigid credit and risk frameworks have limited how banks lend, leaving many viable projects underserved and slowing down decision-making. At the same time, private capital was seeking a more efficient way to access the market—seeing it as a solid alternative to rock-bottom interest rates. Technology was the enabler—allowing us to make faster, more individual credit decisions, offer greater flexibility across propositions and build a platform capable of evolving as market demand changed.

LendInvest became what is widely considered the first ever P2P real estate lending platform in the UK, and it demonstrated that P2P real estate lending could be built at scale, with institutional-grade underwriting, robust security and a technology backbone capable of handling both borrowers and investors. In doing so, it marked the opening act of a broader shift, one that began to prise open the once-exclusive world of real estate credit and extend it, for the first time, to a wider investing public.

LendInvest wasn't alone for long. In the years that followed, platforms like CrowdProperty, CapitalRise, Proplend and Kuflink entered the UK market, each targeting a slightly different niche, from suburban planning gain loans to luxury developments in central London. The formula was broadly consistent: offer individual investors access to short-term loans secured against physical property, typically yielding 6–10% per annum over periods of 6 to 24 months. The risks were real, but so were the returns, and demand surged.

Yet this was never just a British story. Across Europe, similar platforms began to emerge, even in markets where creditor protections were weaker and enforcement frameworks less lender-friendly, a contrast explored earlier in Chapter 1. What united them was not regulatory convenience, but the same structural gap: cautious banks, underserved developers and yield-hungry savers.

In Germany, platforms like Exporo took the model a step further. Retail investors could participate in both debt and equity opportunities with as little as EUR 500, often in smaller-scale commercial or residential developments that fell below the radar of major lenders. Over time, Exporo has channelled more than EUR 1 billion into hundreds of projects, establishing itself as one of Europe's largest digital real estate investment platforms.

As one COO of a European P2P platform put it, 'Digital platforms have made it possible for private investors to participate in real estate financing in a way that was previously reserved to institutions: with transparency, clear risk profiles and tangible assets at the core'.

In France, startups such as Homunity and Fundimmo stepped into the funding void left by increasingly risk-averse regional banks, particularly in the suburban housing market. They specialised in connecting investors with developers looking to raise secured debt for mid-sized residential projects, helping to finance the kind of everyday housing that major institutions often overlook.

Meanwhile, in the Nordics, a cross-border platform called Kameo quietly built a loyal investor base across Sweden, Norway and Denmark. Its focus was SME developers and light industrial assets, deals often considered too small, too bespoke or too operationally intensive for mainstream banks. With target returns of 5–9% and minimum investment thresholds below EUR 250, Kameo attracted a mix of retail and semi-professional investors seeking yield backed by real assets.

To the east, EstateGuru, founded in Estonia, was building one of the most ambitious European platforms. Operating across the Baltics, Finland, Germany and beyond, it offered both retail and institutional investors access to short-term, property-backed loans, often financing commercial or residential redevelopment projects that struggled to secure bank funding. With its minimum investment of just EUR 50, the platform championed accessibility while maintaining a rigorous underwriting approach.

As its co-founder and Chairman, Marek Pärtel put it: 'We exist to close the EUR 300 billion funding gap for SME real estate developers in Europe-and we're doing it one loan at a time'. The mission resonated. By the mid-2020s, EstateGuru had financed over 4,000 projects and attracted tens of thousands of investors from over 100 countries, illustrating just how globalised retail participation in property-backed credit had become.

Even in Spain, platforms such as Housers introduced the concept of crowdlending to a broad retail audience, allowing individuals to invest in development-backed loans with graded risk categories and clear return bands. Legal challenges would later follow, serving as a reminder that democratising credit also needs robust governance. But the innovation itself was undeniable: participation in real estate credit was broadening well beyond its traditional institutional core.

Across the Atlantic, the United States put the model into hyperdrive. There, platforms like Groundfloor, Patch of Land, RealtyMogul and Fundrise emerged at scale, often blurring the lines between debt, equity and structured finance. From bridge loans to large multifamily construction deals, the US P2P and retail private credit ecosystem catered to almost every corner of the real estate market. Technology-enabled platforms lowered entry points to as little as USD 100, an unprecedented level of access to asset-backed lending.

Fundrise went a step further, launching its own family of public, non-traded interval funds, combining retail distribution with institutional portfolio construction. In doing so, it demonstrated how retail capital could be wrapped in vehicles designed to meet regulatory standards, manage liquidity expectations and scale responsibly, bringing private real estate credit closer to the architecture of mainstream investment products.

This wave didn't rise in isolation. It mirrored a broader transformation taking place across financial markets: the democratisation of investing. Retail investors—emboldened by the rise of commission-free brokers like Robinhood, Trade Republic and Revolut—were no longer content to sit on the sidelines. With interest rates at historic lows and bond yields barely keeping pace with inflation, they were hungry for alternatives. Real estate credit, long considered dry, dull and inaccessible, suddenly looked stable, tangible and lucrative.

The platforms evolved too. Some, like Landbay, moved beyond pure P2P models into hybrid structures, combining retail flows with institutional co-investment. LendInvest secured warehouse lines and launched its own securitisations. Exporo began underwriting syndicated deals alongside German banks. Fundraise built in-house asset management capabilities and launched its own real estate funds. As retail capital gained momentum and proved both scalable and resilient, institutional money started to follow it.

Regulation, inevitably, caught up. Regulators in the UK, EU and US introduced tighter rules around transparency, risk disclosure and investor suitability. Some platforms struggled. For example, Lendy in the UK collapsed under the weight of poor underwriting, while Housers faced legal scrutiny in Spain. Yet the broader ecosystem matured. What emerged was not just a retail product, but a new asset class with its own governance standards, risk frameworks and investor expectations.

Today, real estate private credit is no longer the exclusive domain of institutions and insiders. For a growing cohort of middle-class investors, it has become part of a balanced diversified portfolio: a source of income, a hedge against inflation and increasingly, a way to support local development.

> Before platforms like these came along, investing in real estate debt felt completely out of reach—it was something only banks or big funds could do. I never imagined that with just a few hundred euros, I could be part of a real project, earning regular returns backed by real assets. It's given me a way to diversify beyond stocks and savings accounts and to feel like my money is actually working in the real economy—helping developers build homes, not just sitting in a bank. For me, it's about access, transparency and control.
>
> —Retail P2P real estate investor

This story—of platforms, access, technology and trust—is more than a case study in financial innovation. It's a story of inclusion. Of people once shut out of the lending market now playing a role in shaping the built environment around them.

The P2P pioneers didn't just open the gates. They redrew the map.

CHAPTER 4

Why Developers Are Moving Beyond Banks

THE MOMENT BORROWERS LOOKED ELSEWHERE

> *After the 2008 Global Financial Crisis, it became clear that traditional banks were no longer willing or able to support mid-sized developers like us. This forced us to look beyond conventional lending channels. In the early days, however, it was a process of trial and error: we had to 'kiss many frogs' before finding the right partners. The rise of regulated non-bank lenders was by no means an overnight development and like many in the industry, we were initially cautious and even sceptical of these newcomers.*
>
> —Joe McGinnis, Managing Director, Braidwater Group

As we have already explored, in the years since the financial crisis, housebuilders have found themselves confronting a new reality: banks are slower, more constrained and far less willing to accommodate complexity. Projects stall not because they lack demand or viability, but because they don't fit neatly into bank credit boxes: they are non-vanilla, lack market comparable, exceed LTGDV thresholds or need a degree of flexibility that traditional lenders are no longer equipped to offer. That led to the emergence of real estate private credit.

In the previous chapter, we followed the money, tracing how institutional investors, pension funds and family offices have piled into private real estate debt. We examined what draws them in, how they manage risk and where this asset class fits into their broader portfolios. In short, we unpacked the demand side of the equation.

But now, it's time to turn the table. Because you can't have a lending market without someone doing the borrowing.

This chapter flips the lens from capital providers to the people on the ground: the developers, housebuilders and small property firms who are increasingly swapping the familiar, if frustrating, world of bank finance for something altogether more agile. These are the SME operators—often family-run outfits or regionally focused specialists—who once kept their bank relationship manager's number on speed dial. The bank was their first stop and, for a long time, their only one. Over the next few pages, we will explore why private credit—once seen as a last resort or an expensive stopgap—has become, for many, the first call. Through real-world examples, we will explore how speed, certainty of execution and bespoke structuring have reshaped borrower behaviour, and why relationship-driven lenders are winning ground in a market where rigidity kills deals. What emerges is not a story of banks disappearing, but of a fundamental reordering of trust, incentives and expectations in development finance.

THE CHANGING PERCEPTION OF PRIVATE DEBT

That shift from bank to non-bank lending didn't happen overnight. Nor was it driven by developers suddenly waking up and deciding to embrace change. Instead, it's been a slow burn, a decade-long drift triggered by the aftermath of the Global Financial Crisis. As mainstream banks became more risk-averse and less willing to support entrepreneurial, fast-moving development, they pulled back, citing tighter regulations and more conservative lending appetites. The result? Developers found themselves caught in the middle.

As a property developer told me:

> What used to be a relatively straightforward process—a conversation with your bank, a handshake and funding in place—became a bureaucratic maze. Decisions dragged. Covenants tightened. Leverage dropped. And more often than not, the answer was a polite but firm no.

So, quietly at first, developers started looking elsewhere. Alternative lenders—private debt funds, boutique financiers and newer non-bank entrants—began to creep onto the radar. It wasn't love at first sight. These weren't well-worn relationships. The trust wasn't there yet. But when the banks stopped answering the phone, others started picking it up.

But in the early days of the sector, borrowing from a non-bank lender—especially the smaller and less institutionalised ones—carried a serious stigma. These lenders were viewed with suspicion; no self-respecting developer wanted to be seen seeking finance from them, let alone admit to knocking on their door. Many wouldn't even take a meeting with a private credit provider. Private real estate debt was the option of last resort, the preserve of the so-called non-bankable: developers whose plans were too ambitious, too unusual or simply too complex for traditional lenders, as well as those who had gone bust during the Global Financial Crisis or were carrying poor credit histories that made traditional financing all but impossible. If your bank wouldn't touch you, you might—reluctantly—try a non-bank lender. But it certainly wasn't something you boasted about. Private credit was often seen as expensive, opaque and, frankly, a bit dodgy.

As one financial introducer told me, 'There was a time when developers would only approach non-bank lenders as a last resort, —when the bank had said no and they were out of options'. 'It was like pawning the family silver', another senior lending manager at a specialist lender told me. 'You didn't go there unless the banks had already said no, and you never, ever, talked about it afterwards'.

NO LONGER A DIRTY WORD

But that perception has shifted dramatically in recent years, driven both by necessity and by the evolution of non-bank lenders themselves. Over the years, alternative finance providers became not just more visible, but more viable. The private debt space matured. Lenders became regulated, institutionalised and increasingly in tune with the needs of modern developers. More importantly, developers began to see the advantages: speed, certainty, flexibility and an ability to engage with projects on their real-world merits instead of just what ticked a box in a bank's credit matrix.

What was once seen as the financial equivalent of a back-alley deal is now considered a smart, strategic move.

The financial introducer told me:

> Today, non-banks are often developers' first call, not because they have to, but because they want to. Developers value speed, flexibility and a more pragmatic approach to lending. Non-bank lenders have positioned themselves not just as capital providers, but as partners who understand that development doesn't always go to plan, and who are willing to work through the bumps alongside borrowers'.

That has resulted in a significant reordering of the funding landscape. Private debt, once seen as fringe, has moved to the centre. And in the process, it has become something few developers would have imagined a decade ago: their first call.

> The real difference isn't just speed: it's mindset. Banks lend against policy; private lenders lend against judgment. Developers are increasingly choosing partners who understand that real estate projects move in phases, not straight lines. When the capital provider understands risk dynamically instead of mechanically, projects move forward with far greater confidence.
>
> —Theo Kemp, Principal Founding Director, EVOLVE Lending Group

Today, highly respected developers—many of them with long track records and solid balance sheets—are choosing non-bank lenders, not because they've been turned away from banks, but because they value what private capital offers: speed, certainty, commercial pragmatism and an approach to structuring that reflects the reality on the ground. Now, they're not only taking the meetings, but they're also actively cultivating relationships, comparing term sheets and in some cases, bypassing banks entirely. Private credit is now not only respectable, but it's also often the funding route of choice.

> Today's top developers don't see private credit as Plan B: they see it as a tool for execution. They come to us proactively, with deals already mapped out, budgeted and timed. What they want now is a lender who can move at their pace, not slow it down
>
> —Mark Roberts, Relationship Manager, Assetz Capital

There's also the realisation that the cheapest capital isn't necessarily the best capital. Today's developers want capital that moves quickly, comes with fewer strings attached and is provided by people who understand the commercial realities of building and delivering. As Joe McGinnis told me, 'What we've learned is that it's not just about the money: it's about who you're in bed with'. Non-bank lenders are meeting that demand with tailored structures, practical covenant packages and relationship-led underwriting, often delivered within weeks, not months.

As a result, developers are embracing non-bank lending not as a last resort, but as a proactive choice, one that offers partnership, clarity and confidence in an increasingly complex financing environment.

Private credit has shed its old skin. It's no longer a dirty word. It's a new chapter, and more developers are turning the page.

That evolution is really at the heart of this chapter: understanding why so many developers now choose non-bank lenders as their first call, not out of desperation, but by design.

Over the next few pages, we'll explore what they value, not just in capital, but in character. We'll look at why speed, flexibility and tailored solutions matter more than a marginal cost of funds. And we'll hear directly from those on the front lines of development, who've come to see private credit not as a last resort, but as a trusted partner in a world where things rarely go exactly according to plan.

That said, not all private credit is created equal and the journey from banks to non-banks wasn't all smooth sailing. As McGinnis put it with typical understatement, 'We had to kiss a fair few frogs before finding the right funding partner'.

As with any evolving market, the rapid growth of non-bank lending has attracted a wide range of players, some more experienced and reliable than others. Developers still need to tread carefully: to scrutinise funding lines, understand who's really backing the capital and ensure that facilities won't be pulled halfway through a build. The right private lender can be a true partner. The wrong one can be a costly distraction, or worse, a liability mid-project.

In short, while the reputation of private debt has improved, selectivity still matters. Because in this new funding landscape, who you borrow from is just as important as how much you borrow.

TIME KILLS DEALS

> In property, timing really is everything. You can have the best site, the best team and full planning consent, but if your funding isn't in place when you need it, the whole thing can come down crashing. With banks, we were waiting six, eight, sometimes ten weeks just to get through credit committee and that's assuming nothing got kicked back. With non-bank lenders, we're seeing decisions in days, not months. They understand the commercial pressures on the ground, that windows close, contractors walk and costs rise. That speed isn't just convenient: it can make or break a deal.
>
> —Dan Eaton, Director, Pivotal Point Group

In the world of property development, time isn't just money—it's often the difference between a project that gets built and one that dies on the drawing board. That may sound dramatic, but anyone who's ever tried to get a shovel in the ground knows it is true. Delays in funding—especially the kind of delays caused by protracted bank processes—can send even the best-laid schemes into a tailspin. Planning consents can have strict expiry dates. Construction contracts often hinge on locking in material prices or securing labour. Competitive site purchases could fall through if exchange doesn't happen on time. The longer a developer waits for a credit committee to nod a deal through, the greater the chance the deal falls through, because numbers shift, contractors walk away or the seller finds a faster buyer.

Even assuming they're still willing to consider development finance—which, as we've seen, is increasingly unlikely—banks, with their layers of underwriting, risk management and compliance, rarely move at the pace the market needs. Deals typically pass through several internal teams—front office, credit, risk, compliance, legal and sometimes sector-specific committees—each adding friction and time. Take the mysterious credit committees, shrouded in as much secrecy as a Vatican conclave: they usually meet weekly or fortnightly to consider new applications or amend existing finance arrangements. If an application is submitted on a Wednesday and the committee meets on Tuesdays, that's nearly a week lost by default. And if a document is missing or needs clarification, the deal is pushed to the next cycle, adding another week or more. These delays can quickly stack up.

> We once lost a site in Gloucestershire because the bank took eight weeks to get through credit. By the time they gave us the green light, the vendor had walked: sold it to someone who could move faster. That's when it really hit me: banks don't just cost you time: they can cost you the whole deal.
>
> —Dan Eaton

But it's not just credit committees that slow things down. Even getting a foot through the bank's door can be harder than getting an audience with the King. Anyone who's dealt with a bank knows the drill: the application itself is a test of endurance, a rigid, one-size-fits-all template where every detail of the project must squeeze neatly into the bank's tidy little box. And if it doesn't quite fit? Well, everything grinds to a halt while borrowers are politely invited to twist and trim their plans until they match the paperwork, instead of the other way round. And then comes the waiting. They send it off, full of hope, only to watch days turn into weeks while someone, somewhere in the bank, eventually decides to glance at it. There's no urgency on their end; the clock only seems to tick for borrowers. Eventually, if they are lucky enough, the Business Development Manager gives the nod and that's when the real slog begins.

Banks typically require independent valuation and quantity surveying reports, both commissioned at the borrower's own cost and subject to the bank's chosen panel. That takes time. Then, those reports must be reviewed, reconciled with the deal structure and—heaven forbid—if the numbers don't quite line up, the whole process grinds to a halt. Any discrepancy can stall progress.

Then there's the mountain of paperwork: planning consents, contractor agreements, QS reports, financial forecasts, environmental assessments, personal guarantees, all must be up to date and in perfect order. One missing document can send the application back to square one and trigger further delays. It's a system that runs on red tape and patience, and for developers with shovels ready and deadlines looming, neither is in plentiful supply.

Once terms are agreed in principle, legal negotiations begin, and here too, timelines can stretch. Solicitors representing both lender and borrower may spend weeks exchanging documents, especially if the bank's legal team is particularly risk-averse or lacks experience with non-standard development finance projects. On top of that, deals may be delayed by rigid credit models and overly conservative stress testing on sales values, construction costs or interest cover. This can lead to restructuring or a need for further evidence, setting the clock back again.

Then there are the 'computer says no' scenarios. If the project doesn't neatly fit the bank's internal credit box—perhaps it's too small, too unusual or in an unfamiliar location—the deal may stall indefinitely or be declined late in the process.

Other common sources of delay include seasonal bottlenecks and capacity constraints. Bank teams are often overstretched around holiday periods, year-end close or during surges in application volume. Market conditions can also shift mid-process. If interest rates rise or market sentiment sours while a deal is under review, banks may re-price the loan or revisit the fundamentals, leading to further negotiation or delay, something developers experienced frequently during the COVID period.

> During COVID, it was chaos. You'd be halfway through a deal, and the bank would come back with new terms: higher margins, lower leverage, more security. It happened more than once and each time it either killed the deal or forced us back to square one. You couldn't plan with any certainty because the goalposts kept shifting.
>
> —Dan Eaton

And finally, there's the issue of Personal Guarantees (PGs) and security structures. Banks often require PGs or second charges that borrowers may wish to resist or renegotiate, pushing discussions up to senior levels and adding further time.

As a result, delays of several weeks—sometimes even months—are not uncommon. But in that time, a lot can change. Interest rates can rise. Build costs can shift. Buyer appetite can cool. And a deal that once stacked up may no longer make sense. Worse still, developers can be left carrying pre-development costs, servicing expensive bridging finance or locked into exclusivity periods with no progress to show for it.

As Rishi Baungally, Director at Premier Gold Investments, told me:

> Too often in development finance, simple deals become unnecessarily complex at a Bank. Layers of requests and additional information are introduced, even though the underlying risk hasn't changed. The lenders that stand out are the ones who maintain credit discipline without adding friction that ultimately makes no difference to the outcome.

This isn't about impatience. It's about opportunity cost. And in this business, lost time often translates into lost value. That's why more developers now favour funding partners who can move at pace and adapt in real time to the pressures on the ground. A lender who can move in weeks—not months—isn't just convenient. They're the difference between keeping momentum and missing the moment. As Roberts explained to me over a coffee at his Manchester office, 'Non-bank lenders have carved out a vital role in development finance by being able to respond quickly and structure facilities around the realities of each project. Developers value the ability to access capital with a decision-making process that is both pragmatic and closely aligned to their business plans'.

FROM PAPER TRAILS TO DIGITAL RAILS

But for borrowers, the draw of private credit is not only about speed. It is about what the lending experience feels like when it is built for the twenty-first century instead of inherited from the last. Inside many legacy banks, loan origination still runs on ageing siloed systems never designed for modern development finance: data re-keyed across platforms, underwriting models built in Excel and risk reports manually exported from systems that do not speak to one another.

Meanwhile, outside the mahogany boardrooms of the big banks, a new breed of lender is re-writing the rulebook. As we'll explore fully in Chapter 5, digital-first private credit firms are sprinting ahead, unencumbered by legacy systems or manual processes. These tech-native lenders are using AI, automation and real-time data to streamline every single part of the loan journey, from picking up applications almost instantly and setting themselves KPIs around response time, to leveraging modern communication tools to keep lenders, borrowers, brokers, lawyers, surveyors and every other party in the loop without missing a beat.

As one broker said:

> For developers, the real difference with digitally native lenders isn't just speed: it's visibility and control. Applications are acknowledged almost instantly, milestones tracked in real time and communication flows seamlessly between borrower, broker, lawyer and surveyor. Instead of wondering where a deal sits, the developer can see progress as it happens. That clarity reduces friction, builds confidence and allows projects to move forward with far greater certainty'.

Take Automated Valuation Models (AVMs), for instance: platforms such as Hometrack and Geowox allow lenders to generate instant, highly accurate property valuations using machine learning and up-to-date market data, replacing otherwise lengthy RICS surveys and shaving weeks off the application timeline. For development finance, tools like Aprao and LandTech allow lenders and developers to model detailed appraisals and cashflows in real time, allowing immediate adjustments to funding structures as costs or timelines shift. And on the compliance front, AI-driven due diligence platforms like Xapien and Intelligo can complete in minutes the sort of in-depth client and counterparty checks that might take a bank days or even weeks.

As one venture investor focused on real estate technology noted:

> For years, real estate lending relied on fragmented processes: spreadsheets, email chains and relationship-driven sourcing. What's changing now is the growing role of data and intelligent systems. A new generation of tools is enabling lenders to identify risks earlier, streamline due diligence and automate many of the manual workflows that historically slowed transactions down. Tasks that once took weeks can now be completed in a matter of hours. As a result, private credit is becoming less dependent on networks and more driven by access to high-quality data and the ability to interpret it effectively.

Even the dreaded document collation is getting an overhaul. AI-driven systems can now scan, extract and verify borrower information in minutes, cutting through the bureaucracy like a hot knife through butter. Natural language processing and machine vision are doing the heavy lifting in underwriting, cutting time, stress and cost for all involved. While traditional lenders shuffle paper, these platforms are doing deals, quickly, securely and with far fewer hoops to jump through.

In short, the lending landscape is splitting in two: on one side, the legacy lenders weighed down by process; on the other, digital-first lenders laying high-speed tracks where slow-moving paper trails once ran. As the saying goes, you're either on the train or you're on the tracks.

WHEN FLEXIBILITY WINS THE DAY

Speed and tech set the pace, but it's the way non-bank lenders flex around the realities of a project that truly wins borrowers over. These newer lenders approach transactions with a clear intent to make them work, an approach that shapes the project from the outset, not only when it faces turbulence. Traditional lenders, bound by policy and precedent, rarely operate with the same latitude.

Free from the straitjacket of rigid lending models, fixed capital structures and inflexible credit terms, private credit providers have the freedom to look at a deal on its own merits and design capital around the realities of a scheme instead of forcing a scheme to contort itself to fit a pre-set template. That might mean recognising planning gain as part of the equity story, calibrating guarantee levels to reflect track record, tailoring drawdown profiles to phased construction or structuring exits around refinance instead of sales. And that matters, because in property, as any seasoned developer will admit over a pint, things rarely go precisely to plan. Timelines shift, deadlines slip, contractors go bust, suppliers are late, cost inflation creeps in, planning officers take their time, utilities connections drag their heels, the exit strategy wobbles and the weather: well, it never quite behaves. In short, unforeseen hiccups have a way of appearing just when you think you've got everything under control.

For SME housebuilders, who often operate on tight margins and tighter timelines still, the difference between success and collapse can very literally come down to not just whether the lender picks up the phone when things go sideways, but on how intelligently the deal is structured from the outset. A bespoke solution builds resilience into the deal even before the first brick is laid. It anticipates complexity, aligns incentives and creates buffers where they are most needed. And when—not if—challenges inevitably arise, the question is not whether the lender can enforce covenants, but whether they can interpret the nuance of the situation and adjust within a framework designed for real-world development. In a world of so many moving parts, a lender who can structure creatively and bend without breaking isn't just helpful: they can be the difference between a project stalling and a project getting built.

But it wasn't always this way.

In the old days, the bank was both gatekeeper and overlord. Developers borrowed an off-the-shelf product on the bank's terms, danced to the bank's timeline and prayed they wouldn't trip a covenant halfway through a project. There was no such thing as a bespoke facility. Repayment schedules were fixed. Covenant tests were gospel. And if anything slipped—a contractor delay, a planning glitch – they'd find themselves renegotiating with credit officers who'd never set foot on a muddy building site. As Dan Eaton told me:

> In those days, there was no room for real-world messiness. Banks wanted everything to fit neatly into their box and if it didn't, the answer was simply 'No'. You'd be sat across from someone in a suit who'd never seen a live site, trying to explain why the scaffolding was still up and why your QS needed another fortnight. It was like speaking different languages.

This lack of flexibility is the background into which non-bank lenders stepped in. Property developers expected flexibility, they expected their lender to speak the same language, to have walked the site with them and understand the challenges they face. And those non-bank lenders were ready and able to face the challenge by offering flexibility. That was precisely the case with LendInvest, who stepped in when an experienced property developer needed a bespoke facility.

LENDINVEST: ENGINEERING CAPITAL FOR COMPLEX URBAN REGENERATION

COMPLEXITY AS OPPORTUNITY

If ever there were a project unlikely to sail smoothly through a traditional bank's credit committee, this was it.

A Grade II listed building in central Bristol, a regional economic hub in South West England where housing demand, particularly among young professionals and graduates, continues to outstrip supply. A phased conversion and extension programme. A self-delivery contracting model. A mezzanine-backed equity structure. And an exit via refinance into a long-term rental portfolio instead of a straightforward build-to-sell.

For a high-street bank operating within rigid underwriting frameworks, the complexity alone would have set off alarm bells. For a specialist non-bank lender like LendInvest, it was hardly exotic. Not a red flag, but familiar ground, precisely the sort of deal that sits safely within its bread and butter. An opportunity to structure around the realities of the project instead of forcing the project to conform to a template.

THE PROJECT: REGENERATION IN THE URBAN CORE

In August 2022, LendInvest structured a GBP 10.7 million development finance facility to support the acquisition and redevelopment of a site on Redcross Street.

The scheme was ambitious in both scope and character. Phase 1 involved the careful restoration of the listed structure, preserving its historic fabric while

(*Continued*)

(Continued)

delivering 30 units. Phase 2 added a four-storey rear extension and a single-storey roof extension, bringing the total to 61 self-contained co-living studios. Each unit offered private en-suite and kitchenette facilities, complemented by over 2,200 square feet of shared communal space designed for socialising, working and dining, a format tailored to Bristol's growing population of young professionals.

Yet what was unique about this scheme was that the site retained upside potential. Planning dynamics left open the possibility of scaling the scheme to 87 units through additional floors. Embedded optionality, in other words. That sort of upside needed a lender capable of thinking beyond the immediate cost-to-complete calculation and into the longer arc of asset strategy.

To appreciate the scale of the transformation proposed—and the complexity of the site LendInvest agreed to back—it helps to see what the development team were working with (Figure 4.1).

> Traditional lenders often mistake complexity for risk. At LendInvest, we see it differently. The Redcross Street project is exactly the kind of ambitious, multi-layered urban regeneration that we love to support. We pride ourselves on supporting SME developers who understand the realities of the housing market and the agility to back these developers who are thinking five steps ahead.
>
> —Steve Larkin, Managing Director, Development Finance, LendInvest

FIGURE 4.1 Redcross Street—From Dereliction to Designed Regeneration
Source: With permission of LendInvest

WHY BESPOKE STRUCTURING MATTERED

At first glance, the headline numbers looked straightforward. But the capital stack told a subtler story.

Instead of being funded purely through shareholder cash equity, the deal included a mezzanine tranche from joint venture partner Altus sitting beneath the senior debt. In addition, the developer, RenGen, had created what is often described in the industry as sweat equity by securing valuable planning uplifts prior to funding. This layered structure reflected commercial reality: capital efficiency, planning expertise and strategic land enhancement: value generated not by making a payment, but by unlocking planning consent and repositioning the asset.

But here's the thing. Most traditional banks struggle to see sweat equity in quite the same way developers do. In the world of regulated lending, value must be tangible, measurable and immediately loss-absorbing. Cash in. Hard equity. Clear loan-to-cost ratios. Planning gain, no matter how meaningful in the real world, can feel intangible on a credit committee spreadsheet: contingent, revisable, dependent on market conditions and future execution. And so, more often than not, it is discounted or ignored altogether. A deal structured around layered capital and planning gain can quickly begin to look non-standard.

For LendInvest, the question was different. Instead of asking how neatly the structure fitted a pre-set model, the question became whether the value created was real, defensible and aligned. Where a bank might have paused at the complexity, LendInvest leaned into it, structuring around the substance of the deal instead of its form.

The guarantee package illustrates the point. Instead of insisting on a blanket 20% personal guarantee—the market standard—LendInvest agreed a compromise of 10% Personal Guarantee and 10% Corporate Guarantee. This calibrated approach balanced competitiveness with risk control, allowing the lender to remain commercially viable against alternative funders while maintaining sufficient alignment.

It is precisely this willingness to adapt—to structure around the borrower's profile instead of imposing a rigid template—that is drawing developers towards non-bank lenders.

MANAGING NON-STANDARD DELIVERY RISK

The departure from convention did not end there. The scheme was structured as a 'self-build', managed by RenGen's internal contracting team instead of through a traditional JCT main contractor arrangement. For many banks, the absence of a tier-one contractor and fixed-price build contract would raise immediate red flags.

On paper, it was unconventional. In practice, it was anything but if one looked at the context (Figure 4.2).

(*Continued*)

(*Continued*)

FIGURE 4.2 Proposed Scheme for Redcross Street (Architectural CGI)
Source: With permission of LendInvest

RenGen had completed 16 schemes since 2011 under similar structures. The business was led by Iestyn Lewis, a Chartered Civil Engineer and recipient of the James Rennie Medal—an award recognising outstanding engineering achievement—with a total track record of 28 schemes representing approximately GBP 193 million in GDV. The company's particular expertise in listed building conversions across Bath and Bristol added further comfort. Personal and corporate net worth exceeded GBP 17.5 million.

The question, then, was not whether the structure was orthodox. It was whether the team behind it knew what they were doing. Instead of defaulting to checklist underwriting, LendInvest assessed capability. Form gave way to substance.

> Traditional banks are often blinded by the 'form' of a deal: the contracts, the rigid ratios, the standard templates. At LendInvest, we lean into the 'substance'. Whether it's layered mezzanine debt or non-standard delivery, if the underlying logic is sound and the expertise is proven, we'll find

a way to fund it. This project and the facility we provided is a perfect example of why bespoke structuring will always outperform a one-size-fits-all approach.

—Steve Larkin, Managing Director, Development Finance, LendInvest

SECURITY, SUBORDINATION AND EXIT DISCIPLINE

Flexibility, however, was matched by rigour.

LendInvest secured a first-ranking legal mortgage, debentures and share charges. Crucially, a Deed of Subordination ensured that the mezzanine and shareholder loans ranked behind the senior facility, preserving capital stack discipline.

The exit strategy also set the deal apart from speculative development finance. Instead of relying on open-market sales, the planned exit was a refinance into the borrower's existing long-term rental portfolio: a stabilised income-producing asset. To manage timing risk, the facility incorporated a Notification Event trigger at month 15 if satisfactory Heads of Terms for the refinance were not presented. This created a three-month buffer before maturity, ensuring early visibility on exit progress and avoiding last-minute refinancing pressure.

This was not relaxed credit. It was structured credit.

THE BORROWER'S PERSPECTIVE

For developers operating in complex urban environments—particularly those working with listed buildings, phased regeneration or specialist asset classes—price is rarely the only consideration.

Speed matters. Certainty matters. But increasingly, structure matters most.

Banks, constrained by capital rules and internal policy grids, often underwrite to precedent. Non-bank lenders, by contrast, underwrite to project specifics.

In Redcross Street, flexibility in recognising planning uplift, calibrated guarantee levels, acceptance of a non-JCT delivery structure, and a refinance-led exit all combined to unlock a scheme that might otherwise have stalled in committee.

This scheme exemplifies a broader shift. Developers are not moving beyond banks because banks are uncompetitive on price. They are moving because specialist lenders are better equipped to mirror the commercial reality of modern development.

A MICROCOSM OF A WIDER TRANSITION

At its core, this is not merely a story about GBP 10.7 million in Bristol. It is a story about how credit itself is evolving.

As real estate becomes more operationally complex—blending residential, co-living, heritage conservation and institutional rental strategies—financing structures must evolve in parallel. The lender who can interpret nuance, calibrate risk and tailor capital accordingly will increasingly win mandate over the lender who cannot.

In Redcross Street, LendInvest did not simply provide funding. It designed a structure. And in today's development landscape, that quiet distinction makes all the difference.

The LendInvest story is far from unique. Across the market, private lenders are not just offering capital, they're offering partnerships. Structured drawdowns, delayed amortisation, light-touch covenants and clause-by-clause flexibility allow funding to grow alongside the project.

As another specialist lender told me over coffee in Clerkenwell, 'We don't underwrite on an Excel template. We look at the real-world challenges of the build and structure accordingly. Developers don't need headaches—they need headroom'.

It's this kind of thinking that marks the new generation of development finance. Less about box-ticking, more about problem-solving. And it's not just for the big players: in most cases, it isn't designed for them at all. It's built for smaller, nimbler developers navigating imperfect sites, uneven timelines and real-world complexity. SME developers—the lifeblood of regional regeneration across many countries—are increasingly finding that it's not the cheapest lender they need, it's the one who'll sit with them through the messy middle.

Of course, private credit isn't a silver bullet. Not every lender takes a hands-on view and not every term sheet is as friendly as it looks. But when done right—when the lender understands that builds don't run on spreadsheets—the results can be a genuine game changer.

In short, flexibility is no longer a privilege reserved for the biggest players with revolving credit lines and balance-sheet muscle. It has become central to how modern projects get built. And the lenders offering it are no longer operating in the shadows. For many developers, they are fast becoming the default choice.

But does flexibility mean private lenders are taking on more risk? Not necessarily. The best private lenders are forensic in their underwriting. They're staffed by teams who not only understand the numbers, but have walked the sites, spoken to contractors and stress-tested every moving part of the deal. This deep, hands-on understanding allows them to build in flexibility without sacrificing caution. If anything, their terms may be more thorough at the outset than those of a high street bank, precisely because they want confidence the project can carry through, even when plans inevitably shift.

That said, defaults do still happen. But when they do, these lenders aren't scrambling. They typically have clear, pre-agreed routes to resolution and will often step in early to work with the borrower to protect value on both sides. In other words, flexibility here isn't recklessness, it's responsiveness, underpinned by rigorous discipline.

TAILORED SOLUTIONS FOR COMPLEX PROJECTS

> If we try to solve a twenty-first century housing crisis with twentieth century tools, we'll keep falling short. Modular isn't simply a construction technique, it's a delivery system designed for speed, precision and lower carbon. But delivery innovation requires capital that understands different risk dynamics. Private credit has been quicker to recognise that annuity-backed housing, built efficiently and sustainably, is infrastructure as much as development. With the

right partners, we can deliver homes faster, more affordably and with dramatically lower operational and embodied carbon.

—Craig White, CEO, Agile Homes

We've already seen how speed, digital fluency and flexibility have propelled non-bank lenders to the front of the queue for many developers. But there's another, equally compelling reason they're winning business: their knack for crafting funding solutions that are as individual as the projects they back.

Even when a traditional bank is still willing to entertain a development deal—a prospect that's growing rarer under the weight of tighter regulation and the rising cost of capital—they are rarely eager to back anything that strays beyond the neat confines of their lending criteria. The reality is that the most interesting projects are often the ones that colour outside those lines.

In many cities, the squeeze on greenfield land has pushed developers to look elsewhere. Brownfield sites are attracting renewed attention, along with non-traditional plays like converting old churches into stunning new homes and the increasingly popular airspace development model, building above what's already there.

It's an ingenious way to add density without encroaching on greenfield or greenbelt land. London, wrestling with its housing shortage, has become a hotbed for such schemes, with developers eyeing the rooftops as prime real estate. Across the pond, New York has taken the idea a step further with its well-oiled market for tradable air rights, where the 'sky' above a building can be bought and sold, allowing towers to climb ever higher.

THE MODULAR HOUSING REVOLUTION

Another rising star in the development world is modular construction, part of the so-called Modern Methods of Construction (MMC). Modular construction is when components of a building are created off-site, in a factory. When completed, they can be transported to the site, assembled and bolted together in a matter of days. Its appeal is clear: speed, cost control, reduced reliance on scarce labour and the ability to meet increasingly stringent sustainability targets. In short, it's an efficient way to create more homes, in less time and with lower costs. Technology is advancing, the quality gap with traditional methods has narrowed and for many schemes it's becoming the preferred route.

But these kinds of projects—unconventional locations, unusual construction methods, layered exit strategies—often set alarm bells ringing in a bank's credit department. For non-bank lenders, however, such complexity isn't a warning sign; it's an invitation.

By digging deep into the detail and truly understanding the nuances of a scheme, these lenders can shape finance to fit reality instead of forcing reality to fit the finance. That might mean synchronising drawdowns to the quirks of a modular delivery schedule, baking in breathing room for a planning appeal or structuring repayments to dovetail perfectly with phased sales and lettings.

In short, today's non-bank lenders aren't just making payments, they're engineering financial frameworks that keep a project moving from first sketch to final sale, whatever twists and turns the journey takes.

AGILE HOMES: FUNDING MODULAR HOUSING BEYOND THE BANKING TEMPLATE

WHEN HOUSING INNOVATION MEETS BANK CAUTION

In the cautious offices of Britain's high street banks, modular housing is being eyed a bit like a strange new dish on the menu: interesting, but not something they're about to order. Too unconventional, too complex, too untested, too risky, too far outside the templates their systems were built for. Traditional lenders still prefer brick-and-mortar predictability, backed by decades of valuation comparables, in locations that provide a sense of familiarity. Modular, with its off-site fabrication and rapid assembly, doesn't fit neatly into the tick-boxes of bank credit committees.

As one broker put it, 'Some lenders are concerned by what they see as a disconnect between the manufacturer of the modules and the on-site contractor, and who takes responsibility for preparatory works, scaffolding, permits, licences and structural warranty management'.

In other words, before a single spade hits the ground, underwriters want to know exactly who's doing what: and, most importantly, who's on the hook if it goes wrong. When the build is effectively scattered between a factory floor hundreds of miles away and a building site somewhere else, it's not hard to see why some lenders feel a bit nervous.

The modular sector and the institutional underwriting of it, after all, is still maturing. And in an industry where risk is about as welcome as rain on a bank holiday, there are still too many 'what ifs' floating around. What if the factory goes bust halfway through production? What if the module supplier collapses before the walls and roof panels ever make it to site? As the broker notes, even the insurance world hasn't quite caught up. Standard policies may exclude modular builds altogether or attach so many endorsements they're barely worth the paper they're printed on.

Then there's the simple geography of it. With still relatively few modular factories dotted around the country—each with their own bespoke designs—replacing one with another mid-project isn't exactly like swapping out a bricklayer. If the original manufacturer folds, the developer might be left with a very expensive half-finished jigsaw and no matching pieces in sight.

But the real issue isn't caution: it's structural mismatch. Bank credit models were built for short-cycle, build-to-sell housing schemes, not long-duration, indexed annuity structures or vertically integrated modular delivery platforms.

That structural mismatch has left parts of the market underserved, and it is into that space that non-bank capital has increasingly stepped, with Agile Homes positioned to serve that demand.

A FACTORY-LED MODEL BUILT FOR WHAT COMES NEXT

Founded in 2019 by Craig White, an architect, entrepreneur and senior lecturer at the University of West England, Agile Homes was built around a simple but radical proposition: that Britain's housing and climate crises cannot be solved with yesterday's construction methods or the financial structures that underpin them. From their headquarter in Bristol, Agile develops scalable, low-carbon homes using factory-built, precision-engineered modular systems designed to reduce build time, cost volatility and embodied carbon.

Agile's modular homes can be deployed even on challenging terrain, illustrating the adaptability that traditional construction methods struggle to match (Figure 4.3).

FIGURE 4.3 Modular Homes Installed on Complex Terrain
Source: With permission of Agile Homes

(*Continued*)

(*Continued*)

For someone who combined architectural practice, research and development, manufacturing and academia, Craig has built anything but an academic project. His entrepreneurial flair has already attracted senior political support, with cabinet-level backing and draft lease documents now being passed between legal and funding partners as live schemes push towards delivery.

At the heart of Agile's model is the combination of deep social purpose and financial innovation, uniquely enabling access to both institutional private capital and new revenue models such as Carbon & Social Value Trading (CSVTs). Figure 4.4 shows one of Agile's completed low-carbon homes in situ, demonstrating how the finished product integrates seamlessly into existing communities.

> For me, this isn't just about modular or finance. It's about aligning speed, sustainability and social need and impact. When capital is structured around long-term public benefit rather than short-term exit cycles, you create space for better housing decisions, better materials, better design and better outcomes for the people who live there.
>
> —Craig White

The model is compelling from a technical and a policy point of view. But it is less straightforward from a bank's credit perspective.

Factory production reduces construction timelines and alters cashflow dynamics. Figure 4.5 highlights how precision-engineered modules are craned into position on-site, reducing disruption and compressing build schedules.

FIGURE 4.4 Completed Low-Carbon Modular Homes Integrated into the Community
Source: With permission of Agile Homes

FIGURE 4.5 Precision-Manufactured Modules Craned into Position
Source: With permission of Agile Homes

Biogenic materials such as timber, straw and hemp challenge conventional valuation benchmarks. Social housing tenures introduce local authority counterparty exposure. Layered revenue streams—including carbon and social value monetisation—sit well outside standard lending frameworks.

> We work in parts of the housing system that are under the greatest pressure: vulnerable residents, stretched local authorities and communities that need certainty, not delay. Modular allows us to deliver at pace. Private capital allows us to structure that delivery around long-term, indexed income streams with clear statutory backing. This isn't about novelty. It's about reliability, proven build systems, durable cashflows and aligned partners. When those elements come together, you don't just build homes; you strengthen the resilience of the wider housing ecosystem.
>
> —Craig White

(*Continued*)

(*Continued*)

For many banks, that combination creates hesitation. Credit policy is built around precedent. Modular delivery, carbon tokenisation and annuity-backed supported housing rarely feature in historical data sets.

That's where private capital stepped in, equipped to assess forward-looking cashflows and structures that fall outside traditional bank templates.

> The real shift isn't from banks to private debt, it's from project-by-project development to platform-based housing infrastructure. When income is long-term, index-linked and underpinned by statutory need, housing starts to look less like speculative property and more like social infrastructure. That's the lens institutional capital understands. Our role is to align construction, policy and finance so that long-duration capital can support long-duration community outcomes.
>
> —Craig White

INSTITUTIONAL CAPITAL STEPPED IN WHERE BANKS WOULDN'T

In the summer of 2025, Agile entered a joint venture with Aether Energy, an impact-led capital structuring platform. Together, they secured a GBP 500 million institutional mandate from Phoenix Capital to deliver housing across two urgent need categories: Specialised Supported Housing (SSH) for vulnerable adults with complex needs and Temporary Accommodation (TA) for individuals experiencing homelessness.

The structure looked nothing like traditional SME development finance. Instead of relying on senior bank debt supported by speculative open-market sales, the capital was structured around quasi-governmental annuity income streams, underpinned by local authority statutory obligations to provide housing under UK housing legislation.

This was not short-dated development risk. It was long-duration, income-backed credit. Rents are long-term, index-linked (CPI+1%) and designed to look like and to behave like liability-matching assets sought by pension funds and insurers: exactly the sort of exposure that banks' short-cycle development models aren't built to underwrite.

For traditional banks used to build-to-sell cycles, this structure felt unfamiliar. But private debt funds are increasingly comfortable underwriting these structures because they assess risk differently. Instead of focusing just on construction volatility, they analyse counterparty strength of local authorities, stability of supported housing cashflows, indexation protection and portfolio-level diversification.

Furthermore, Agile's vertically integrated model—from land assembly to modular manufacture to alignment with specialist care providers—materially reduced execution risk and strengthened the credit case.

BUILDING AN EXPANDED REVENUE STACK

But Agile's model goes further than rental income alone.

Through its Carbon & Social Value Trading (CSVT) model, Craig and his team capture and monetise measurable environmental and social outcomes generated through its modular system.

On the one hand, carbon locked into biogenic materials is verified and tokenised as credits. On the other hand, social value—including employment initiatives such as its 'Prisoners Building Homes' programme—is quantified using established proxy metrics linked to national frameworks.

For lenders, these additional revenue layers function as a resilience enhancer: lowering effective leverage, improving debt-service coverage and widening exit optionality. But they are treated conservatively, never as primary security.

Banks often discount such upside entirely because it sits outside their eligibility rules. Private credit can incorporate it, prudently and transparently.

The result is not looser credit, but broader credit (Figure 4.6).

FIGURE 4.6 Agile's Low-Carbon, Timber-Framed Modular Homes in Operation
Source: With permission of Agile Homes

(*Continued*)

(*Continued*)

A DIFFERENT DEVELOPMENT MODEL AND A DIFFERENT FUNDING PARTNER

Agile's delivery model also challenges traditional assumptions.

Public land secured at discounted rates, modular construction that reduces labour reliance, and distributed manufacturing—including prison workshops and community facilities—help reduce concentration risk.

Unlike a typical SME developer reliant on plot sales, Agile behaves like a pipeline originator for institutional capital: assembling land, structuring projects and delivering homes through a scalable platform.

Private credit is better suited to underwriting that kind of repeatable, platform-driven pipeline than banks reliant on prescriptive build-to-sell models.

CIRCULAR FINANCE AND LONG-TERM CAPITAL

Agile's partnership with Jeremy Leggett under the Nature Prosperity banner pushes the model even further, linking regenerative forestry, carbon sequestration and modular housing into a circular supply chain.

From 'field and forest to front door', UK-grown materials are integrated into ultra-low-carbon homes. Carbon is stored physically within the built asset. Social and environmental outcomes are measured, monetised and reinvested.

For private debt investors, the appeal lies not in novelty but in risk diversification: regenerative land strategies support long-term asset resilience, carbon monetisation enhances revenue stability and policy alignment reduces regulatory risk.

The result is a blended-value structure capable of supporting long-duration, income-focused capital, the kind increasingly allocated by insurers, pension funds and impact-led private credit vehicles.

Agile's story underlines a recurring theme in modern development finance: innovation in the built environment rarely fails for lack of demand: it fails for lack of flexible capital. Modular housing, social impact, off-site manufacture and unconventional delivery models all sit uncomfortably within traditional lending frameworks. Non-bank capital, by contrast, has shown a growing willingness to fund ideas that don't yet have decades of precedent behind them, provided the logic, governance and execution stack up. And modular construction is only one frontier where this matters. In dense cities, the next challenge is not how to build faster, but where to build at all. That question has led developers to look upward, into the unused air above existing buildings, a space banks have been just as reluctant to finance.

THE RISE OF AIRSPACE DEVELOPMENT

One of the fastest-growing—yet most bank-shunned—trends in property development is airspace building. It has all the makings of a clever urban solution: take the unused air above an existing block and turn it into homes worth a small fortune. On paper, it's brilliant. In reality, it's a bit like trying to renovate your loft while the family's still eating dinner downstairs: intricate, delicate and riddled with opportunities for things to go wrong.

> For developers working on airspace and non-standard builds, traditional banking simply isn't structured for the practical realities of today's market. Banks were designed for predictability; they underwrite what they know, not what is novel. In contrast, non-bank and specialist lenders understand the nuanced risk and value in complex property deals. They move faster, tailor finance to real project timelines and are willing to underwrite ideas conventional lenders still struggle to price. That is why developers are increasingly choosing them: they offer clarity and certainty when the product itself is anything but standard.
>
> —Richard Benson OBE, Director, Tay Developments & Investments

Airspace development is notoriously tricky due to a combination of technical and legal hurdles. Structurally, many buildings simply weren't designed to carry the weight of extra floors, meaning engineers must assess, reinforce and essentially teach the old building a few new tricks before any bricks can be laid. Then there's the fiddly business of extending electricity, gas, water and telecoms up into the new space, all while keeping the original occupants happy and, preferably, still on speaking terms with the developer.

The legal side is no gentler. Negotiating with freeholders, wrangling 'rights to light' from leaseholders, securing party wall agreements with prickly neighbours: and that's before you even get to the Byzantine maze of planning permission. Each stage is a potential banana skin, capable of sending a project sliding weeks, months or even years behind schedule.

With all this in mind, it's no surprise high street banks won't go anywhere near these projects. The combination of risk, complexity and the absence of a tidy precedent means airspace schemes are firmly in the 'computer says no' category. For developers without a proven track record in this niche, bank funding is about as likely as hitting the lottery jackpot twice in a row.

KHK CAPITAL: TURNING EMPTY AIR INTO PRIME HOMES

> Airspace developments are a perfect example of value hiding in plain sight. The land is already there: it's simply above our heads. But unlocking it requires lenders who are comfortable with unconventional structures, complex planning frameworks and the practical realities of building above occupied homes.
>
> —Scott Harris, Director, KHK Capital

(*Continued*)

(*Continued*)

UNLOCKING VALUE ABOVE THE ROOFLINE

In the quiet suburban streets of Pinner in North West London stood Cornwall Court, a typical 1960s apartment block comprising twelve flats arranged across three floors (Figure 4.7). The building sat in a desirable residential neighbourhood known for its village atmosphere, green spaces and convenient access to central London.

Yet what Cornwall Court lacked in architectural distinction, it possessed in something far more valuable: unused air.

Like many buildings of its era, the block had a pitched roof and significant structural capacity. Above the top floor lay a roof void and airspace that represented latent development potential.

For decades it remained untouched. But by the early 2020s—as London's housing shortage intensified and development land became scarcer—developers began to look upward. And Cornwall Court offered exactly that opportunity.

AIRSPACE OPPORTUNITY

Planning permission was granted by Harrow Council in February 2021 for an additional storey to be built above the existing building. The proposal involved removing the existing roof, extending the building's elevations upward and building a new residential floor before reinstating the roof structure above.

FIGURE 4.7 Cornwall Court Before Airspace Development
Source: Photo by KHK Capital

The new level would provide four apartments, each designed with a gross internal area of approximately 61–64 square metres and configured as two-bedroom homes with open-plan living spaces.

Importantly, the development required no additional land purchase. The entire scheme would sit above the existing building footprint. This is why airspace development has gained momentum across cities like London. It allows developers to create new housing without consuming greenfield land, intensifying urban density while utilising infrastructure that are already in place.

Yet despite its conceptual simplicity, airspace development is rarely straightforward.

COMPLEXITY ABOVE THE ROOF

Building above an occupied residential block presents a whole set of technical and financial challenges.

Structurally, engineers need to confirm that the existing building can support additional loads or determine what reinforcements are needed. Planning authorities also need to assess impacts on neighbours, natural light and visual appearance. Additionally, developers need to manage construction logistics while residents continue living below.

Even accessing the construction site can be complicated. At Cornwall Court, the plan was to scaffold the building externally and use a goods lift to move materials, minimising disruption to residents while works carried out above them.

These factors contribute to the unique risk profile of airspace schemes. They are rarely large developments. They often involve specialist structural work. And construction takes place within the constraints of an existing building instead of on an empty site.

For traditional lenders, this complexity can make underwriting very challenging. For specialist lenders and development financiers, however, these constraints are precisely where opportunity lies.

FINANCING THE SKY

Before construction began, the roof space itself had to be valued as a development asset. The valuation undertaken in 2023 assessed the market value of the 999-year leasehold interest in the roof space and airspace above the building, assuming the benefit of planning permission and vacant possession.

This type of asset is unusual. Unlike conventional land, its value depends almost entirely on the feasibility of the proposed development. Surveyors therefore relied on a residual development appraisal, estimating the completed value of the proposed flats and deducting construction costs, professional fees and developer profit to arrive at a residual value for the airspace.

(*Continued*)

(*Continued*)

The appraisal assumed construction costs of roughly GBP 600,000 to deliver the additional floor and a build programme of nine to ten months. Local market conditions were supportive, with strong demand for owner-occupied flats in the area and an anticipated sales period of around three to six months once the homes were completed.

The valuation concluded that, despite the niche nature of airspace developments, demand from developers for such opportunities was robust. Sites like Cornwall Court could be sold to alternative developers within six to nine months, even though the market remained relatively specialised.

FROM AIRSPACE TO HOMES

Construction started with the removal of the original roof structure. The building's elevations were then extended upward, creating a new top floor before the roof was rebuilt above it. When completed, the additional storey blended visually with the existing structure while delivering four modern apartments, as shown in Figure 4.8.

FIGURE 4.8 Cornwall Court After Airspace Development

By late 2024, the homes were finished and brought to market. Each flat offered contemporary interiors and open-plan layouts designed to appeal to both owner-occupiers and the rental market. The units were completed to a high specification and quickly attracted tenants.

The four apartments achieved a combined market value of approximately GBP 1.55 million, with individual units valued between GBP 400,000 and GBP 415,000.

Rental demand was also strong. Together the flats generated a total annual rental income of GBP 103,200, with individual rents ranging between GBP 2,400 and GBP 2,500 per month.

For a development that had effectively begun as unused roof space, the transformation was remarkable.

THE ECONOMICS OF AIRSPACE

What makes projects like Cornwall Court particularly compelling is the relationship between land cost and value creation. Because the development takes place above an existing building, the 'site' can often be acquired at a fraction of the cost of traditional development land. At Cornwall Court, this meant four new homes could be created without purchasing additional land, while the new floor added significant capital value to the building itself. Once completed, the flats not only enhanced the overall asset value but also generated both rental income and sale potential.

For cities struggling with housing shortages, this model has clear advantages. It increases housing supply while preserving scarce land resources and existing neighbourhood character.

WHY BANKS HESITATE

Despite the clear economics, airspace developments remain difficult to finance through traditional lenders.

The reasons are familiar. Projects are often too small relative to the size of bank lending programmes. Construction risks are atypical, involving structural adaptation instead of ground-up development. And planning frameworks vary between boroughs, introducing further complexity.

From a credit committee perspective, these deals rarely fit standard underwriting models. Specialist lenders and private credit providers, however, tend to approach them differently. Instead of relying solely on historical comparables, they assess the engineering feasibility, planning certainty and local market demand. In other words, they underwrite the project itself, not just the template.

(*Continued*)

(Continued)

WHY THIS CASE MATTERS

The Cornwall Court development illustrates an important shift in modern real estate finance. In mature cities where land is scarce, the most valuable opportunities increasingly lie not in empty plots but in re-imagining existing buildings.

Airspace developments represent one of the clearest examples of this shift. They require imagination from developers, flexibility from planners and—perhaps most importantly—lenders willing to fund projects that fall outside conventional development models.

For KHK Capital and similar investors, the lesson is simple. Sometimes the most valuable development land isn't land at all. Sometimes it's the empty air above a roof.

Airspace schemes like this underline a broader truth about modern development finance: value increasingly lies in complexity not conformity. As cities grow denser and sites grow scarcer, the most compelling opportunities are often the ones that don't fit legacy lending models. Non-bank lenders, by structuring capital around the realities of the build instead of the comfort of precedent, are making these projects possible.

NEW LIFE FOR OLD CHURCHES

But modular builds and airspace schemes aren't the only projects that get a swift 'No', from the banks. With greenfield plots harder to find than an empty lounger at a pool in high season, more developers are casting their eyes towards church conversions. It's a trend that ticks both the practical and the fashionable boxes: reimagining existing buildings while tapping into the growing appetite for homes with character. And with their soaring windows, vaulted ceilings and architectural quirks, former churches can command a handsome premium.

But while buyers may be queuing up, lenders rarely are. Converting a church is not for the faint-hearted, nor for the risk-averse credit committee. As one developer quipped to me—and he wasn't being metaphorical—'once you start digging under a church, God knows how many skeletons you'll find'.

The next case study shows how lenders sometimes have to look backwards as well as forwards. Converting historic religious buildings into homes demands a different kind of judgement: balancing heritage preservation with modern housing needs, and financing projects where architectural sensitivity and community impact matter as much as bricks, mortar and spreadsheets.

LOWRY CAPITAL: CONVERTING CHURCHES INTO HOMES

A CHURCH WITH A SECOND LIFE

In Manchester, an enterprising developer acquired an old Methodist church at auction, a building with real character and a clear path to residential reuse. Planning permission was already in place to transform the structure into eight flats, but there was a ticking clock: the developer had financed the site purchase with angel capital and that funding now needed repaying or risk derailing the entire project (Figure 4.9).

That's where Lowry Capital, a Manchester-based specialist non-bank lender, stepped in with precision and speed. Within just 18 working days, Lowry advanced GBP 117,000 to clear the angel investment, giving the developer the breathing room necessary to push ahead with construction without compromising timelines.

WHEN HERITAGE MEETS LENDING CONSTRAINTS

> Some of the most socially valuable schemes are also the hardest to finance. Converting a church into homes or community space can breathe new life into a building that has stood empty for years, preserving heritage, revitalising high streets and adding much-needed housing.

FIGURE 4.9 Former Methodist Church in Manchester Prior to Residential Conversion
Source: https://www.lowrycapital.co.uk/case-study/funding-for-the-conversion-of-a-former-church-into-8-flats-manchester

(*Continued*)

(*Continued*)

Yet these projects rarely fit neatly into standard lending criteria. The irregular layouts, the listed status and the layered planning conditions make them complex to underwrite. Many traditional lenders simply don't have the appetite for that kind of nuance. Specialist private lenders, however, are often willing to engage with the detail, and that willingness can be what turns a boarded-up building into a working asset again.

—Property developer

UNLOCKING HERITAGE THROUGH FLEXIBLE CAPITAL

By unlocking liquidity quickly and aligning financing with the rhythm of the redevelopment, Lowry enabled a heritage asset to be given a new lease on life as much-needed housing. For the developer, it meant continuity and momentum; for the neighbourhood, it meant a piece of the city reborn instead of left to languish.

The stories told so far are not outliers. They are just the most visible edge of a much wider shift that has been unfolding across the development landscape. Modular housing, airspace schemes and church conversions may grab the headlines, but they are not alone in relying on private capital to get off the ground. As we saw in Chapter 2, there is a growing list of projects that would never have made it beyond the drawing board without non-bank finance stepping in. Care homes, once a staple of relationship banking, are nowadays considered too operationally challenging for banks. Old factories are being reborn as housing only because specialist lenders are willing to look past soot-stained bricks and see future value. New living formats—co-living, micro-living, purpose-built student accommodation—regularly fall foul of outdated credit templates.

In each case, it is not a lack of demand that holds projects back. It is a lack of lenders willing to engage with anything that doesn't look like yesterday's deal. And increasingly, it is private capital—flexible, forensic and commercially minded—that fills the gap where banks once stood.

Which brings us back to the question at the heart of this chapter: why are developers turning away from banks? The answer is disarmingly simple. In today's market, the most viable opportunities in real estate no longer sit within the neat boundaries traditional lenders were built to serve. And when capital won't stretch to meet reality, developers don't wait around. They turn, instead, to specialist non-bank lenders and private capital, not out of preference, but out of necessity.

A BROADER TOOLKIT FOR DEVELOPERS

For many developers, the shift away from banks hasn't just been about access to capital. It's been about the experience of getting it. In contrast to legacy lenders—where financing can feel like a slow, opaque process conducted through layers of intermediaries—today's private lenders increasingly offer something closer to a toolkit than a term sheet—part capital, part technology, part insight—designed to help developers move faster, make better decisions and understand their own projects more clearly along the way.

One mid-sized developer I spoke to, active across the Midlands, put it simply: 'With the bank, I spent months explaining my own project back to them. With the private lender, the system showed me what worked, what didn't and why, before we'd even agreed the loan'. What surprised him most wasn't the speed of the credit decision, but how clearly the process surfaced the pressure points in his scheme: cost overruns, sensitivity to delays and the impact of different exit timings on cash flow.

This contrasts to the journey with legacy lenders. It's the opacity. The paper trails. The weeks of silence followed by a last-minute credit committee decision that bears little resemblance to the conversations held on site months earlier. The sense that the lender never quite understood the project, or worse, never really tried to.

That clarity offered by non-banks is increasingly delivered through technology. Many digital-first lending platforms have built proprietary credit analytics tools that allow lenders—and borrowers—to model downside scenarios in real time. Developers can see how changes in build costs, interest rates or sales velocity affect debt service and covenant headroom long before those risks materialise on site. Instead of discovering problems six months too late, they're stress-tested upfront.

Digital drawdown platforms now link funding releases directly to verified build milestones, reducing friction and uncertainty. Live dashboards track loan-to-cost, interest accrual and contingency usage, replacing retrospective reporting with real-time visibility. Some lenders even integrate planning timelines and sales pipelines into their monitoring tools, aligning finance more closely with the realities of development instead of forcing projects into rigid schedules.

From the borrower's perspective, this shift is tangible from day one. Digital onboarding replaces endless document chases. Real-time dashboards show where a loan sits, what's been drawn, what's available and what milestones are coming next. Drawdown requests are tracked transparently, not lost in inboxes. Covenants are visible, measurable and—crucially—explainable.

But the real value goes deeper than convenience.

By structuring their platforms around granular, project-level data, specialist lenders often end up giving developers clearer visibility into their own businesses than they've ever had before. Cashflow sensitivity, interest roll-up, build-cost inflation, exit assumptions, all laid out in a way that allows developers to stress-test decisions before the market does it for them.

That transparency changes behaviour on both sides of the table. Developers arrive better prepared, clearer on their own assumptions and constraints. Lenders, in turn, can underwrite with greater confidence: not because they're taking less risk, but because they can see it earlier and manage it more intelligently.

In some cases, these platforms even help developers articulate financing needs they hadn't fully crystallised. A scheme that initially looks like it needs a simple bridge may, once modelled properly, benefit from staged funding, interest deferral or a hybrid structure that aligns more closely with sales velocity or planning risk. The technology doesn't replace judgement, it sharpens it.

This is where the borrower's experience begins to diverge most starkly from traditional banking. Instead of being handed a take-it-or-leave-it term sheet late in the process, developers are increasingly co-creating funding structures alongside lenders, informed by live data, evolving assumptions and an honest assessment of what the project actually needs to succeed.

For developers operating in a world of tighter margins, political planning risk and construction uncertainty, that support can be as valuable as the capital itself. It reduces friction. It saves time. And it restores a sense that the lender is working with the project, not simply judging it from afar.

In that sense, the shift away from banks is not just about who is willing to lend. It is about who is equipped to engage with the modern realities of development. Capital still matters. But increasingly, it's the tools wrapped around it that make the difference between a deal that drags—and one that gets built.

RELATIONSHIP-DRIVEN LENDING IN A TRANSACTIONAL WORLD

> What really distinguishes non-bank lenders in development finance is the relationship-driven approach. By focusing on the project's vision and understanding the challenges developers face, they provide not just funding but a sense of partnership that helps projects move forward confidently'.
>
> —Mark Roberts

Dan Eaton is not your run-of-the-mill property developer. For starters, he's a strikingly young man in a field still dominated by men old enough to remember the last three housing cycles, men with decades of bricks-and-mortar experience behind them. His own professional pedigree couldn't be more different: an ex-military communicator turned management consultant, with a career focused on business transformation and large-scale IT change. Dan was far more at home building operating models and reshaping organisations than pacing around a muddy construction site in steel-toe boots.

Yet he walked away from that high-flying career to start from scratch in property. When I first met him in 2018, he was taking his first tentative steps in the sector. Fast-forward to today and Dan's built a multi-million-pound portfolio across the East Midlands, specialising in something both practical and profoundly human: turning tired, derelict industrial and commercial buildings into high-quality co-living spaces for young professionals.

His funding journey has been as unconventional as his career path.

'At the start', he recalls, 'I had no choice but to go to non-bank lenders. My lack of experience meant the banks wouldn't even entertain me. It wasn't that I chose them, it was that they were the only ones who'd give me the time of day'.

But success changes the game. As his projects started winning awards, the same banks that once turned him away began courting his business. He borrowed from a few, and promptly went back to non-bank lenders. This time, not because he had no options, but because he preferred them.

The difference, he explains, is night and day. Where banks keep borrowers at arm's length, with layers of opaque process and box-ticking, many non-bank lenders invite the developer straight into the room with the decision-makers. There's a conversation, not just a checklist. A meeting of minds, not just a submission of forms.

This approach is increasingly being supercharged by technology. At some non-bank lenders, ML, vast datasets and cloud computing are slashing the time and cost of in-depth credit analysis, the kind of forensic work that used to be reserved for multi-billion-pound corporations. Now, underwriters can spend less time buried in spreadsheets and more time 'under the bonnet' of a borrower's business.

The result? Facilities that are genuinely built around the project's quirks and timelines, not bent to fit rigid templates. Lenders walk into meetings with a deep understanding of the business and its sector. Conversations are sharper. The focus shifts from bureaucratic back-and-forth to the heart of the matter: structuring the right deal, at the right time, for the right borrower.

For developers like Dan, that's more than a better borrowing experience: it's a partnership.

CHAPTER 5

How Technology Reshaped Private Credit

FROM HANDSHAKE TO PLATFORM

Joseph Safra, the Lebanese-Brazilian billionaire often described as the world's richest banker, was known to approach banking with advice passed down from his father: 'Always look customers in the eye, for eyes tell more than balance sheets'. That philosophy shaped generations of lenders. Banking was built on judgement, conservatism and an instinctive distrust of anything that appeared to distance the decision-maker from the borrower.

Nowhere was this more palpable than in property finance. For decades, real estate lending was defined less by technology than by relationships. Innovation was often considered a dirty word, viewed with suspicion, even disdain. Economists famously labelled real estate 'the backward industry', a sector slow to modernise and reluctant to digitise processes that relied on human assessment and local knowledge. The industry has long worn the tag conservative, and in many corners, it still fits.

As we have already seen, traditional lenders were institutions encumbered by legacy systems whose processes were fraught with inefficiencies, manual workflows and lengthy approval timelines that frustrated borrowers and credit teams alike. Things have of course evolved, but even today, property lending remains one of the least digitally disrupted pockets of global finance. Ask most developers and they will tell you how credit decisions are still largely shaped by local knowledge, personal relationships and the quiet judgement of experienced financiers who know their borrowers, their markets and—crucially—their collateral.

But the industry is slowly changing. The retreat of banks from real estate lending did more than create a funding gap. It exposed a deeper structural challenge: modern real estate markets had become too complex, too fragmented and too fast-moving to be intermediated using analogue tools. As private capital stepped in to fill the gap left by bank balance sheets, it didn't just replicate those old structures with different capital. Instead, it arrived with an ambition to modernise lending itself. In that sense, the rise of real estate private credit and the integration of technology into credit markets have evolved tandem. A new generation of private credit lenders is steadily rewriting the rulebook: digital-first firms unburdened by legacy systems, paper-based processes and institutional inertia.

PROPTECH COMES OF AGE

Private lenders had the advantage of starting afresh. Without decades of inherited processes, each step in the lending chain was open to redesign. Origination, underwriting, due diligence, documentation and end-to-end case handling no longer had to rely on paper files, email trails and institutional memory. Instead, they could be rebuilt around data, automation and platforms designed for speed and scale.

FinTech platforms, AI and data-driven tools for origination, underwriting and portfolio management have moved from the margins of real estate finance to its operational core. Not as substitutes for judgement, but as force multipliers that allow private credit to operate at institutional scale while retaining discipline, transparency and speed.

The shorthand term that has come to describe this shift is PropTech. At its simplest, PropTech refers to the application of technology to real estate, but in practice, it is less about shiny front ends and more about infrastructure. It is the plumbing underneath modern property finance: the systems that pull in the data, bring consistency to decision-making, flag risks and connect borrowers, brokers, lenders and investors in real time.

In the context of private credit, PropTech includes platforms that automate deal origination, decision engines that encode credit policy, analytics that monitor portfolios continuously and digital workflows that compress months into days. These tools have become integral to how non-bank lenders compete.

In retrospect, real estate private credit was always a natural candidate for this kind of technological disruption. The asset class is tangible, repeatable and deeply data-rich, even if much of that data historically sat unused. What PropTech, FinTech and modern analytics have done is not replace judgement but extend it: bringing structure to intuition and scale to experience.

This chapter explores how that transformation is disrupting each link in the lending chain—how tech is reshaping origination, underwriting, due diligence, portfolio monitoring and asset management—and why technology has become the quiet infrastructure underpinning the next era of real estate private debt.

THE PLATFORMISATION OF DEAL ORIGINATION

For decades, real estate loan origination was largely about being in the right rooms. Opportunities came about through broker networks, repeat borrowers or long-standing banking relationships. As one lender once put it, much of the business 'happened over a few pints at the pub'. It was a system that rewarded loyalty and friendship, and put real strain on the industry's livers. Not coincidentally, it was a highly male-dominated industry.

That is now changing as technology has quietly widened the room, and moved dealmaking out of the pub and into the platform. Marketplaces, APIs, aggregators and workflow platforms with matchmaking features are emerging as the primary drivers of this transformation by streamlining the entire process of creating and processing new loans, from initial application through funding. Digital marketplaces and data-driven sourcing tools can now streamline application processing by aggregating opportunities that once sat in local inboxes and informal conversations. Developers who previously relied on a handful of trusted broker or lenders are now able to submit the same deal to multiple lenders. What was once an opaque, relationship-driven funnel has become wider, more transparent, and unsurprisingly more competitive.

As Ian Humphreys, Founder and CEO at Brickflow, observes, the shift has not replaced relationships but scaled them. 'Technology hasn't removed trust from origination', he notes. 'It's allowed lenders and borrowers to engage earlier on substance instead of access'. In other words, platforms have changed who gets into the room, not the fact that a real conversation still needs to happen once they are there.

Underpinning this shift is a fairly simple but powerful tech stack. APIs pull data from broker systems and borrower portals into centralised platforms. Cloud-based Customer Relationship Management (CRM) tools track repeat borrowers and intermediaries at scale. Rule-based engines pre-screen deals against lender mandates on leverage, asset type, geography, risk appetite and pricing. Machine Learning (ML) models are layered on top, trained on historical deal outcomes to flag combinations of borrower profile, location and structure that deserve closer attention. AI tools extract key data from credit packs, valuation reports and financial models in seconds, compressing what once took hours into minutes.

Crucially, none of these tools decide whether a deal should be funded. But they ensure that human judgement is applied to a far better-curated universe of opportunities. For lenders, it's a game changer. It means technology acts as the first filter, so originators now spend less time finding deals and filtering them and more time applying judgement where it actually adds value.

BRICKFLOW: FROM THE PUB TO THE PLATFORM

THE OLD NETWORK-DRIVEN DEAL FLOW

For much of modern real estate finance, access was everything. Not access to data or platforms, but to people. Deals circulated through familiar channels: a trusted broker, a long-standing lender, a conversation had quietly and informally long before any credit paper was written. For those inside the network, it worked well enough. For those outside it, opportunity could remain frustratingly out of reach.

Brickflow was built to challenge that dynamic, not by removing relationships from the process, but by widening the doorway through which deals could enter.

Founded with the explicit aim of modernising how bridging loans, commercial mortgages and development finance is sourced, Brickflow operates as a digital origination platform connecting brokers, borrowers and specialist lenders in one central marketplace. At its core is a simple proposition: take the fragmented, relationship-heavy front end of real estate lending and give it structure, visibility and speed, without stripping away human judgement.

(*Continued*)

(*Continued*)

> We're not trying to replace relationships, those remain central to property finance. What we're doing is giving those relationships better information. By analysing hundreds of thousands of data points every week on lender mandates and deal characteristics, the platform becomes better at matching opportunities with lenders who genuinely want them.
>
> —Ian Humphreys

FIXING THE ORIGINATION BOTTLENECK

The inefficiency of the traditional process is striking. Lenders typically fund only one in every 25 to 100 deals they review, meaning the vast majority of time spent by brokers and credit teams is absorbed by opportunities that never proceed. Dozens of conversations, emails and credit packs circulate before a lender with the right mandate is even identified.

Brickflow's model is designed to solve precisely that problem. In practice, that means replacing dozens of parallel conversations with a single, standardised digital submission. Brokers upload a deal once onto a digital data room—including asset details, capital stack, location, exit strategy and borrower track record—and Brickflow's platform instantly matches it against the live mandates of a wide panel of lenders. Criteria that once lived in lenders' heads or PDF credit guides—leverage limits, asset preferences, geographic constraints, appetite for planning or development risk—are codified into the platform's logic.

What used to take days of phone calls now happens in minutes.

DATA-DRIVEN MATCHMAKING

Behind the scenes, Brickflow's technology stack does much of the heavy lifting. APIs pull in deal data and distribute it securely across lender dashboards. Rule-based engines pre-filter opportunities so lenders only see transactions aligned with their mandate. Document-handling tools standardise submissions, reducing the friction that often slows early-stage underwriting.

And as volumes grow, the platform becomes smarter. Brickflow now processes and stores more than 200,000 data points every week on lender preferences, deal characteristics and transaction outcomes. That constantly expanding dataset allows the platform to refine how deals are matched to lenders, improving the quality of introductions and increasing the likelihood that a project lands with a funding partner whose mandate genuinely fits.

> For decades, development finance has operated through informal networks: a broker calling around, lenders reviewing dozens of deals that were never really a fit in the first place. When you consider that most lenders fund only one in every 25 to 100 deals they see, the inefficiency becomes obvious. Brickflow's goal is simple: get the right deal in front of the right lender the first time.
>
> —Ian Humphreys

UNDERWRITING IN THE DIGITAL AGE

For lenders, underwriting acts as the gatekeeper for sound lending decisions. It is the credit decision-making process where the lender forms a view on whether to lend, how much, on what terms and at what price. In other words, it is the part where the lender asks: 'Is this a risk we are willing to take and if so, under what structure?'

Underwriting is the most delicate craft in real estate lending: part instinct and part science. It involves a complete assessment of potential lending opportunities to determine their risk/reward profile. The best underwriters, the ones who command outsized trust (and paycheques), are valued because they understand nuance. They know how to read a sponsor's track record between the lines, sense when a location's risks are understated, form a view on exit strategies, get a feel of asset liquidity or recognise when a valuation that looks ok on paper feels overstretched in practice.

As one senior underwriter told me: 'There's no piece of tech powerful enough to replace the power of walking a site with the developer and assessing the risks'. Indeed, there are myriad elements that could impact the outcome of a property project that would be very hard for tech to pick up. For example, he told me, site access:

> I recently worked on a deal that looked perfect on paper: location was great, valuation stacked up, build cost sounded reasonably conservative. But once I started walking the site with the developer, I instantly picked up a major issue that wasn't immediately obvious at first: site access. The site had a very narrow access and was adjacent to a government-run supported living facility for vulnerable individuals. This could cause clear issues and indeed affected the way we saw the deal. Ultimately, we still funded the project, but we offered a lower LTV to mitigate the risks.

It is precisely because underwriting is so judgement-led that one question has long lingered over the industry, asked quietly and often sceptically: can—or should—algorithms ever replace the judgement of an experienced underwriter?

The answer, at least so far, is a clear no. But that doesn't mean technology has left underwriting untouched. Its influence has simply been more subtle, or in banking jargon, back office led. Technology is helping human underwriters make better, faster decisions, not replacing them. For example, platforms like nPlan have developed machine learning software designed to enable lenders to predict the outcomes of construction projects and de-risk them accordingly. Others, such as LandTech, centralise planning data, comparables, ownership records and local policy into a single system, giving lenders clearer early-stage visibility and allowing underwriters to assess planning and development risk with far greater confidence and speed.

That said, one of the main uses of technology in underwriting has focused on doing something deceptively simple: pulling everything together. That is because real estate underwriting has always been data-heavy, but historically that data was fragmented and cumbersome: valuation reports locked in PDFs, lease schedules spread across spreadsheets, cash-flow assumptions buried in email chains, borrower information stored in half-remembered folders on shared drives. Decisions were not slow because underwriters lacked insight, but because assembling a coherent deal picture took time and effort. That is why platforms such as nCino began centralising property, borrower and market data into single, structured systems. The impact was immediate. Friction fell, timelines compressed and credit committees became faster and more consistent. Deals were no longer lost in translation between teams or reshaped by whichever spreadsheet happened to be most recently updated.

As one senior product lead at a digital workflow management platform puts it: 'We're not trying to tell lenders what the right answer is. We're trying to make sure everyone is looking at the same facts, at the same time, with the same assumptions, so judgement is exercised deliberately, not accidentally'.

Only once the data was organised did analytics begin to layer on top. Comparable transactions, market-rent trends, vacancy dynamics, planning and zoning risk and sponsor behaviour across cycles were surfaced alongside the core underwriting case. Increasingly, integrations with external data providers and project-management platforms allow construction progress, cost overruns and leasing velocity to feed directly back into credit files in near real time. What emerged was not an automated yes or no, but a more complete picture of risk.

In this new model, technology acts like a second set of eyes: tireless, unemotional and capable of spotting patterns that human judgement might miss. It flags anomalies, highlights correlations and stress-tests assumptions across multiple scenarios at once. But it stops short of making the decision. That responsibility still sits with the human underwriter, whose role has subtly shifted from assembling information to interrogating it.

In that sense, tech has not replaced underwriting; it has professionalised it. Judgement remains at the centre of the process, but it is now supported by cleaner data, broader context and tools designed to reduce blind spots. In a market where speed matters but mistakes are costly, that balance has become one of private credit's quiet, but decisive, competitive advantages.

LANDBAY: FAST DECISION SERVICE

TECHNOLOGY AS INFRASTRUCTURE

As we've already seen in Chapter 3, Landbay began life in 2014 as a P2P lender. Today, it is a technology-led institutional platform through which pension funds, insurers and asset managers deploy billions into residential mortgages. How did Landbay get here? When I met the company's Chief Operating Officer, Julian Cork, it was immediately clear that the answer is partly technology. At Landbay, tech is not a support function built onto a lending business; it is the infrastructure that makes the business viable at scale. The sheer size of the company's tech workforce makes the point clearly: nearly 40% of its employees sit in technology roles, a ratio that would look unusual in a traditional property lender, but entirely logical here.

At the centre of this architecture sits one of Landbay's most important pieces of intellectual property: its proprietary decisioning service. It ensures that every case entering the system is assessed against the same rules, data sources and product parameters, long before an underwriter even becomes involved. In a market where delays typically stem not from big decisions but from thousands of small administrative frictions, the decisioning engine creates consistency: bringing order to the inputs, highlighting instantly what's missing and cutting out the endless back-and-forth. Its purpose is simple but powerful: to turn what is normally a fragmented, manual front end into a coherent, orderly process and to present underwriters with a clean, consistent file. In effect, it operates as an always-on triage system, quietly doing the heavy lifting so that human judgement can be applied where it truly adds value.

DECISIONS IN MILLISECONDS

In traditional mortgage lending at legacy banks, eligibility is worked out through a comprehensive underwriting process that focuses on the Five Cs of Credit: Capacity, Capital, Collateral, Credit and Conditions. It's a slow, often frustrating process, one that can drag on for weeks, if not months.

By deploying machine-learning tools and rule-based automation, Landbay inverted that experience.

Its decision engine pulls in thousands of data points as the case is being submitted—from brokers, applicants, valuers and third-party sources—and assesses eligibility in under 30 milliseconds. Not minutes. Not hours. Milliseconds.

The mechanism is by no means intended to replace human judgement, but to clear the path for it, flagging inconsistencies, highlighting missing information and presenting underwriters with a clean, streamlined case file in real time.

For brokers, this unlocks what Landbay calls decision as you go. Instead of waiting days for an underwriter to manually review documents, the system immediately runs the case through a series of rules, risk tolerances, historic decision patterns and pricing parameters. If something falls outside policy, the system doesn't simply reject it: it explains why. Loan-to-value too high? Property type misaligned? Rental coverage just short? The feedback is immediate and specific, allowing brokers to adjust parameters and structure the case correctly before submission.

The effect is subtle but powerful. Time is saved on both sides. Brokers submit fewer unviable cases. Underwriters receive applications that are already closer to policy fit. And crucially, the friction and frustration that so often define lender–broker interactions are materially reduced.

BUILT FOR LENDERS, NOT JUST ENGINEERS

What makes Landbay's decision engine unique is not just its speed, but who controls it.

(Continued)

(*Continued*)

Instead of hard-coding credit logic deep into software—a common flaw in legacy banking systems—Landbay built the engine around decision tables. This allows complex rules to be managed transparently and be changed quickly by business users. Each time a configurable rule—from credit policies to fee structures—is changed, the system dynamically rewrites the code and deploys the executable, thus allowing for hard-coded performance alongside the agility of configuration.

In practical terms, this means Landbay can evolve its lending criteria without multi-month development cycles or risky system rewrites. When market conditions shift, products change or risk appetite tightens, the rules can be updated quickly, tested safely and deployed cleanly. All the while importantly retaining the platform performance and scalability expected of a leading FinTech.

This flexibility matters. In volatile markets, speed of policy adaptation can be as important as speed of credit approval. Landbay's architecture allows it to respond in days where traditional lenders might take quarters.

DECISIONING BEYOND CREDIT APPROVAL

But Landbay soon realised that the power of its decisioning capability could be leveraged far beyond just underwriting. Once the system proved it could bring order and clarity to the chaos of initial applications, the team began extending its reach across the entire lending journey.

What followed was less a reinvention than a quiet re-engineering of dozens of small tasks that traditionally slow a case down. The engine now establishes, in real time, which checks a case genuinely needs and which can be safely omitted. It generates tailored document requests so brokers know exactly what to upload instead of navigating generic, catch-all lists. It verifies whether those documents actually satisfy the requirements, cross-checking dates, formats and content long before a human underwriter ever begins their review.

Even at the legal stage—normally one of the most manual parts of the process—the same system now drafts offer conditions automatically, reducing the rework that often happens when information becomes inconsistent across teams.

Each of these steps seems small in isolation. But taken together, they dismantle the friction that has defined mortgage lending for decades. And they free underwriters to focus on the handful of decisions that truly require human judgement, instead of chasing paperwork or reconciling versions of documents that never quite match.

As one Landbay executive put it, 'Every minute an underwriter spends checking whether a document is dated correctly is a minute they're not spending thinking about risk'. The decision engine, in that sense, doesn't replace judgement, it protects it.

TECHNOLOGY AS QUIET DISCIPLINE

What stands out about Landbay's approach is not technological showmanship, but the quiet discipline behind it. There is no attempt to replace underwriters with algorithms or handing credit decisions over to artificial intelligence. The ambition is narrower, and more credible.

Technology is used to enforce consistency, surface clarity and compress timelines. It acts as a discipline layer: making sure the right rules are applied every time, that brokers understand those rules upfront and that underwriters are freed to focus on judgement instead of admin tasks.

The result is a system in which clarity replaces ambiguity. Where consistency replaces the idiosyncrasies of individual underwriters. And where speed does not come at the expense of rigour, but emerges naturally from cleaner inputs and sharper data.

For institutional investors, the impact ripples far beyond the front end. Faster decisioning improves capital deployment. Cleaner origination improves portfolio quality. Better data improves portfolio-level oversight. And the same infrastructure that underpins origination now feeds directly into monitoring, reporting and risk analytics, strengthening the entire credit chain.

Landbay's technology story is, in many ways, a microcosm of the wider evolution of real estate private credit. The edge no longer lies in saying yes faster for its own sake. It lies in having the systems that allow lenders to say yes—or no—with confidence. And increasingly, that confidence is being engineered quietly, behind the scenes, a few milliseconds at a time.

DIGITISING DUE DILIGENCE

Once a deal has been originated and underwritten, due diligence kicks in. That is when underwriters ask: 'Do the facts support the underwriting case we've agreed in principle?' Due diligence has long been the slowest, lengthiest and most delicate part of the lending process. It sits at the centre of credit decision-making, and is where otherwise viable deals often lose momentum. One 'computer says no' moment and the entire deal can go back to square one.

Historically, due diligence didn't need to rely on so many moving parts. Fewer counterparties, simpler structures, less regulatory scrutiny. But today, due diligence is asked to shoulder a far heavier burden. Nowadays transactions are way more complex, ownership structures more layered and less transparent, funding sources more global and regulatory expectations much higher. At the same time, credit timelines have compressed. Borrowers expect answers in days, not months. The result is a growing mismatch between the complexity of what due diligence is meant to capture and the manual, linear processes traditionally used to perform it.

This is why due diligence has become the most document-heavy and process-driven part of the lending chain, and one where things can really go wrong. Not because the risks are new, but because the volume and interconnection of those risks have outgrown the tools used to manage them. What was once a relatively straightforward verification exercise has become a multidimensional and multilayered challenge: connecting disparate facts, spotting weak signals early and understanding how legal, financial, operational and regulatory risks interact.

In the old model, that synthesis depended on static documents. Valuation reports frozen at a point in time, even as prices shifted. QS reports and construction schedules captured in a single moment. Excel models built on fixed assumptions. Long chains of documentary verification passed from inbox to inbox. Source of funds and ownership structures. Anti-Money Laundering (AML) and sanctions checks. Title and lease analysis. Security enforceability. Parallel technical, legal and environmental reports—flood risk, contamination, structural condition—commissioned separately and stitched together late in the process. By the time a credit committee reviewed the pack, parts of it were already out of date, internally inconsistent or based on assumptions that no longer held, particularly in volatile markets or cross-border transactions where data quality and transparency varied widely by jurisdiction.

Technology is now transforming this layer. Modern due diligence platforms are shifting the process from periodic review to ongoing assessment. Automated data pipelines pull in market comparables, leasing and occupancy data, planning records, ESG indicators, climate-risk overlays and borrower histories in near real time. AI-driven tools then work across that information: stress-testing assumptions, flagging inconsistencies, highlighting gaps and highlighting correlations that would be difficult for human reviewers to identify under time pressure.

This is particularly evident in borrower and counterparty due diligence. Platforms such as Onfido have industrialised digital identity verification, using biometric analysis, document authentication and ML models to verify principals and beneficial owners in minutes instead of days. Meanwhile, solutions like NorthRow (now part of Featurespace) support Know Your Customer (KYC) and AML screening across complex ownership structures, sanctions exposure and adverse media.

'Our aim isn't to replace human diligence, it's to remove the noise', a senior manager at a digital identify verification platform told me. 'When teams spend less time chasing documents and reconciling versions, they have far more capacity to focus on what actually matters: where real risks sit'.

The result of this tech integration is not faster rubber-stamping, but deeper interrogation. Due diligence has become a live process instead of a static hurdle, particularly valuable when underwriting transitional assets, development risk or assets exposed to regulatory, ESG or planning uncertainty. Human judgement remains central, but it is exercised with broader context, cleaner data and far fewer blind spots.

In that sense, due diligence is moving decisively beyond the checklist. It is no longer simply about confirming what is already believed to be true, but about continuously testing whether that belief still holds: a subtle but powerful shift in a market where assumptions can change faster than closing timetables.

ONFIDO: AUTOMATING BORROWER VERIFICATION

THE COMPLIANCE BOTTLENECK IN TRADITIONAL LENDING

Founded in 2012, Onfido became a pioneer in digital identity verification. It's AI-driven and ML technology, including optical character recognition and face detection, allowed businesses to verify an applicant's passport or ID to prevent fraud.

At a time when real estate private credit was starting to emerge, Onfido's technology quickly became a game changer for the real estate lending industry. In traditional real estate lending, identity verification was slow, manual, cumbersome and surprisingly fragile. Confirming a borrower's identity meant physical forms, certified copies of passports or licences that were often emailed as PDF attachments, utility bills that often arrived out of date and back-and-forth with brokers, all adding days, even weeks, to applications. Compliance teams spent days reconciling documents, chasing missing pages and escalating edge cases that rarely added insight but frequently delayed deals.

AUTOMATING IDENTITY VERIFICATION WITH AI

Onfido set out to industrialise this process using AI. Its platform combines document authentication, biometric analysis and ML models trained to detect fraud patterns across millions of identity checks globally. Borrowers upload documents digitally. Onfido verifies their authenticity, matches facial biometrics and flags anomalies in seconds instead of days.

So, real estate private credit providers started using Onfido. One of the earliest adopters was LendInvest. In 2018, as developers and brokers increasingly demanded speed and simplicity, LendInvest recognised the perennial bottleneck in the credit process and partnered with Onfido.

Instead of reverting to paper and couriered documents, a broker or borrower could now upload a snapshot of a passport and a selfie via LendInvest's online portal. Behind the scenes, Onfido's AI analysed the document and the facial biometric in seconds, enabling secure, compliant identity checks without in-person visits.

TRUST AT SCALE IN DIGITAL UNDERWRITING

This meant faster onboarding, less paperwork and a sense that the loan journey could finally match the pace of digital customer expectations.

For private credit lenders like LendInvest, the impact was less about speed alone and more about confidence. Automated identity checks reduced false

(*Continued*)

(*Continued*)

positives, surfaced genuine risk earlier and allowed compliance teams to focus on judgement instead of paperwork. Crucially, the system creates auditable trails that satisfy regulators without paralysing deal teams. As Christian Faes put it:

> From the outset at LendInvest, we believed that technology would fundamentally change how real estate lending operated. Identity verification was one of the biggest bottlenecks, slow, manual and full of human error. What Onfido gave us was the ability to build trust at scale. Automated checks meant we could verify who we were dealing with in seconds, not days and with a level of accuracy no manual process could match. That confidence allowed our teams to focus on lending decisions instead of paperwork and it set a new standard for what modern underwriting should look like.

In a market where complex ownership structures, cross-border sponsors and heightened AML scrutiny are now the norm, platforms like Onfido illustrate how AI can remove friction without lowering standards, transforming due diligence from a blunt gatekeeper into a sharper risk signal.

DATA-DRIVEN DOCUMENTATION

If there is one part of real estate lending that has stubbornly resisted modernisation, it is documentation. Loan agreements, QS reports, security packages, title reviews, schedules of condition, all still passed around as PDFs and Word files in endless email chains, each version slightly different from the last. For years, banks tolerated the friction as the price of caution. But for private credit managers trying to move at pace, it quickly became unsustainable.

One London-based private debt manager described a moment that reveals just how antiquated real estate documentation workflows still are. Midway through a live development deal, the borrower emailed asking which version of the facility agreement they should be responding to: the one titled Final_NovUpdate_v2 or Final_NovUpdate_v3. Three separate law firms had updated the document in parallel, each saving their edits onto an email thread that had splintered into multiple versions. By the time the lender pulled everyone onto a call to reconcile the differences, it took two hours just to establish which clauses were current and which had been overwritten by mistake.

No one had done anything wrong, it was simply the result of a paper-heavy system built on email chains, manual edits and documents living in inboxes instead of structured workflows.

A similar story was recounted to me by another lender. Before adopting digital clause libraries and document-comparison tools, one pan-European lender described its loan book as 'four versions of the truth': slightly different enforcement rights in different jurisdictions, subtly inconsistent covenants and documentation drift that only became obvious when a workout exposed the gaps. Standardising the spine of the documents—while preserving local nuance—not only made execution faster; it materially improved the portfolio's risk profile.

What technology is really doing here is preserving institutional memory. A covenant that proved too loose in one deal doesn't vanish when the team turns over: it gets quietly corrected in the next template. Mistakes stop repeating. Knowledge compounds.

For borrowers, the benefit is far less friction: fewer rewrites, fewer last-minute surprises and legal processes that don't feel like a paper chase. For lenders, the gain is consistency, deals that are not just quicker to close, but structurally more robust.

In a sector long weighed down by documents, binders and PDFs titled FINAL_v5_reallyFINAL, this quiet documentation shift is proving one of private credit's most meaningful upgrades, not flashy, not visible, but transformative all the same.

THE DIGITAL FRONT DOOR OF CREDIT

Real estate has long been one of the economy's most heavily intermediated markets. Property transactions are complex and expensive, often requiring a small army of professionals to shepherd a deal from its introduction to its completion. Yet for all that intermediation, the mechanics of the market remained surprisingly old-fashioned until very recently.

For years, a typical property deal began the same way. A broker sent a long email or made a phone call. Shortly afterwards, a credit pack landed as a sprawling PDF attachment. Then came the waiting. Progress updates depended on the familiar ritual of chasing, nudging and waiting for someone on the other side to respond.

Information gaps were inevitable. Brokers often had little visibility on where a case sat, why it had stalled or what might unlock the next steps. For lenders, the experience was no better: duplicated data entry, inconsistent submissions and valuable underwriting time spent clarifying basic information instead of assessing risk.

Digital broker portals have quietly begun to transform that front door of credit. What started as little more than a document upload point has evolved into a structured origination environment, and increasingly, a competitive advantage for lenders that offer them.

Today, brokers enter deal information once, through standardised fields that map directly into a lender's credit systems. Mandatory inputs reduce incomplete submissions. Embedded logic flags potential issues upfront—loan size, leverage, asset type—before the case ever reaches an underwriter.

The shift may seem subtle, but its effects are significant. Instead of acting as intermediaries frustratingly ferrying PDFs back and forth, brokers become participants in a shared workflow. They can see, often in real time, whether a case has been credit-approved, conditionally accepted or paused pending clarification. Feedback that once arrived days later now appears instantly: which assumption needs revisiting, which document is missing.

For lenders, the improvement in signal quality is immediate. Applications arrive cleaner, more consistent and easier to compare. Origination teams now spend less time triaging applications and more time discussing structure, pricing and risk. For brokers, the opacity that once strained relationships with both borrowers and lenders begins to fade.

And for borrowers, the benefits are just as tangible: greater visibility, faster responses and a sense that the process is moving forward instead of disappearing into an email inbox.

Perhaps most importantly, broker portals change behaviour. When eligibility criteria are visible and feedback is immediate, deal quality improves upstream. Brokers learn what works. Borrowers adjust earlier. And credit conversations begin with substance instead of process.

The result is not just faster origination, but better origination, something email-driven workflows struggled to achieve.

AUTOMATING CASE MANAGEMENT

If broker portals rewire the front door of lending, case management portals reshape everything that happens once a deal is inside. Historically, loan applications fragmented the moment they were submitted. Credit teams worked off internal spreadsheets, legal teams tracked conditions separately and borrowers were left navigating a maze of requests with little sense of priority or progress. The case existed everywhere, and nowhere-in particular.

Modern case management portals collapse that fragmentation. Each loan becomes a single, living workflow: application data, underwriting notes, due diligence checks, legal conditions, valuation updates and correspondence all anchored to one digital spine. Tasks are assigned, dependencies are mapped and progress is visible to everyone, subject to permissioning.

For borrowers, this is a game changer. Instead of receiving piecemeal requests by email, they interact with a clear checklist: what's outstanding, what's been approved and what is blocking completion. Uploading documents becomes purposeful instead of speculative. For developers juggling multiple schemes, this clarity reduces cognitive load at exactly the point where time and attention are most stretched.

For lenders, the benefits compound quickly. Underwriters can see at a glance which risks are resolved and which not. Credit committees receive cleaner, more current information. Operations teams gain visibility over bottlenecks—whether in valuation, legal review or borrower responsiveness—allowing resources to be reallocated in real time instead of after the fact.

Over time, these portals become repositories of institutional knowledge. Patterns emerge: which conditions typically delay closing, which borrower types require more intervention, where assumptions most often break down. That feedback loop rarely existed in legacy processes, where deals closed or didn't, and the learning dissipated with the emails.

The broader implication is cultural as much as operational. Case management portals shift lending away from episodic decision-making and towards continuous oversight. A loan is no longer something assessed, approved and filed away; it is something actively managed from first contact through drawdown and beyond. In an asset class defined by long timelines and evolving risk, that shift may prove as important as any algorithm or credit model.

BEYOND ORIGINATION: TECHNOLOGY AND PORTFOLIO INTELLIGENCE

If technology has transformed the front end of lending, its next frontier lies further downstream.

Historically, once a loan was originated, monitoring relied on periodic reports, borrower updates and spreadsheets maintained by asset managers. Information arrived slowly and often unevenly. By the time a problem surfaced, it had usually been building for months.

Today, a new generation of portfolio monitoring tools is changing that dynamic. Data feeds, automated covenant tracking and real-time dashboards allow lenders and investors to see risk evolving across an entire portfolio as it happens.

Taken together, these technologies do not represent a single breakthrough moment. There was no sudden revolution, no single platform that transformed real estate credit overnight. Instead, the change arrived gradually, almost quietly, through a thousand incremental improvements across the lending process.

Origination has moved from personal networks and email chains to structured digital marketplaces. Underwriting increasingly draws on live data instead of static documents. Due diligence and documentation are becoming automated and standardised. Broker portals and case management platforms now allow lenders, borrowers and intermediaries to operate within shared workflows instead of disconnected inboxes.

None of this removes the human element at the heart of credit. Lending remains a business built on judgement. But technology is steadily clearing away the friction that once surrounded that judgement: the delays, duplication and uncertainty that slowed decisions and obscured risk.

In doing so, technology is quietly reshaping the operating system of private credit.

For lenders, the prize is scale without losing discipline. For borrowers, it is speed and transparency in a process long known for neither. And for investors allocating billions into real estate debt, it offers something the industry has historically struggled to provide: clarity.

Private credit did not grow simply because banks retreated. It grew because new participants built a system that could operate differently. Technology has been central to that shift.

And as the industry continues to expand, the lenders who master this new digital infrastructure will not only move faster than their competitors. They will understand risk better—and in credit, that is what ultimately defines success.

CHAPTER 6

What Comes Next for Private Real Estate Debt

THE END OF THE EASY YEARS

The appeal of private credit and other alternatives is undeniable in a low-yield world, but investors must be realistic about trade-offs. Diversification isn't free: it costs in terms of liquidity and operational complexity. Properly assessing those trade-offs, instead of assuming high yields come without consequence, will determine whether these strategies earn their place in a long-term portfolio.

—Dan Kemp, Founder, Portfolio Thinking

Throughout this book, we've traced private real estate debt back to the aftermath of the Global Financial Crisis, when bank retrenchment, tighter regulation and dislocated capital markets created a vacuum that was quickly filled by a new generation of lenders operating outside the traditional banking system. That context remains essential, but it no longer tells the whole story. What began as a response to absence has now moved beyond filling a gap to building an asset class, complete with its own institutions, operating models, tech stack and investor expectations.

As Dan Kemp notes, investment history is 'a graveyard of asset classes that grew too fast for their own good'. His warning lands sharply in today's market. Private real estate debt has grown from what was once opportunistic niche into a multi-trillion-dollar cornerstone of global finance: a fully-fledged ecosystem spanning origination platforms, service providers, risk analytics and increasingly layered capital stacks. But rapid inflows always carry a cost. When too much capital chases too few opportunities, decision-making quality tends to erode, underwriting standards slip and late entrants 'pay a premium for assets that quickly evaporates when the cycle turns'. Growth has brought scale, but also vulnerability.

Unsurprisingly, this evolution has attracted more scrutiny and higher expectations. Investors now ask tougher questions about how managers source deals, how risk is being underwritten and priced, how portfolios behave under stress and whether governance frameworks are robust enough to withstand a turn in the cycle. They wonder: is there too much money chasing too few deals? Are underwriting standards slipping? And as Kemp stresses, the managers who endure are those with intellectual honesty: the discipline to mark assets to market and confront reality early instead of smoothing volatility with optimistic models.

Borrowers, too, have become more probing and selective. They compare lenders not just on price, but on certainty of execution, quality of engagement and the ability to support a project through its inevitable hitches. And regulators, carefully watching the sector scale at speed, are also beginning to ask their own uncomfortable questions about concentration risk, systemic exposure and whether parts of private credit are drifting towards a 'too big to fail' status.

These are fair questions, but they are often framed the wrong way. The issue is not whether private real estate debt will endure, or whether it has peaked, but how it will evolve as it moves from a period of rapid expansion to one of maturity and institutionalisation.

What is becoming increasingly clear though is that the easy phase for private credit is now firmly behind us. The years in which capital was plentiful, margins were forgiving and the rising tide lifted all boats are unlikely to return. Funding is now scarer, valuations more uncertain, exit assumptions under pressure and execution risk now fully exposed.

This is where Kemp's remaining hallmarks of long-term winners become crucial: operational robustness and alignment. As cycles turn, the winners will be those with real workout capabilities—the teams that know how to restructure a loan long before default occurs—and those who invest their own capital alongside clients, ensuring underwriting discipline is not a slogan but a lived practice.

What comes next for private real estate debt will be less forgiving, and far more interesting. Three major forces will shape the next chapter for the sector: consolidation across an increasingly crowded non-bank landscape; a gradual rebundling of banks, private lenders and technology platforms into hybrid models; and a regulatory framework that is beginning—cautiously and unevenly—to tighten. Together, these forces will determine not just who survives, but how the market itself evolves.

THE ERA OF CONSOLIDATION

The first decade of private real estate debt was defined by proliferation. Hundreds of new lenders entered the market, largely positioning themselves as substitutes for banks: stepping in where traditional lenders would not, funding the awkward, the transitional and the non-standard. Many were founded by alumni of retrenching banks; others backed by opportunistic capital eager to deploy quickly. Barriers to entry were low, track records were short and, in a market awash with liquidity, momentum often substituted for depth.

That role still matters, but it no longer defines the market. That phase is coming to an end.

The inflection point came in the early 2020s, coinciding with the most severe global shock in modern financial history. Beyond its human cost, the Covid pandemic marked the end of cheap money. Between March 2022 and July 2023, the Federal Reserve increased its policy rate more than a dozen times, taking it from near zero to over 5.25% as it battled inflation. The Bank of England raised rates 14 times over the same period. Across the continent, the European Central Bank embarked on an extended tightening cycle, delivering around ten consecutive rate hikes to bring its main rates up from negative territory to historic highs. Other central banks followed.

As liquidity retreated, capital became more selective, pricing tightened and regulators started paying closer attention. As a result, signs of consolidation began to appear.

The consequences were predictable. Smaller platforms with narrow funding lines, limited technology and fragile risk frameworks began to struggle. Rising costs—from compliance and reporting to data infrastructure—favoured scale. So too did the growing preference among institutional investors for fewer, deeper relationships with managers that could deploy capital consistently across cycles.

The consolidation we are seeing among non-bank lenders has taken several forms. Some lenders are being acquired outright by larger platforms seeking origination capacity, servicing capability or geographic reach. Others are merging to achieve scale in risk management, operations or fundraising. A third group is quietly exiting the market, unable to refinance warehouse facilities or raise successor funds on acceptable terms.

The result is not contraction, but concentration. Fewer lenders, but stronger ones. Platforms with deeper balance sheets, more institutional governance and the resources to invest in technology, people and process. In many ways, private real estate debt is beginning to resemble other mature asset classes: still competitive, still innovative, but less fragmented and far less forgiving.

OAKNORTH BANK & ASK PARTNERS: SCALING SPECIALIST LENDING

FROM PARTNERSHIP TO STRATEGIC INVESTMENT

In October 2022, OakNorth Bank acquired a 50% stake in ASK Partners, formalising a long-standing relationship between two complementary lenders. OakNorth—a digital-first UK bank founded in 2015—had already built a reputation for providing tailored lending to mid-sized businesses often overlooked by high-street banks. ASK Partners, by contrast, had emerged as a specialist property lender focused on structured real estate credit, working closely with developers on complex or transitional projects.

The two firms had collaborated on transactions for several years before the acquisition, combining OakNorth's balance sheet capacity with ASK's agile deal structuring and close relationships with property sponsors. Together they funded SME developers and property entrepreneurs quickly and creatively, stepping in where mainstream lenders often hesitated.

The investment therefore represented less a new relationship than the formalisation of an existing one.

(*Continued*)

(*Continued*)

More importantly, it reflected a broader trend within the private credit market. As alternative lenders matured and institutional capital flowed into the sector, partnerships between specialist lenders and regulated banks increasingly became a mechanism for scaling operations while maintaining the flexibility that had initially defined the sector.

The transaction allowed OakNorth to deepen its exposure to real estate lending without building an entirely new origination platform from scratch. For ASK, it provided long-term capital support and access to a stable funding partner capable of underwriting larger transactions.

COMBINING BALANCE SHEET STRENGTH WITH LENDING AGILITY

Both organisations share a focus on credit discipline, customer experience and speed of execution—characteristics that have become increasingly important in a market where developers often require swift decision-making and tailored financing structures.

By integrating their capabilities, the two firms sought to combine OakNorth's regulated bank balance sheet with ASK's specialist lending platform and investor network, which channels institutional and private capital into property-backed debt.

The result is a hybrid model that sits somewhere between traditional banking and private credit. OakNorth contributes funding capacity, regulatory infrastructure and balance sheet strength. ASK contributes deal origination, structuring expertise and a flexible approach to underwriting that is often better suited to complex development or transitional projects.

Importantly, ASK retained operational independence following the investment. Its investment process, deal sourcing and borrower relationships remained intact, while the partnership with OakNorth allowed it to expand the scale and range of transactions it could support.

SCALING ORIGINATION AND EXECUTION

Over the year following the transaction, the partnership delivered more than GBP 270 million in financing across a range of projects. Among these were a GBP 62 million development loan supporting the delivery of 133 residential apartments in Canary Wharf and a GBP 41.5 million refinancing of a Grade A office building in central London.

These transactions illustrate the types of projects that increasingly fall outside traditional bank lending criteria. Developments in prime but complex urban locations often involve planning risk, construction timelines or capital structures that require a degree of flexibility that many large banks are reluctant to provide.

For OakNorth, the investment reinforced its strategy of serving what it calls the missing middle: businesses and property developers that are too large for small business lending but too small or complex for global banks.

For ASK, the partnership provided the capital stability and underwriting capacity required to scale its lending platform while continuing to structure bespoke solutions for developers.

WHAT IT ILLUSTRATES

The OakNorth–ASK partnership is a textbook example of consolidation within the private real estate credit market.

As the sector matures, successful specialist lenders increasingly find themselves partnering with larger institutions that can provide funding capacity and balance sheet stability. At the same time, banks are discovering that working alongside specialist platforms allows them to access deal flow and underwriting expertise without abandoning the regulatory discipline imposed after the Global Financial Crisis.

In other words, rather than replacing banks entirely, private credit is gradually becoming integrated into the wider financial ecosystem.

The partnership therefore illustrates an emerging model in real estate finance: a blended structure in which regulated banks, specialist lenders and institutional investors collaborate to deliver capital more efficiently.

For developers, this hybrid approach can provide the best of both worlds: the financial strength of a bank combined with the speed, flexibility and creativity traditionally associated with private credit.

THE REBUNDLING OF BANKS AND NON-BANKS

The second major shift is more subtle and counter intuitive. After more than a decade of disintermediation, the lines between banks and non-banks are blurring.

For years, the narrative was one of replacement: banks retreat, non-banks step in. In reality, what is emerging now is a process of rebundling. Banks are not disappearing from real estate finance: they are repositioning themselves. Increasingly, they are partnering with, funding, white-labelling or embedding non-bank platforms instead of competing with them head-on.

Some banks provide leverage, hedging or balance-sheet capital to private lenders. Others distribute loans originated by non-banks to institutional investors. A growing number consume non-bank technology—underwriting tools, broker portals, monitoring platforms—to modernise their own lending operations without rebuilding systems from scratch. And then there are the merger and acquisition (M&A) deals where banks have been acquiring non-bank lenders.

At the same time, leading private lenders are adopting more traditionally bank-like features: regulated deposit-taking entities, long-dated capital, dedicated risk teams and increasingly sophisticated treasury functions.

The old binary distinction between banks and alternative lenders is giving way to a more modular ecosystem, where capital, origination, risk and technology are recombined in new ways. What matters now is not the label on the door, but where each player sits in the value chain, and how effectively they collaborate.

THE NEW REGULATORY LANDSCAPE

A third force looms in the background: regulation. One of the drivers of private credit's rapid growth since the Global Financial Crisis was its relative freedom from bank-style heavy-handed regulation. While banks grappled with capital requirements, stress tests and leverage caps, private lenders operated with far greater flexibility. That asymmetry created opportunity, but it also created blind spots.

But as private real estate debt has grown and matured as an asset class, regulatory scrutiny has followed. This is inevitable. Regulators are now paying closer attention. Not because private real estate debt is inherently unstable, but because it has become systemically relevant. Expectations around transparency, reporting standards, valuation discipline, governance, liquidity management and risk oversight are rising, even if formal regulation remains fragmented across jurisdictions.

One sign of this shift came in December 2025, when the Bank of England announced a system-wide exploratory scenario exercise focused on private markets, including private equity and private credit. The initiative was not a traditional bank stress test, but rather an attempt to understand how risks might propagate across the broader financial system in periods of market stress. The exercise will bring together banks, insurers, pension funds, asset managers and other financial institutions to examine how exposures to private markets interact with leverage, liquidity and valuation dynamics during severe economic shocks.

In effect, regulators are beginning to ask the same question they once asked about banks: what happens if a large, opaque corner of the credit system comes under pressure at the same time?

The significance of the exercise lies less in the immediate regulatory consequences and more in what it signals: private credit is now large enough to warrant macro-prudential attention. What was once considered a niche corner of the financial system is increasingly viewed as part of the core plumbing of modern finance.

Another emerging focus for regulators is the growing web of connections between banks and private credit funds themselves. While private lenders often sit outside the regulated banking system, they frequently rely on banks for subscription lines, warehouse facilities, leverage financing and hedging arrangements.

As private credit has expanded, supervisors have begun examining whether these links could transmit stress back into the banking system during periods of market disruption. The concern is not that private lenders resemble pre-crisis banks, but that the boundaries between banks and non-banks are becoming more interconnected.

Increasingly, regulators are asking not only how risky private credit might be, but how risks might travel across the wider financial system if conditions deteriorate.

Upcoming changes to the EU's AIFMD II framework—including specific rules for loan-originating funds—signal a tighter perimeter. In the US, the Securities and Exchange Commission has sharpened its focus on valuation, disclosure and retail exposure. Some policymakers still resist over-regulation, but over a 10-year horizon, greater oversight appears inevitable.

At the same time, regulators are grappling with a second structural shift: the gradual opening of private markets to a broader investor base. Historically, private real estate debt funds were largely the preserve of institutional investors such as pension funds, insurers and sovereign wealth funds.

But regulatory reforms are beginning to change that dynamic. In Europe, the revised ELTIF 2.0 framework is designed to make long-term private market strategies more accessible to wealth managers and retail investors. Similar structures are emerging elsewhere, including semi-liquid private credit funds aimed at high-net-worth investors.

While this expansion could unlock a new pool of capital for real estate lending, it also introduces new supervisory questions around liquidity management, valuation practices and investor disclosure when illiquid assets are distributed to investors accustomed to more liquid products.

The likely outcome is not a wholesale importation of bank rules, but incremental tightening. More disclosure. More scrutiny of leverage and funding mismatches. More focus on who ultimately bears the risk. For well-run platforms, this is not an existential threat, it is a competitive advantage. Regulation tends to reward those already investing in infrastructure, governance and data.

Of course, the unintended consequence of that will be a higher cost of doing business. Greater transparency, reporting standards and governance expectations will increase operating costs, but they will also reinforce credibility. The lesson from banking is not that regulation kills markets, but that poorly designed regulation distorts them. The challenge for policymakers will be to recognise the diversity of private credit models, instead of treating the sector as a single, uniform bloc.

For lenders, the implication is clear: those who invest early in compliance, data integrity and governance will find themselves ahead of the curve instead of reacting to it.

A MORE SELECTIVE MARKET

If the early years of private real estate debt were defined by growth, the next phase will be defined by selection, not only among lenders, but among the investors who back them.

Not every lender that entered the market will remain. Some have already folded, others will. Capital will continue to consolidate around platforms that demonstrate disciplined underwriting, robust servicing and credible performance under stress.

This selectivity applies equally to the investors backing them. As Dan Kemp cautions, there is 'no free lunch' in investing. Higher returns come with hidden costs—usually liquidity and complexity—and the most dangerous phrase in finance is the seductive promise of 'equity-like returns with bond-like risk'. In private credit, the premium investors earn is not a windfall; it is compensation for the very real constraints of being unable to change your mind when conditions shift.

For years, many investors have treated private debt as a near-substitute for public fixed income, attracted by the stability of valuations and the higher yields. But as Kemp stresses, the trade-offs are fundamentally different. In public markets, volatility is the toll you pay; in private markets, it is illiquidity. Problems arise when investors want the best of both worlds: the steadiness of mark-to-model valuations combined with redemption terms that look like a mutual fund. It is precisely in this mismatch that silent risks start to stack up.

As the cycle turns and liquidity tightens, these distinctions will matter more. Investors with multi-decade horizons can harvest the illiquidity premium; those who may need access to capital during downturns can quickly discover that a long-term allocation becomes an illiquid headache at exactly the wrong time.

This is why the next phase of private real estate debt will be more than a culling of weaker managers: it will be a broad recalibration of expectations. Investors will gravitate towards lenders that price risk honestly, manage liquidity conservatively and resist the temptation to engineer smooth, unrealistic return profiles. Lenders who understand and communicate these trade-offs clearly will earn the trust of long-term capital providers; those who obscure them will be exposed when stress starts to show.

This shift is already visible. Some funds have wound down quietly. Others have pivoted strategies, extended maturities or repriced risk to reflect new conditions.

TECHNOLOGY AS INFRASTRUCTURE, NOT ADVANTAGE

Alongside these structural forces, another transformation is becoming impossible to ignore: the normalisation of technology.

What once differentiated lenders—digital origination, automated underwriting, real-time monitoring—is now becoming basic infrastructure. Technology is no longer an overlay; it is the infrastructure of modern private credit.

Lenders that fail to invest in data architecture, workflow automation and analytics will struggle to compete on cost, speed or risk management. By contrast, those that embed technology deeply will gain resilience, not just efficiency.

But technology doesn't eliminate judgement. If anything, judgement becomes more valuable, but it is exercised later, on better information and with greater accountability. The future belongs to lenders who combine human discretion with institutional-grade tooling.

A BROADER DEFINITION OF 'REAL ESTATE'

Another quiet shift is underway: the boundaries of what constitutes real estate lending are expanding. Private credit is increasingly active in sectors that sit adjacent to—or overlap with—traditional property finance: life sciences, data centres, energy-linked infrastructure, operational real estate and hybrid asset classes that defy old labels.

These assets require lenders who understand not just bricks and mortar, but operating risk, regulation and long-dated cash flows. Banks, constrained by templates and capital rules, often struggle here. Private lenders, with flexible mandates and specialist teams, are better positioned.

As Dan Kemp observes, this expansion into niche, future-themed sectors is also a reminder that the narrative machine in finance is powerful. A data centre fund or a life sciences strategy sells easily because the story is seductive. But compelling narratives do not necessarily translate into compelling returns. Kemp argues that the industry must invert the usual logic: instead of asking whether a specific asset class is fashionable or whether a particular deal aligns with the zeitgeist, the starting point should be the portfolio itself. What role does this cash flow play? How does it behave through the cycle? What risks does it add, or mitigate?

Seen through that lens, labels matter far less than fundamentals. What looks like 'real estate' on the surface often behaves more like infrastructure, or operating business credit, or something in between. Student accommodation, for example, tends to be defensive and less correlated with GDP growth; hotels are cyclical; care homes face regulatory exposure; older data centres may be vulnerable to technological obsolescence. A portfolio-based approach forces investors to treat these assets not as thematic buckets, but as cash-flow streams with specific behaviours under different scenarios.

Kemp's view, that investors should be 'agnostic about the asset type and obsessed with valuation and covenant strength', reflects the broader maturation of the market. As private real estate debt enters new sectors, the challenge is not classification but integration. Moving beyond product-led thinking means evaluating strategies by their contribution to the resilience of the whole, not by the attractiveness of their narrative. The strongest portfolios are not built around good stories; they are built as engines capable of surviving a wide range of futures.

THE AGE OF BORROWER CHOICE

Perhaps the most overlooked transformation lies with borrowers.

Developers and sponsors are no longer turning to private lenders as last resort. For many, non-bank capital is now the first call, not because banks are unavailable, but because specialist lenders better understand the realities of modern development, planning risk and execution complexity.

As competition deepens, borrowers will benefit from greater choice, but also face clearer differentiation. The best lenders will be those who combine certainty of capital with flexibility of structure and clarity of communication. Relationships will still matter, but they will be built on delivery instead of proximity.

BEYOND THE BOOM

Private real estate debt is no longer in its adolescence, but it is not yet a mature asset class. Most importantly, it hasn't yet been fully tested by a deep, protracted credit downturn. The coming years will test business models, underwriting assumptions and operational resilience.

What is clear is that the market has crossed a threshold. It is no longer defined by what banks no longer do, but by what private lenders do differently, and increasingly, better.

Time will of course tell, but I deeply believe that beyond the boom lies something more durable: a credit market shaped not by nostalgia for old models, but by adaptation to a more complex, data-rich and demanding world. The lenders that thrive will be those who recognise that private credit's real advantage lies not in speed alone, but in judgement, supported, scaled and sharpened by technology.

The next phase will be less about explosive growth and more about shape: who survives, who scales and who quietly disappears; how capital, technology and regulation re-align; and whether private real estate debt can do what banking once did—provide stability through cycles—without losing the flexibility that gave it an edge in the first place.

That question, more than any headline about stress or excess, will define what comes next.

Conclusion: The Quiet Rewriting of the Financial System

The journey traced through this book is not one of sudden revolutions or headline-grabbing disruptions, but of something quieter, steadier and ultimately far more profound: the gradual rewriting of how credit is created, distributed and deployed across the built environment. Real estate private debt didn't emerge with a bang. It emerged through multiple incremental shifts—each a response to a gap, a friction, a retreat, a bottleneck or a failure within the traditional banking system—until, taken together, they formed the new architecture of modern finance.

For years after the Global Financial Crisis, the prevailing narrative was that banks had stepped back temporarily and would eventually return to 'normal service'. Yet the reality of the last two decades tells a different story. Instead of snapping back, bank lending has shifted permanently. Not gone, but transformed. Capital adequacy rules hardened; risk appetites shrank; regional imbalances widened. In that space—the space where banks once dominated development finance, SME lending, bridging loans and specialist projects—private lenders stepped in, at first cautiously, then with growing conviction.

What began as marginal now sits at the centre. Private credit is no longer a niche allocation pursued only by the most adventurous investors on the fringes of institutional portfolios. It has become one of the most significant capital flows shaping how homes, workplaces, logistics hubs and urban regeneration projects are financed, now embraced even by the most risk-averse institutional investors. The case studies in this book—from Northern Ireland to Germany, London to California—show how this shift ripples through every tier of the market. It affects the small developer fighting to survive. It influences the institutional allocator balancing long-term liabilities. It shapes the lender designing a new product, adapted to a more flexible, evolving financing landscape.

Interestingly, while post-crisis policy reforms helped set this transformation in motion, the quiet rewriting of the financial system is no longer being driven by governments, regulators or central banks. It's happening in investment committees, credit teams, underwriting desks and the daily decisions of thousands of market participants who rarely make headlines. It's visible in the ability of a small developer in Belfast to secure real estate-backed financing when banks step back; in the conviction of an asset manager in Stuttgart deploying patient capital into secured lending strategies; and in the steady repositioning of pension funds towards resilient, collateral-backed income.

What is remarkable is not just the scale of the transformation, but how technology is enabling it. Technology has redrawn the boundaries of what is measurable, monitorable and modelled. Data has narrowed the gap between perception and risk. Platforms have redefined speed and accessibility. Meanwhile, the rise of ESG and impact frameworks has added new layers of accountability: a recalibration of not just how we lend, but why.

Across the industry, a quiet rebalancing is underway. Lenders who once relied primarily on networks and instinct now augment both with analytics and real-time insight. Investors once content with listed fixed income now seek yield, security and transparency beyond public markets. Developers once dependent on their local bank manager and personal networks to secure funding now navigate a broader ecosystem of funds, platforms and specialist lenders who can structure creatively in ways banks increasingly cannot.

What ties these threads together is not disruption for its own sake, but a pragmatic response to a world in transition, a world of more volatile interest rates, more unpredictable economic cycles, tighter regulation and deeper social need for housing and infrastructure. In such an environment, private debt has become a bridge: between capital and communities, between institutions and real assets, between liquidity and long-term value.

This is not to romanticise the asset class. Private debt brings its own risks: opacity in parts of the market, the need for rigorous governance and the danger of capital being deployed too aggressively in search of yield. History offers a sobering reminder that financial innovations rarely expand in a straight line. As Dan Kemp notes in Chapter 6, investment history is 'a graveyard of asset classes that grew too fast for their own good'. Private credit will not be immune to that reality. As capital continues to flow into the sector, weaker underwriting, overconfidence in rising collateral values and competition for deals may test the resilience of some lenders: it already has. There will be cycles ahead that separate prudence from exuberance, and not every platform that enters the market today will still be standing tomorrow. Yet periods of correction are not a sign of failure but of evolution. They are the moments when stronger institutions refine their processes, sharpen their discipline and demonstrate why this form of lending has become an enduring feature of modern credit markets. But the overall trajectory is clear: private credit—and real estate private debt in particular—is becoming a structural pillar of modern finance.

This book has aimed to document that shift: to show not just what is changing, but why and through whose hands the change is being shaped. Real estate private debt is no longer the answer to the question, 'Where do you go when the bank says no?' It has evolved, moved centre stage, quietly rewriting the script of how credit flows through the real economy.

But this story is far from complete. If the past decade was about emergence, the next will be about consolidation, institutionalisation, integration and partnerships. Private credit will become more transparent, data-driven and globally connected. The practitioners building this market—from founders to credit officers to the institutional allocators steering billions—will play an increasingly central role in defining the financial architecture of the future.

What comes next will not be defined by noise, but by the steady, disciplined expansion of a system that has already begun to reshape how the world builds, finances and sustains its real estate. The quiet rewriting is already underway. And it is far from over.

Acknowledgements

Writing a book of this scope is never a solitary endeavour, and *Beyond Banks* is no exception. It has been shaped by the generosity, insight and encouragement of many people who gave their time, expertise and patience along the way.

My sincere thanks go first to the outstanding editorial team at Wiley—Gemma Valler, Sherri-Anne Curtis and Alice Hadaway—whose support helped transform early ideas into a coherent manuscript.

I am particularly grateful to Dr. Ben Bernanke, former Chair of the US Federal Reserve, for generously sharing his reflections on the post-crisis regulatory landscape, insights that helped frame the conditions in which private credit began to flourish. My thanks also go to Lord Adair Turner, former Chair of the UK Financial Services Authority, whose thinking on credit cycles and financial stability helped sharpen several of the book's central themes, and to Lina Morales for facilitating the conversation with Lord Turner.

Many practitioners across the industry generously contributed their perspectives to the discussions throughout this book. I am especially grateful to Christian Faes, Co-Founder and Chairman of LendInvest and CEO at Faes & Co.; Benn Zemek, former CFO of Battersea Power Station and Director at Locate Living Co.; Julian Cork, COO at Landbay; Vincent Nobel, Head of Asset Based Lending at Federated Hermes, and the Federated Hermes communications team, specially Roanna Leung and Hannah Bellfield; the team at CalPERS: Marcie Frost, CEO, Brad Pacheco, Deputy Executive Officer, and Johnette Flores; Shabir Randeree CBE; the team at LendInvest: Rod Lockhart, CEO, Steve Larkin, Development Finance MD, and Erik Niewiarowski, Content and Communications Manager; Eugenio Sangermano, CEO at BF.capital, and Samuel Duncombe for facilitating that introduction; Daniel Sutton, Operations Director, and Ermir Sefolli, MD at OEH Group; Joe McGinnis, MD at Braidwater Group; Dan Eaton, Director at Pivotal Point Group; Theo Kemp, Principal Founder Director at EVOLVE Lending Group; Matthew Dailly, MD, and Mason Ward, Head of Origination at Tiger Financial; Dan Kemp, Founder at Portfolio Thinking; Craig White, CEO at Agile Homes; Albane Poulin, Head of Private Credit at Gravis Capital; Richard Benson, Managing Director at Tay Developments; Scott Harris, Director at KHK Capital; Rishi Baungally, Director at Premier Gold Investments; Mark Roberts, Relationship Manager at Assetz Capital; Ajay Sharma, Commercial Finance Director at CS Finance; Dr Naz Nathani, Director at MACC Group; Ian Humphreys, Founder and CEO at Brickflow, and Sabinder Sandhu for facilitating that introduction; Justin Cartwright, National director at the Chartered Institute of Housing Northern Ireland; Peter Unwin, Head of Middle East Private Wealth and Family Office at IQEQ; and the team at Thomas London Day Schools.

My heartful thanks also go to Andrew Wilde and Olivia Evans at Edelman Smithfield for their early belief in the project and for facilitating important conversations.

I would also like to acknowledge the Private Debt Investor team, particularly Wassyl Abdessemed, for providing access to datasets and market intelligence that have informed several sections of this book.

Beyond those named here, this book benefited from conversations with many lenders, developers, investors and policymakers, some of whom preferred not to be quoted directly, but whose candour and insight shaped my understanding of how private credit has evolved.

Finally, my deepest gratitude goes to my family. To my husband, thank you for your unwavering support and for providing the steadiness that allowed me to write with clarity and purpose. And to my sons, one already exploring the world with boundless curiosity and the other who joined us as this manuscript was born. Thank you for bringing perspective and joy to every day.

To all of you: thank you.

About the Author

Roxana Mohammadian-Molina is a financier, investor and strategist specialising in private credit, real estate finance and financial innovation. Over a career spanning more than fifteen years, she has worked at the intersection of capital markets, technology and real estate, advising private and institutional investors on capital allocation and investment strategy.

She began her career in investment banking, serving as Vice President at Morgan Stanley and Barclays, where she advised institutional investors, hedge funds and family offices on trade ideas and portfolio diversification strategies in commodities markets. She later became Chief Strategy Officer at Blend, a UK FinTech and private credit platform backed by institutional investors, where she worked with the board on corporate strategy, capital raising and partnerships.

Roxana serves as Vice Chair of the Saudi British Joint Business Council, where she supports investment dialogue and economic cooperation between the UK and the GCC region.

A frequent speaker at global conferences, she is known for translating complex financial systems into clear strategic insights.

Roxana lives in Switzerland with her family.

Bibliography

Allen, F., & Gale, D. (2007). *Understanding Financial Crises.* Oxford University Press.

Allen, F., Carletti, E., & Marquez, R. (2011). Credit market competition and capital regulation. *Review of Financial Studies* 24(4): 983–1018.

Albertazzi, U., Ponte Marques, A., Abbondanza, A., & Travaglini, G.L. (2025). *The impact of capital requirements on bank capital.* ECB Working Paper Series No. 3128. European Central Bank.

Altman, E.I., & Benhenni, R. (2019). The anatomy of distressed debt markets. *Annual Review of Financial Economics* 11(1): 21–37.

Anjum, M., & Bharucha, N.H. (2025). US *Pension Funds Lag in Private Debt Allocation.* S&P Global Market Intelligence.

Apollo Global Management (2023). *Apollo and Mubadala Investment Company expand partnership.*

Arner, D., Barberis, J., & Buckley, R. (2016). *The Evolution of FinTech: A New Post-crisis Paradigm.* University of Hong Kong Law Research Paper.

Baily, M., Litan, R., & Johnson, M. (2008). *The Origins of the Financial Crisis.* Brookings Institution.

Bank for International Settlements (2005). *BIS Working Papers No. 150.*

Bank for International Settlements (2018). *Structural changes in banking after the crisis (CGFS Papers No. 60).*

BBC News (2014, April 15). *Anglo Irish Bank: From world's best to nationalised.*

BlackRock (2025). *BlackRock Family Office Survey 2025.*

Blackstone (2014). *Blackstone announces sale of IndCor Properties to GIC.*

Blackstone (2025). *Blackstone announces $8 billion final close for latest real estate debt strategies fund.*

Blinder, A.S. (2013). *After the Music Stopped: The Financial Crisis, the Response, and the Work Ahead.* Penguin Press.

Bloomberg News (2014, March 20). *Fed stress test shows 29 of 30 banks meet or top capital target.*

Bridges, J., Gregory, D., Nielsen, M., Pezzini, S., Radia, A., & Spaltro, M. (2014). *The impact of capital requirements on bank lending.* Bank of England Working Paper No. 486.

Brookfield Asset Management (2024). *The Future is Debt: Brookfield's Kingston on the Rise of Real Estate Credit.* PERE Credit.

Brunnermeier, M.K. (2009). Deciphering the liquidity and credit crunch 2007–2008. *Journal of Economic Perspectives* 23(1): 77–100.

CalPERS (2022). *Annual investment report: Fiscal year ended June 30, 2022.*

CalPERS (2025). *Private Debt Annual Program Review.*

CalPERS (2026). *Investment Committee Report.*

CapitalRise (2025, February 26). *Bank lending to SME property developers has almost halved since 2017.*

Cassidy, J. (2010). The Volcker Rule. *The New Yorker.*

Complementa, A.G. (2024). *Alternative assets for Swiss pension funds.*

Cordell, L.R., Hopkins, M., & Huang, Y. (2011). *The trust preferred CDO market: From start to (expected) finish*. Federal Reserve Bank of Philadelphia Working Paper.

Covucci, G.E., & Weisel, S.J. (2010). *The long and winding road: A short tour of the Dodd–Frank Act and its impact on real estate*. Pipeline Magazine.

Cresset Capital (2024). *The meteoric rise of private credit*.

European Commission (2023). *Regulation (EU) 2023/606*.

European Parliament and Council (2019). *Law No. 2019-486 (PACTE Law)*.

Equity Development (2021). *LendInvest plc: Profitable fintech disrupter in property finance*.

Federal Reserve Bank of Boston (2010). *$1.25 trillion is still real money*.

Federal Reserve Bank of New York (n.d.). *Large-scale asset purchases*.

Federated Hermes (2023). *The power of diversification: Real estate debt and portfolio construction*.

Ferguson, N. (2008). *The Ascent of Money*. Penguin Press.

Financial Stability Board (2018). *Global shadow banking monitoring report 2017*.

Financial Stability Board (2024). *Global monitoring report on non-bank financial intermediation 2024*.

Financial Times (2021, August 4). *Bond rally pushes global stock of negative-yielding debt above $16tn*.

Garner, C.A. (2008). Is commercial real estate reliving the 1980s and early 1990s? *Economic Review* 93: 89–115.

Geanakoplos, J. (2010). The leverage cycle. *In NBER Macroeconomics Annual 2009* 24(1): 1–66.

Gennaioli, N., Shleifer, A., & Vishny, R. (2015). Neglected risks. *American Economic Review* 105(5):310–314.

GIC (2023). *Realty Income establishes strategic partnership with GIC*.

Goldstein, M. (2013). Not so fast on Volcker Rule. *The New York Times DealBook*.

Gorton, G. (2010). *Slapped by the Invisible Hand*. Oxford University Press.

Gorton, G., & Metrick, A. (2012). Securitized banking and the run on repo. *Journal of Financial Economics* 104(3): 425-451.

Gravis Capital Management (2024). *Three reasons to invest in private credit*.

IFA Magazine (2025). *Guiide warns of looming pension sustainability crisis*.

Investment & Pensions Europe (2018, August 10). *Allianz and Brookfield refinance Blackstone's St Katharine Docks*.

JLL. (2023). *Global real estate outlook*.

JPMorgan Securities Services (2023). *Private market boom in French pension funds*.

King, M. (2016). *The End of Alchemy*. W.W. Norton & Company.

KPMG. (2024). *Private Debt Fund Survey 2024*.

Landbay Partners Limited (2025). *Technology @ Landbay: An introduction*.

LendInvest plc. (2023). *Annual Report and Accounts 2023*.

Macfarlanes (2023). *The growth of real estate debt*.

Mian, A., & Sufi, A. (2014). *House of Debt*. University of Chicago Press.

Morgan S. (2025). *Investing in European private credit*.

Northampton Chronicle & Echo (2023). *Grade II listed former shoe factory conversion*.

Oaktree Capital Management (2020). *The case for private debt in real estate investing*.

Ontario Teachers' Pension Plan (2023). *Investing in infrastructure*.

Ostrum Asset Management (2016). *Solvency II for real asset debt*. Research Paper.

PE (2025). Swiss pension fund boosts private assets. *Investment & Pensions Europe*.

PitchBook (2024). *2023 Annual Global Private Debt Report*.

Place North West (2011, March 30). *Peel agrees £205m debt with Aviva*.

PREA (2024). Private real estate credit. *PREA Quarterly*.

Preqin (2023). *Preqin Global Report 2023: Private Debt*.

Property Week (2018, August 10). *Blackstone refinances London's St Katharine Docks.*
Private Debt Investor (2025). *Investor Report 2025.*
Rajan, R.G. (2010). *Fault Lines.* Princeton University Press.
Reuters (2009). *Fed MBS purchase program seen extending into 2010.*
Reuters (2024). *Cheyne capital wins investment from ADIA.*
Reinhart, C.M., & Rogoff, K.S. (2009). *This time is different.* Princeton University Press.
Richardson, C.J. (2023–2024). *Dodd–Frank's Unintended Consequences for Housing.* Regulation.
Rosenfeld, B.Z. (2024). *Credit and Usury in Jewish Society.* Brill.
Shiller, R.J. (2008). *The Subprime Solution.* Princeton University Press.
SUERF (2025). *Do we still need banks?*
Taylor, J. (2009). *The financial crisis and the policy responses.*
Thakor, A.V. (2015). The financial crisis of 2007–2009. *Review of Corporate Finance Studies.*
The Conversation (2022). *A brief history of the mortgage.*
Turner, A. (2015). *Between Debt and the Devil.* Princeton University Press.
U.S. Congress (2010). *Dodd–Frank Wall Street Reform and Consumer Protection Act.*
Vuong, H. (2024). Private real estate credit. *PREA Quarterly.*
World Bank (2020). *Global Financial Development Report.*
Zions Bancorporation. (2013). *Preliminary assessment of the Volcker Rule.*

Index

Note: Page numbers in *italics* and **bold** refer to figures and tables respectively.